P9-BAV-872

Immigration Phobia and the Security Dilemma

Russia, Europe, and the United States

Immigration phobia is a paradoxical global phenomenon: Neither theories that link conflict to "symbolic" and "realistic" threats nor the "contact hypothesis" can systematically explain intense antimigrant alarmism and exclusionism toward marginally small migrant minorities. Through a careful comparative study of immigration attittudes in the Russian Far East, the European Union, and the United States, this book is the first to demonstrate that concerns about national identity and economic interests associated with migration are themselves ignited by a unique perceptual logic of the security dilemma. Regression analysis and case studies trace support for expulsion of migrants to human yearning for preemptive self-defense under uncertainty. Alarmism and hostility arise from ambiguities about immigration consequences and migrants' motivations. Framing migration as a national security problem is therefore logical, but counterproductive. The book instead recommends managing migration through economic incentives and new institutions at the global, national, and local levels.

Mikhail A. Alexseev is an associate professor of political science at San Diego State University. A former Kremlin correspondent of the *News from Ukraine* weekly, Alexseev was the first Soviet citizen to receive a Reuters' Fellowship at the University of Oxford and the NATO Democratic Institutions Fellowship in 1990. He is the author of *Without Warning: Threat Assessment, Intelligence, and Global Struggle* (1997) and the editor of *Center-Periphery Conflict in Post-Soviet Russia: A Federation Imperiled* (1999). His articles have appeared in numerous journals, newspapers, and magazines, including *Political Science Quarterly*, *Journal of Peace Research*, *Political Communication*, *The New York Times*, *Newsweek*, *USA Today*, and *The Seattle Times*.

Immigration Phobia and the Security Dilemma

Russia, Europe, and the United States

MIKHAIL A. ALEXSEEV
San Diego State University

CAMBRIDGE UNIVERSITY PRESS
Cambridge, New York, Melbourne, Madrid, Cape Town, Singapore, São Paulo

Cambridge University Press
40 West 20th Street, New York, NY 10011-4211, USA

www.cambridge.org
Information on this title: www.cambridge.org/9780521849883

First published 2006

Printed in the United States of America

A catalog record for this publication is available from the British Library.

Library of Congress Cataloging in Publication Data

Alexseev, Mikhail A., 1963–
Immigration phobia and the security dilemma : Russia, Europe, and the United States/Mikhail A. Alexseev.
p. cm.
Includes bibliographical references and index.
ISBN 0-521-84988-8 (hardback)
1. Russia (Federation) – Emigration and immigration. 2. Europe – Emigration and immigration. 3. United States – Emigration and immigration. 4. Immigrants – Russia (Federation). 5. Immigrants – Europe. 6. Immigrants – United States. I. Title.
JV8190.A45 2006
325′.1–dc22 2005004771

ISBN-13 978-0-521-84988-3 hardback
ISBN-10 0-521-84988-8 hardback

Contents

Acknowledgments

This book may be traced to the time around 1997 when Chechnya achieved *de facto* independence from Russia, when the leaders of Russia's constituent regions and republics became popularly elected and claimed increasing autonomy from the Kremlin, and when eight time zones away from Moscow Russia's Far Eastern provinces had been intensifying economic, political, and cultural exchanges with their dynamic East Asian neighbors. This set the backdrop for my focusing on Chinese migration – first as a possible tangible threat to Russia's security and increasingly as an imagined and overrated threat. It would be impossible to remember all the people who shaped this project, but I must acknowledge first and foremost the profound intellectual stimulation and encouragement at the most important turning points in this project by Stephen Hanson, Herbert Ellison, Ronald Grigor Suny, Robert Jervis, Wayne Cornelius, and Richard Hofstetter. This work would not see the light of day if it were not for a lot of help from my colleagues and friends in Russia when I conducted fieldwork there: Tamara Troyakova, Viktor Larin, Yevgenii Plaksen, and Liudmila Romanova in Vladivostok and Volodya and Liuda Vagin in Moscow. I am also indebted to all those whose support and whose comments sustained my fieldwork, writing, and public presentations of research that culminated in this book (listed in no particular order): Nykola Mirylovic, Phil Roeder, Bruce Acker, Dominique Arel, Deana Arsenian, Jere Bacharach, Akihiro Iwashita, Rajan Menon, Blaire Ruble, Charles Ziegler, Pavel Minakir, Nadezhda Mikheeva, Sergei Chugrov, John Davies, Boris Tkachenko, German Dudchenko, Valery Tishkov, Aleksei Voskresenskii, Bob Huber, Jonathan Mogul, Kimberly Righter, Andreas Wenger, Jeronim Perovic, Oleg

Alexandrov, Jinichiro Tabata, Hillary Appel, Richard Pape, Balazs Szelenyi, Yulia Shevchenko, Andrei Znamenskii, Les Vogel, James Billington, Sergey Khrushchev, Dipak Gupta, Lei Guang, Kristen Maher, Farid Abdel-Nour, Ronald King, Brian Loveman, Lyndelle Fairlie, Jonathan Graubart, Dennis Grady, Lou Terrell, Sergey Golunov, and members of my intellectual family – the Program on New Approaches to Russian Security of the Center for Strategic and International Studies (PONARS) – Celeste Wallander, Astrid Tuminez, Ted Gerber, Bear Braumoeller, Matthew Evangelista, Fiona Hill, Nikolai Petrov, Ivan Kurila, Georgi Derlouguian, Mark Kramer, Yoshika Hererra, Andrew Kuchins, Andrei Makarychev, Nikolai Sokov, Vladimir Popov, Yekaterina Stepanova, Edouard Ponarin, Vladimir Gel'man, and Dmitry Gorenburg. The project would have been impossible without the dedication and professionalism of the Primorskii survey interviewers Olga Funtusova, Irina Tikhonova, Nadezhda Romanova, Yevgenii Plaksen, Jr., Svetlana Plaksen, and Yelena Larina. Research was made possible, in large part, by generous support of the United States Institute of Peace, the Pacific Basin Research Center of the John F. Kennedy School of Government and the Soka University of America, the National Council for Eurasian and East European Research, and the John W. Kluge Center at the Library of Congress, where most of the first draft of the book was written in 2002 and 2003. I am also grateful for travel and fieldwork support to the Kennan Institute for Advanced Russian Studies of the Woodrow Wilson International Center for Scholars, the International Research and Exchanges Board, Appalachian State University, and San Diego State University. I am thankful for being able to present my earlier writings at the Council on Foreign Relations, the National Bureau of Asian Research, the Center for Comparative Immigration Studies at the University of California–San Diego, the PONARS conferences, the Wilder House of the University of Chicago, the Kluge Center at the Library of Congress, the Keck Center for International and Strategic Studies at Claremont McKenna College, the Slavic Research Center of the Hokkaido University, the Kennan Institute at the Center for Security Studies and Conflict Research of the ETH Zentrum in Zurich, and the Korea Research Institute for Strategy. Limitless gratitude goes to the woman of my dreams and passions, Cindy Machen. My parents, Lyudmila and Anatoli Alexseev, helped greatly in Moscow. The book was written with love for my daughter, Leah Alexseev, whose generation, I hope, will be able to harness the benefits of international migration more than its predecessors.

1

Immigration Phobia and Its Paradoxes

As an Aeroflot flight attendant served a baked salmon meal on one of my six trips to the Russian Far East between 1999 and 2001, a woman sitting next to me started talking about problems facing her hometown of Livadia – a small coastal resort with sandy beaches a few miles away from Russia's largest Pacific trade port of Nakhodka. When she said "problems," I expected to hear another deeply troubling personal account of post-Soviet Russia's social ills, such as unpaid wages and pensions, collapsing education and medical care services, and violent organized crime. But the first problem she mentioned was different: "We have too many Chinese." In fact, she said, this was more than a problem. It was a threat – potentially a mortal threat to Russia's sovereignty over its provinces stretching along the Russia-China border from Lake Baikal to the Pacific: "The way things are going, it won't be long before they claim all of our lands back." Having by then researched Chinese migration in the Russian Far East for more than a year, I knew that the number of Chinese nationals, legal and illegal, in my fellow traveler's home province of Primorskii was no more than about 1.5 percent of the local Russian population (Alexseev 2001). I also knew that the county where my fellow traveler lived was not among locations within that province that attracted disproportionately large numbers of Chinese migrants. More importantly, my information – from government sources, opinion surveys, and field observations – suggested that most migrants went back and forth and had no intent to settle in Primorskii krai and to reclaim it for China. So I asked the woman troubled by the rising "yellow tide" if she knew what motivated the Chinese migrants – perhaps they had little interest in Russia's Far East given harsh economic conditions and climate. "Oh, they will have a lot of interest," she insisted. "They will just keep coming, and then what are we going to do? Look, our young people try to go and study in Moscow or Central Russia – and they are not coming back. In fact, whoever can do it, leaves." She obviously contradicted herself: If the Russians were not all that eager to live in the Far East, why would the Chinese? Nevertheless, I knew from the opinion survey I conducted with my Russian colleagues in Primorskii krai in September 2000 that my fellow traveler's alarmism was widespread among local Russians. Survey respondents on average overestimated the number of Chinese migrants by a factor of ten. When asked what proportion of Primorskii population was Chinese, 46 percent of them said it amounted to 10–20 percent. This was also what in statistical terms is known as the *modal response* – a response reflecting the central tendency among those polled. Given all this knowledge, I still found it striking that someone in a casual conversation, unprompted, would bring up a numerically marginal migration and talk about it as a more tangible and in-your-face threat than massive economic and social problems facing the region. I soon found these common-person's apprehensions incipiently shared in the Russian academic community. In Vladivostok, one of the research fellows at the Institute of History, Archeology, and Ethnography of the Peoples of the Russian Far East, was selling self-published books warning that the Chinese were proverbially coming and ready to settle and claim Russian territory. He admonished this author and other Russian colleagues to write about this threat. This scholar later received a special award from the Primorskii krai governor for precisely these publications. Back in Moscow, during a long discussion of alarmist perceptions of Chinese migration in the Russian Far East, one of the most perceptive and knowledgeable Russian specialists on migration affiliated with the Academy of Sciences agreed with me that the scale of Chinese migration and its putatively threatening implications had been stubbornly exaggerated by the Russian officials and the public. This cool-headed assessment notwithstanding, the same expert at the very end of the conversation gave a deep, uneasy sigh and pointed to the map on the wall: "Yeah, but in the end, no matter what we do, our Far East will go to China."

Meanwhile, more than 5,000 miles to the west, local officials in Krasnodar krai, one of Russia's border regions in the North Caucasus, continued to warn Moscow and the local public that Russia's territorial integrity was gravely challenged by the Meskhetian Turk refugees. The Meskhetian Turks had been deported from their homeland in the former Soviet Georgia to Central Asia on Stalin's orders at the end of the Second World War. In the late 1980s, under Mikhail Gorbachev's policies promoting political openness (*glasnost*), the Meskhetians were allowed to go back to Georgia, but they "got stuck" in transit in Krasnodar after the Soviet Union collapsed in late 1991 and now faced crossing international borders into a newly independent state that itself became engulfed in political turmoil and civil war. That reality aside, the leader of the local legislature in Krasnodar in the late 1990s was imputing threats to Russian sovereignty from the fact that some of the Meskhetian Turks settled near Russia's Black Sea port and oil terminal of Novorossiisk. Humanitarian aid coming from neighboring Turkey in the form of vegetables, fruit, and clothes was cited as another reason to fear the refugees. Guiding these settlement patterns and the humanitarian aid were arguably the same unidentified, but sinister and deadly, global actors who allegedly subsidized armed separatists in Chechnya. The same incognito – and therefore deadly – forces now, according to the legislative chief, presumably aimed at establishing "an Islamic Republic of Kuban" in Krasnodar, with a longer-term goal of forcing Russia to collapse the same way that the Soviet Union did in 1991 (Radio Free Europe/Radio Liberty 2001). Meskhetian Turk settlements became the target of violent pogroms and antiimmigrant rallies. The popular slogan ran: "We Won't Let the Kuban Become Another Kosovo!" Never mind that even judging by the "worst-case" assessments provided by local government agencies and sociologists, Meskhetian Turks comprised less than 0.3 percent of Krasnodar's more than five million residents from the early 1990s to the early 2000s (Kritskii, Nistotskaia, Remmler 1996: 67; Perov 2004).

This exaggeration of migration scale and imputed threats to sovereignty and security – the fear of being "swamped," "overrun," "overwhelmed," "absorbed," "consumed," "driven out," or "conquered" by "tidal waves," "swells," "hordes," "armies," "flows," "multitudes," and "flocks" of ethnic others, no matter how marginal their numbers in proportion to the incumbent population size – is also strikingly illustrated in studies of ethnic conflict in South Asia and Oceania by Donald Horowitz of Duke University. Horowitz (1985: 178) recorded cases in which precisely this kind of "apprehensions about survival, swamping, and subordination" arose when actual demographic trends were *favorable* to incumbent ethnic groups. The Fijians raised alarms in the 1970s and 1980s about the incoming Indians even though their population grew at least as fast. The Sikhs continued to express fears of going extinct even though their population had increased fastest in Punjab and one-third faster than any other ethnic group in India in the preceding decades. Anti-Chinese alarmism endured among the Malays despite their population having a persistently higher rate of increase than the Chinese migrant population – and regardless of Malays's proximity to the more populous and fast-growing ethnic kin population of Indonesia. Threatened as they said they were by swarming migrants, the Hausa of Northern Nigeria and the Telanganas of Andhra Pradesh enjoyed demographic trends that precluded them from becoming ethnic minorities.

In the United States, the mayor of Lewiston, Maine, sent an open letter in September 2002 to the elders of the local Somali community pleading with them to discourage fellow ex-Somalis elsewhere in the United States from moving to Lewiston. The mayor's plea was couched in familiar language of alarmed desperation, saying "we have been overwhelmed" and "we need breathing room," because Lewiston got "maxed-out financially, physically and emotionally (http://pressherald.mainetoday.com/news/immigration/021005raymondletter.shtml). Never mind that by late September 2002 the cumulative influx of new residents of Somali origin to Lewiston amounted to about 1,000, or less than 2.8 percent of the town's incumbent population of 36,000. And never mind, as the Somali community leaders pointed out in response to the mayor, that at the time the letter was written, the influx of ex-Somalis declined and completely stopped. Besides, the elders expressed surprise with the alarmist tone of the letter. In their extensive dialog with other local government officials, they were told the new arrivals were welcome because the area was sparsely populated and could use more workers and voters (ibid.).

Highlighting the same paradox is the reverse tendency – absence of widespread antiimmigrant alarmism and political campaigns in countries experiencing disproportionately large influxes of migrants. My extensive search of powerful electronic databases comprising hundreds of news sources, LexisNexis and ProQuest, for stories similar to those described in the preceding text and coming from the United Arab Emirates, Kuwait, and Oman yielded precious little, beyond reports of prejudice and workplace discrimination and use of racial and ethnic slurs that are also commonly reported in societies experiencing no significant in-migration. And yet, the UN Population Division (2002a: 3) estimated that the number of residents born abroad had reached 74 percent in the United Arab Emirates, 58 percent in Kuwait, and 27 percent in Oman – among the highest such proportions in the world.

One also consistently finds that variation in migration rates within host states has little direct and systematic relationship with immigration attitudes. In Canada, combined results of ten Angus Reid surveys from

1996 to 1998 illustrate these persistent inconsistencies. Thus, in Ontario and Alberta about the same proportion of survey respondents (45 and 43 percent, respectively) said their provinces received too many immigrants. Yet, in Ontario the immigrant inflow per 100 local residents was estimated at 1.11 percent and in Alberta at less than half that rate (0.51 percent). In both cases, however, we again register widespread alarmism about numerically marginal migration. Similarly, in Quebec and the Atlantic provinces of Canada, exactly the same proportion of survey respondents (39 percent) felt that immigration levels were too high, while the actual inflow of migrants was twice higher in Quebec than it was in the Atlantic Provinces (.40 per 100 vs. .20 per 100) (Palmer 1999: 5–6).

Furthermore, in many cases where population trends tangibly threaten the majority status of ethnic incumbents, they do not necessarily engender hostility and violence. Even when current or projected changes in the ethnic population balance raised fears of ethnic "swamping," hostility and violence manifested themselves with greater intensity in some cases (e.g., the Mudarese workers in West Kalimantan; the Chinese in Indonesia; Georgians in Abkhazia; Jewish settlers in the West Bank) than in others (e.g., Russians in Estonia and Kazakhstan; the Koreans and the Vietnamese in Russia; Brazilians in Paraguay; Mexicans in California). Both the former Soviet Union and former Yugoslavia faced a Muslim population explosion – in Central Asia (d'Encausse 1979) and in Bosnia (O'Balance 1995: 197), respectively. In the Soviet Union, this trend by the mid-1980s was literally changing the face of the Soviet Army. Yet ethnic Russian military commanders stationed in Soviet Central Asia did not authorize the use of force on behalf of their ethnic kin living among the Muslims in these republics at the breakup of the Soviet Union, as some top Serb military commanders in Bosnia did at the breakup of Yugoslavia. Nor did Russian ethnic communities – especially in vast and predominantly Russian-populated expanses of northern Kazakhstan – pursue hostile mobilization and deadly violence under the pretext of countering this demographic threat, to the extent that many Bosnian Serb communities did – especially in or around the enclaves with sizeable Serb population.

At the global level, no empirical evidence suggests that between the late 1980s and the early 2000s the number of migrants intentionally or involuntarily undermining the security and economic performance of the host states increased at all in proportion to the total number of international migrants around the world. The United Nations (2002a: 3) data continued to show that economic motivation predominantly explained global migration patterns. People kept leaving poorer and less economically stable states in search of livelihood in richer and economically more stable states. And yet, a tectonic conceptual shift in immigration research had been afoot since the late 1980s, with a disproportionately large and growing number of studies framing migration as a security issue. This is evidenced by studies that I discuss further in this volume with respect to Russia, Europe, and the United States and by my survey of academic and mainstream media publications archived in electronic databases. The "Academic Universe" (EBSCO) database – widely used by the international scholarly community and accessible on the Web through most university libraries in the United States – listed no articles published prior to 1990 in which the words *migration* and *security* appeared together in an article abstract without being accompanied by words related to *economy* or *economic*. The search of the ProQuest dataset retrieved eleven articles matching the same search criteria, but none focused on international, national, or group security. Of these eleven articles, nine dealt with the Social Security program as an economic issue in the United States, one with the health of migrant workers, and one with migration of electronic data. For the same time period, the EBSCO search retrieved fifty-nine article abstracts and the ProQuest search retrieved 266 articles in which *migration* appeared together with the words related to *economy* or *economics*, but not together with *security*. These articles predominantly focused on economic aspects of human migration within and across international boundaries. By October 2004, EBSCO had eighty-four abstracts and ProQuest had fifty-one abstracts of academic journal articles related to migration and security – but not economics. These articles focused on security implications of migration in the same way as the studies of war, conflict, or crime did (e.g., Ivakhniouk 2004, Schloenhardt 2001).[1] At the theoretical level, scholars within what would become known as the Copenhagen School heralded widespread legitimation and normalization of viewing migration through the prism of a "societal security" in a symptomatically titled book, *Identity, Migration, and the New Security Agenda in Europe* (Waever et al. 1993). Grounding the concept in theories of society, identity, the nation, and the individual with references to Rousseau, Tönnies, Giddens, Weber, Wallerstein, Lasswell, Walker, Foucault, and Durkheim, the authors defined *societal security* as socially constructed perceptions of threat "in identity terms" that are predominant within

[1] The number of scholarly articles dealing with economic aspects of migration also increased, with 654 retrieved on EBSCO and 1,173 on ProQuest.

human collectivities (ibid.: 17–23). Migration therefore could become categorized as a security threat to the extent that host societies would perceive it as a challenge to individual, group, or national identity. Terms such as *new security* and *common security* also emerged in the academic and policy literature to encompass diverse social and economic phenomena such as migration – with some scholars pointing out their elasticity, looseness, cliché-like nature, and symbolic popularity in official discourses (Butfoy 1997: 21–2). Outside the academe, the inclusion of migration into security studies appeared to become significantly more widespread by late 2004. My search of articles from all sources with ProQuest in October 2004 retrieved 2,023 entries for *migration* and *security* – almost half as many as 4,834 entries on *migration* and *economy* – a monumental shift in the ratio since 1990. Whereas migration may pose clear and present threats to security and sovereignty of nation-states, however, such challenges by no means occur even half as often as socioeconomic challenges. Interpretation of predominantly economic challenges as challenges to national security would thus constitute qualitative threat exaggeration even if the scale of migration is estimated accurately and its trends are not exaggerated. Such qualitative overrating of threats would be especially puzzling in cases of marginal migration driven by economic motives.

Despite "securitizing" migration, authoritative reviews (Checkel 2004; Choucri 1974; Koslowski 2002; Krebs and Levy 2001; Weiner and Teitelbaum 2001) of scholarly literature suggest that neither bottom-up sociological perspectives nor top-down international relations perspectives have provided us with a comprehensive conceptual assessment of the relationship between migration and national security.[2] And this is notwithstanding the inclusion in the reviews of work by Azar and Farah (1984); Brown 1997; Eberstadt (1991); Freedman (1991); Goldscheider (1995); Homer-Dixon (1994); Tapinos (1978); Teitelbaum and Winter (1998); Weiner (1971); and Zimmermann (1995). The Failed States Project, financed by the U.S. government, did not focus on changes in ethnic demographics or migration data (Esty et al. 1998). The field of migration research still awaits studies similar in scope and rigor to

[2] Checkel (2004: 242–4) also showed that research projects linking international relations theory and migration – Soysal (1994) on transnational spread of immigrant rights and Freeman (1998) on interest groups' impact on immigration policy – have not systematically addressed the social and psychological sources of antimigrant alarmism and hostility in host populations. Hollifield (1992) turned the question around, asking why migration into industrialized democratic states persisted in the 1970s and 1980s despite increasing public hostility in receiving states.

Schmeidl's (1997) pooled time-series analysis of the effects of mass violence on forced migration – but the ones that would reverse causality and assess the longer-term effects of demographic trends.

Challenge to Intergroup Conflict Theories

The systematic evidence presented previously is more than an assortment of counterintuitive empirical trends. The sum of these puzzles – the apparent disconnect between the scale and nature of migration on the one hand and the urge within host states to "securitize" migration on the other – has profound theoretical implications. While it may not seem intuitively obvious, the antimigrant hostility paradox confounds the predominant academic perspectives of intergroup conflict – that is, theories that emphasize the role of either "realistic" or "symbolic" threat or some combination of both. The principal challenge to the literature arises from one underlying commonality: Whether scholars emphasize "real" competition for resources and power or concerns about cultural identity, most research on antimigrant hostility and support for exclusionist policies in North America and Europe is grounded in theories that ultimately interpret interethnic animosity as a "linear function of a single out-group size" (see Oliver and Wong 2003: 567–8 for a review). More broadly, Bhagwati (2004: 35) argued that backlashes against the "international flow of humanity" require as a precondition "a rapid and substantial influx of immigrants." As the following sections will show, it is precisely this underlying commonality and assumption of the size–hostility linkage that is challenged by rampant antimigrant alarmism and mobilization in regions with marginal migration and by the absence of mass antimigrant mobilization in regions where migration significantly changed the face of local population.

Antimigrant Alarmism and Realistic Threats

Dating back at least to Aristotle, the "realistic threat" hypothesis associates interethnic hostility with clashes of material interest (especially see Hardin 1995). This perspective is consistent with broader arguments about zero-sum competition for resources and living space as the principal driver of intergroup and interstate conflict that had been advanced by classical political realists (Morgenthau 1947). It also encompasses the rational choice theory emphasis on private self-interest as the determinant of political behavior (Downs 1957; Page 1977) and the underlying public attitudes (Campbell et al. 1960; Lipset 1960). In contemporary sociological and political science research, migration size is directly, although not necessarily explicitly, associated with an individual sense of realistic threat. Such threats are typically conceptualized as threats to majority group status and privileges (Blumer 1958) or threats of economic competition (Olzak 1989, 1992), or both. One of the best exponents of the size–hostility linkage in the realistic-threat paradigm is Susan Olzak's analysis of the relationship between immigration patterns and interethnic violence in major American cities at the turn of the nineteenth and twentieth centuries. Olzak (1992: 78, 242–3) found that change in overall immigration rates had a significant effect on anti-Black violence. In Olzak's studies, migration size is a crucial underlying component of "competitive exclusion" and intergroup violence, because size was the principal driver of socioeconomic "niche overlap and competition," of which one of the most explicit manifestations was the physical length of "a racial job queue" (ibid.: 209–10). Olzak's studies also reflect theoretical insights of ecological competition theories (notably, Barth 1969). Bobo (1999), Bobo and Hutchings (1996), Fosset and Kielcolt (1989), Giles and Herz (1994), Glaser (1994), and Quillian (1995) directly inferred racial threat from statistically significant relationships they found between the concentration of ethnoracial minorities and antiminority and antimigrant attitudes. In this sense, they linked antimigrant attitudes in theory to the same socioeconomic competition factors that would make little sense if the influx of migrants were marginal and did not tangibly affect economic conditions. This intrinsic dependence of realistic or real competition threat on migration size is cogently summarized by McLaren (2003: 916): "[I]f there are not many immigrants with whom to compete, it is less likely that citizens will be threatened by them, and thus willing to expel them." Due to this fundamental inferential linkage between migration size and hostility, the realistic threat explanation is confounded in places like the Russian Far East, where this author found no Russian–Chinese job queues and no sizeable concentrated settlements of ethnic Chinese. Moreover, one of my earlier analyses of the Primorskii 2000 survey revealed that sensitivity to ethnic population balance tipping in favor of the Chinese, perceptions that the Chinese migrants were winning economic competition against the local Russians, and location of respondents in counties bordering directly on China were not related directly to hostility. Some perceptions were significantly related to general fear of Chinese migrants, but not to support for hostile responses to migration (Alexseev 2003). Yet somehow, fears of Chinese takeover had a lot to do with considerations of the economic impact of migration – a paradox that requires explanation outside the logic of real-life resource competition. Another major putative dimension of realistic threat – competition for political influence – was also absent in Primorskii, where no ethnic Chinese migrant rose to any position in the executive, legislative, or judicial branch from the early 1990s to the early 2000s.

Research elsewhere also indicates that the sense of realistic-threat competition – even where it is related significantly to antimigrant hostility – is not necessarily a linear function of migration scale and the corresponding economic pressures. In Europe, statistical and opinion survey data compiled by Lincoln Quillian (1995: 607–8) showed that levels of antiimmigrant prejudice were about the same in France, Germany, and Denmark around 1993 – despite the fact that the proportion of non–European Union (EU) immigrants differed markedly in these countries with about the same levels of gross domestic product (GDP) per capita. At the same time, in Belgium and the Netherlands as well as in Portugal and Greece both GDP per capita and percentage of non-EU immigrant population were about equal, but levels of antiimmigrant prejudice were sharply higher in Belgium than in the Netherlands and in Greece than in Portugal. A popular argument that economic strains on host countries arose from refugees and asylum claimants seeking public assistance is also hard to sustain with real-world data. The Eurobarometer survey in 1997 (discussed in detail in Chapter 6) showed, for instance, that support for wholesale deportation of all immigrants was approximately 50 percent higher in Germany than in Austria and France. Yet, between the end of 1995 and the end of 1997 – approximately two years prior to the survey – the total refugee population declined in Germany by 217,000, increased in Austria by about 57,000, and remained largely unchanged in France (decreasing by 4,000) (United Nations High Commissioner for Refugees 1998: Table 2). Adding to these puzzles, a survey on racism and xenophobia in the EU in 2000 found that approximately 25 percent of EU respondents were "ambivalent" on immigration, holding both positive and negative views about minorities at the same time, yet without systematic association with migration levels (Thalhammer et al. 2001a: 35).

In Canada, from the late 1980s to the late 1990s, representative Angus Reid surveys registered increasing tolerance of immigration. The number of respondents agreeing with the statement "Non-whites should not be allowed to immigrate to Canada" – a small minority to begin with – dropped even further from 1989 to 1996 (Palmer 1998: 2). One intuitively plausible interpretation of this trend was that the erosion of intolerance toward migrants paralleled the improved performance of national economy and the decline in unemployment (ibid.). However, the same study revealed significant, yet unexplained, puzzles. For example, unemployment rates in Vancouver after dropping in the mid-1980s climbed from about 7.3 percent in 1989 to 8 percent in 1996, while peaking at 9.3 percent in 1993 (BC STATS 2004). In Toronto, the number of full-time and part-time jobs declined continuously from approximately 1.36 million in 1989 – also following an economic boom and employment growth to 1.15 million in 1996 (Toronto Urban Development Services 2000: 3). In Montreal, job availability decreased by approximately 3 percent from 1989 to 1993, but then rose by 5 percent toward the end of 1996 (Ville de Montreal 1997). Despite palpable variation in employment trends, support for "racist exclusion" failed to change in all three cities and differed significantly (Palmer 1998: 4). Another study of immigration perceptions in Canadian cities (Schissel, Wanner, and Friederes 1989) found that city-level unemployment rates were only weakly associated with individual attitudes toward immigrants.

In the United States, an analysis of the American National Election Studies (ANES) data for 1992 and 1996 established that assessments of personal and national economic well-being were only weakly related to immigration policy attitudes. This suggests that the realistic-threat interpretation of antimigrant exclusionism is problematic regardless of whether *pocketbook* or *sociotropic* (national economy) valuations play a larger part in the formation of political attitudes among individuals (this literature is reviewed in Chapter 3). More counterintuitively, in 1992, but not in 1996, the worse the respondents' personal outlook on the economy was, the more they favored increased immigration (Burns and Gimpel 2000). In other words, negative economic valuations were found to cue both pro- and antimigrant sentiments in the United States at different times. While Hoskin (1991) and Feltzer (2000) found that Americans who felt that immigrants threatened their economic position also favored restricting immigration, Sorenson and Krahn (1996) reported that among young Canadians job prospects had little relationship to immigration attitudes. In U.S. counties where a higher concentration of immigrant minorities posed a tangible threat of job competition, Hood and Morris (1997) found that approval of immigrant presence by majority group members was actually higher than in counties with lower or no threat of job competition. In one of the strongest empirical challenges to the realistic-threat theory, Diamond (1998) identified fourteen independent studies reporting that African Americans in the United States were more supportive of immigration than Americans of Caucasian origin – despite the fact that African Americans generally lived in communities that experienced larger job losses to migrants.

At the global and national levels, the realistic-threat perspective is challenged by persistent public fear of migrants bearing economic gifts. Most immigrants clearly demonstrate commitment to "making it" in the receiving countries – something that inevitably requires harder effort from the migrants than from the locals to adjust to the host states' political and socioeconomic conditions. The well-known willingness of migrants to work harder and longer hours doing lower-paid jobs and to uproot themselves moving where workers are scarcest (*The Economist* 2002: 14) is in itself a credible signal of their commitment to contribute to the host state's economy. An exhaustive study of immigrant economic behavior in the United States in the 1970s and 1980s by Simon (1999: 364–74) found that immigrants had higher participation in the labor force, higher savings rates, stronger proclivity to start new businesses, commitment to working more intensively, and law abidance. Immigrants in the first five years received about half what the natives received in welfare services (in constant 1975 dollars) and contributed more in taxes – including illegal Mexican immigrants (see also Clark et al. 1994: 8).

Macroeconomic analyses suggest that on the whole migration yields net economic gains for receiving states and for the global economy. Alan Winters, an economist at the Sussex University, estimated in 2002 that if the states in which relatively richer economies attract migrants from poorer states raised the proportion of temporary guest workers to 3 percent of their workforce, the world economy would net a gain worth more than U.S.$150 billion – bigger than projected gains from any single policy measure of global trade liberalization (*The Economist* 2002: 14–15). Dani Rodrik, a Harvard economist, reached essentially the same conclusion independently, arguing that unlike gaps in the prices of traded goods, gaps in the wages of similarly qualified workers failed to become smaller after decades of increasingly freer global movement of goods and capital (*The Economist* 2002: 15). Based on these findings, *The Economist*'s survey of international migration in November 2002 concluded that tearing down the barriers restricting global movement of labor would constitute the most effective strategy for rapidly increasing the growth of the global economy.

It is puzzling why it has taken so long for policy makers and the public in receiving states to embrace primarily economic strategies for accommodating migrants and regulating migration flows. For example, migration still lacks a multilateral rule-setting body such as the World Trade Organization (WTO) that existed under different names for decades – reflecting lack of a similar push for such an institution by the economically and politically influential states. Also, immigration restrictions are still based on quotas and bans, unlike trade restrictions that shifted to more transparent tariffs in the second half of the twentieth century. And unlike globalization of trade, where the principal actors have inexorably moved toward lifting tariff and nontariff barriers, the major migrant-receiving states in the 1990s tightened immigration restrictions, emphasizing border enforcement and security. The United States government, for example, funded the construction of a triple metal wall along the border with Mexico south of San Diego that makes the Berlin Wall inconsequential, rather than allowing the labor market to regulate migrant flows.

All in all, the principal paradox embedded in these findings is why responses to migration in most receiving states – ostensibly enacted to address public concerns over economic costs of illegal immigration – expressly discount tangible net economic gains? If the realistic threat of economic losses appears to drive antimigrant sentiment, why shouldn't appreciation of economic gains from migration drive more accommodative migration policies with delegation of the power to control migrant flows to the labor markets? In broader theoretical terms, why would economic benefits fail to assuage fears of population change?

Antimigrant Alarmism and Symbolic Threats

A seemingly more flexible and powerful explanation of public alarmism about being "swamped" or "overwhelmed" by outsiders – no matter what their numbers – would have to do with concerns about racial, religious, linguistic, and cultural identities in host societies (Weiner 1995: 3–8) and with the ways these identities are actualized in symbolic public discourse and practices (Kaufmann 2001). Yet, although less directly, persistent cases of alarmist and hostile exclusionism toward marginal migrant minorities around the world challenge not only the "realistic threat," but also the "symbolic threat" conception of interethnic conflict. At first glance, migration size is not the issue for the symbolic-threat logic, given its emphasis on the clash of social identities between host societies and migrants. This emphasis is also found in some forms of what is described as *traditional racism* – such as negative stereotyping or affect and the sense of out-group inferiority. Predominantly, the symbolic-threat view draws on the *social identity theory* (reviewed in Brown 1995), and it is empirically grounded in experimental analyses of the Bristol School (notably,

Tajfel 1970, 1981 – a more detailed review of this literature is in Chapter 2). The principal variable affecting in-group favoritism and out-group hostility in these experiments was what later became known as *social categorization* – essentially the assignment of symbolic group distinctions to subjects and observing their implications for behavior within and between the designated groups. In theory, out-groups would be symbolically threatening not necessarily and not primarily due to out-group size, but largely due to intergroup distinctiveness. However, none of the experiments modeled interactions in situations that would resemble marginal migration because the designated groups (e.g., the "blues" and the "reds") were typically of equal and small size. In fact, the most powerful experiments concerned the so-called minimal intergroup situations, involving groups with only two participants in each. To model the social context in Primorskii krai in the late 1990s, however, such experiments would have to juxtapose a group of two people representing the Chinese migrants and a group of 150 people representing the Local Russians – a setting that would also fundamentally challenge the methodology of the minimal intergroup paradigm and complicate inferences. If a group of two can appear threatening to another group of two because they are designated as the "reds" and the "blues," it does not follow that a group of 150 should be equally threatened by a group of two for the same reason. In the framework of social identity theory, the marginal migration puzzle outlined at the start of this chapter would be equivalent to a hypothetical experimental finding that "red" groups the size of 100 felt more threatened by "blue" groups the size of two than "red" groups the size of fifty felt threatened by "blue" groups the size of fifty – all other groups characteristics being equal. Thus, whereas empirical tests of the Bristol School scholars suggest that group identity is a powerful behavioral microfoundation, they do not offer a systematic theoretical explanation of identity effects in widely asymmetric group situations that one could apply to marginal migration contexts.

To the extent that one would trace the emergence of in-group identities and out-group "anti-identities" – or internalization of ethnic group symbols or markers – to childhood and adolescence, the migrant minority paradox would also challenge, although not necessarily to the same degree, a variant of symbolic politics theory developed by David Sears and his collaborators. In their analysis of American whites' opposition to school busing – designed to bring together students of diverse racial and ethnic backgrounds in the same classrooms – Sears, Hensler, and Speer (1979) found that "residues of pre-adult socialization" such as political conservatism and racial prejudices were significant predictors, but not narrow self-interest, such as living in neighborhoods more affected by busing. Formulating the perceptual microfoundations of "symbolic racism," Kinder and Sears (1981: 416, quoted in McLaren 2003: 916) show that the symbolic-threat logic is intrinsically grounded in valuations of ethnic or intergroup balances: "Symbolic racism represents a form of resistance to change in the racial status quo based on moral feelings that blacks violate such traditional American values as individualism and self-reliance, the work ethic, obedience, and discipline." One unanswered question is whether the same logic would explain intergroup hostility if "change in the racial status quo" is not presumably an issue, as it would be in the case of marginal minorities. An even broader problem is: How do individuals decide whether the racial or ethnic or any group status quo is at risk of changing in the first place? Finally, given the grounding of both social identity and socialization theories in emotional experiences associated with group differences, one is inclined to ask why emotional value of self-differentiation from a marginal minority should matter as much as or sometimes higher than differentiation from larger minorities that tangibly threaten an ethnic or racial status quo?[3]

In fact, a large literature in environmental psychology and sociology that deals with the effects of overcrowding on intergroup aggressiveness suggests that the reverse should be the case. Research on overcrowding established that perceived population pressures give rise to stress and proneness to aggression – arising from "a unique source of discontent" grounded in human cognition and emotions (Kelly and Galle 1984: 115). Other studies challenged this interpretation, however, establishing that

[3] Sniderman and Tetlock (1986) challenged the very notion of "symbolic racism." They argued that its two principal components – old-fashioned or segregationist, "Jim Crow" racism and individualism – influence attitudes independently and that therefore "symbolic racism" adds no new theoretical knowledge. Two points are noteworthy with respect to this challenge. First, in response to the Kinder/Sears-Sniderman/Tetlock debate, Hughes (1997) used the American National Election Survey (ANES) data to test the effects of "symbolic" versus "old-fashioned" racism with respect to the Whites' attitudes toward affirmative action. In particular, Hughes (1997: 69–71) put to rest the Sniderman/Tetlock critique by finding that (a) survey items representing symbolic and old-fashioned racism, although intercorrelated, did not measure a single underlying dimension, but constituted two separate factors and (b) measures of symbolic racism turned out to be more strongly related to opposition to affirmative action than measures of old-fashioned racism. Second, the term used in this study is *symbolic threat,* defined as threat to group identity – and this term would encompass all of the opinion measures that in the Kinder/Sears-Sniderman/Tetlock debate would relate primarily to either symbolic or old-fashioned racism. In this sense, the implicit linkage between threat theories and migrant group size would be relevant to both sides of the debate.

perceptions of overcrowding depended strongly on such factors as perceived predictability and controllability of social situations (Averill 1973; Cohen, Glass, and Philips 1979) and on perceived meanings communicated by sources of stress (Lazarus 1966). However, these and other correlates of perceived overcrowding, including variation of personal space requirements by individuals, were also found to vary significantly across cultures (Hall 1962). But specifically with regard to the central paradox of alarmism about marginal migration, these studies fall short of generating systematic explanations as to why perceptions of overcrowding might be consistently exaggerated across cultural contexts. For example, what is it about the communicated meanings of population stress that would drive residents in the Russian Far East to overestimate the number of Chinese migrants by the factor of ten or the Telanganas in Andhra Pradesh to express fear of "swamping" despite favorable demographic trends? Indeed, environmental psychologists have demonstrated that "environmental or social stimulation per se does not induce human stress and therefore the potential for conflict, but the *interaction* of various physical, social, cultural, and individual logic" (Proshansky 1984: 70). And yet, research in environmental psychology is yet to generate a theory that would identify parameters of precisely this "interaction of logics" to explain variation in immigration phobia cross-nationally.

Regarding research on immigration attitudes, the identity-threat arguments implicitly rely, once again, on interpretations of migration size and its trends. In the United States, one of the best exponents of the identity-threat logic has been a Harvard political scientist, Samuel Huntington (1996, 1997, 2000, 2004a, 2004b). In his view, the migration of Latinos and especially Mexicans to the United States poses a threat to the survival of the United States as a nation, because the migrants' desire to maintain a distinct social identity predicates putative lack of commitment to U.S. national security interests.[4] Yet, valuations of group size appear to be a major factor in the linking of group distinctiveness and the magnitude of perceived symbolic threats. Thus, Huntington argues that Mexican migration is a threat to America's national identity, because (a) Mexico and the United States share a long border that encourages immigration; (b) Mexican migrants, as a consequence, continue to arrive in larger numbers than other groups, reaching 25 percent of total legal migration to the United States in the 1990s – in contrast to dispersed

[4] Empirical studies, however, indicate that Huntington's argument with respect to Latino patriotism and cultural adaptation are incorrect (de la Garza 2004: 110–11).

sources of immigration from the 1860s to the 1960s; (c) the rising number and concentration of Mexicans creates incentives for them to forgo the American Creed and establish their own cultural enclaves that would translate into "hispanization" of the West and the Southwest of the United States as the number of persons of Mexican origin rises to a projected 25 percent of U.S. population by 2040; (d) the reluctance of Mexican migrants to assimilate into the American Creed has been evidenced by salsa outselling ketchup in the United States and by *José* replacing *Michael* as the most popular name given to newborn boys in Texas and California (Huntington 2004a: 223–56; Huntington 2004b: 38). Without these and other pieces of evidence regarding migration size, Huntington's (2004a: 246) reassertion of Morris Janowitz's (1983: 128–9) claims that Mexican migration threatens "a bifurcation in the social-political structure of the United States" would be unsustainable – even with selective and confirmatory use of evidence upon which Huntington bases the argument.

In the Sears et al. (1979) study, the symbolic racist attitudes – an interactive mixture of prejudice and political conservatism embedded in one's preadult socialization – seemingly had little relationship to ethnic balances within the neighborhoods into which minority children were bused. It may thus appear that the symbolic racism theory is not predicated on migration size estimates. Yet, the opinion survey sample upon which the study was based came from a social context of the late twentieth-century United States, in which the principal minority (African Americans) comprised a sizeable 10 percent of the population. More importantly, the study examined social attitudes toward a phenomenon that stood to increase racial and ethnic intermingling and, in this sense, magnify the exposure of the majority group to members of already sizeable minority groups. In addition, the symbolic racism's emphasis on early socialization in ethnic prejudice suggested that white opposition to busing should be higher in the American South – yet regression analysis of the survey found no significant relationship (ibid.: 375). Nevertheless, despite these caveats and the immediacy of busing effects on community life (which is not necessarily the case with immigration), the Sears et al. (1979) findings have important lessons with respect to alarmism about marginal migration. At the time of the survey upon which the study relied (1972), only about 4 percent of school children in the United States were bused for the purposes of school integration. Yet, Sears found that 24 percent of respondents said busing was affecting ethnic interactions in their neighborhoods and another 13 percent expected busing to affect their neighborhoods.

Although less explicitly related to ethnic transitions, empirical tests of symbolic-threat theory in other studies have been typically done in the same demographic contexts as the tests of the realistic-threat theories – and typically where migrant groups or ethnic minorities were nonmarginal (comprising more than 5 percent of the total population). Huddy and Sears (1995), for example, found that "hard work" values translated into opposition to spending on bilingual education of Latino immigrants in the United States in 1980 – with a study based on a nationwide sample of 1,700 with 400 overdrawn from four "heavily Latino" areas in California, New York, and Texas. Would the same logic explain threat perception in societies where no heavily populated minority areas emerge as a result of migration, yet antimigrant alarmism and hostility are intense? Wilson (2001) examined the impact of perceived threats to economic and cultural interests of Americans on opposition to policies benefitting immigrants. Drawing on the 1994 General Social Survey data using a probability sample of the U.S. population – comprised of sizeable ethnic and racial minorities – Wilson found that threat to identity mattered beyond traditionally conceived self-interest and ethnic prejudices. Gibson and Gouws (2000) found that strong in-group positive identities among South Africans significantly related to their antipathy toward political opponents representing ethnic out-groups. The study was based on a survey of 3,031 respondents, 17 percent of whom identified themselves as "white" and about 9 percent each as "colored" or "Asian origin." Each group comprised a sizeable population segment, and the combined minority population exceeded one-third of the sample, reflecting, to a degree, South Africa's demographic composition. Interestingly, Gibson and Gouws (ibid.) found that group solidarity was significantly associated with negative perception of out-groups ("anti-identities") only among respondents who self-identified as "colored" – the smallest of the groups. In other words, respondents appeared to perceive stronger identity threat with respect to groups that were relatively larger in size in relation to their own. (At the same time, however, minority group size also exhibited elusiveness as an identity-threat predictor, because no relationship between in-group solidarity and out-group hostility was found for groups of Asian origin). In Europe, as Chapter 6 will show, symbolic threats have been generally attributed in public discourses and academic analyses to the largest migrant groups such as the Turks in Germany or the North Africans in France and Spain.

To summarize, population size is implicitly factored in the conception of symbolic threat in a simple fashion: It is perfectly commonsensical that marginal minorities by definition are too small to "dilute" or destroy the cultural identity of any host society. That they would pose a threat to identity or national unity is counterintuitive. True, marginal minority leaders may evoke powerful symbols of their group identity that may offend the incumbent majority population. However, if such hostile displays seriously challenged the survival of majority group identity, the value- and symbol-conscious majorities would be expected, in theory, to quickly and resolutely quash them. With the source of symbolic challenge thus eliminated or plausibly "eliminatable," alarmism should not be expected to spread widely among majority populations. On the contrary, one would rather expect marginal minorities to be apprehensive about promulgating offensive symbols in fear of backlash reprisals. One would also need to account for cases such as the Russian Far East or the North Caucasus where symbolic-threat perceptions emerged with respect to marginal migrant groups such as the Chinese and the Meskhetian Turks that did not arrive in the host communities aggressively brandishing their ethnic symbols and that, in most cases, even lacked coherent ethnic elites who would activate these symbols to enhance collective identity. That symbolic threats may become strongly linked with marginal migrant minorities therefore has to be explained by something other than the logic of group identity and group symbols.

Threat Perception and Contact

Another theoretical perspective that does not directly relate immigration attitudes to migration scale is the "contact hypothesis" going back to Williams (1947). Are people more fearful of and hostile toward migrants if they interact with them less? Does contact across ethnic divides – in and of itself and independently of group status, goals, and political, social, economic, and cultural context – mitigate mutual animosities and prejudice? The strongest arguments in favor of the unconditional contact hypothesis emphasize the role of "acquaintance potential" (Cook 1962) or "friendship potential" (Pettigrew 1998). The notion of "potential" is central here. Friendship with one out-group member would logically create expectations that friendship with other out-group members is acceptable, if not desirable. Ethnic others would thus appear less threatening as a collectivity. Potential for friendship would reduce hostility. Despite the deployment of nonrecursive path models by Pettigrew (1998) and Wilson (1996) – a statistical technique enabling one to assess indirect and interactive effects of multiple causal variables on the outcome variable – the contact hypothesis continues to face the reversed causality challenge. Even with nonrecursive models, which ultimately depend on specification of linkages between variables that any researcher could draw differently, it is hard to rule out the claim that less-prejudiced people are more likely to seek friendship across ethnic lines in the first place. Regardless of what comes first, however, the contact hypothesis potentially offers a solution to at least one part of the threat perception versus marginal migration puzzle. Because contact is more likely if migration size is larger, this perspective may explain why hostility toward immigrants may actually diminish when migration levels increase or stay high. Other studies (Forbes 1997) found, however, that more-frequent and -widespread contact between culturally dissimilar groups is likely to increase intergroup hostility in many social contexts. Perhaps one of the most serious objections to the political relevance of contact comes from the experiences of massive brutality in the former Yugoslavia and in Rwanda, where thousands of lifelong friends ceased contact and became enemies in a matter of months or even days. These objections and disagreements aside, the contact hypothesis faces a serious methodological challenge with respect to the marginal migration puzzle: Variation in the relationship between realistic and symbolic threats and antimigrant hostility – in cases where migration rates are similarly low and contact unlikely – would still have to be explained by something other than friendship potential.

To sum up at this point, alarmism about national security arising from marginal migration is the principal paradox. And it raises an intriguing conceptual question: If putative causes of hostility toward marginal minorities vary from one context to another, while overreaction persists, does it mean that there is an independent exaggeration logic that drives threat perceptions? In fact, it is hard to imagine fear without exaggeration – as the Russian proverb puts it, "fear has humongous eyes" – meaning that the person who is scared would inevitably exaggerate the ostensible causes of fear. The very posing of this question suggests that powerful perceptual constants must come between variation in the demographic, political, and socioeconomic context of migration and variation in conflict proclivities. What are these putative constants? How and why would their effects vary from context to context? How much variation in antimigration hostility may they explain?

Immigration Phobia: The Phenomenon under Investigation and Its Dimensions

To begin addressing these questions, I defined the principal phenomenon under investigation in this study as immigration or migration phobia. The first part of this term refers to any movement of people across nation-state, provincial, county, municipal, or neighborhood boundaries – either for permanent resettlement or for temporary but prolonged stay. The term *migration* in this study thus encompasses legal and illegal immigrants, permanent and temporary settlers, all types of refugees, rural–urban migrants, traders, guest workers, migrant farmers, students, smugglers, and those tourists who also engage in trade or business on the side. In this interpretation, the emphasis is on two dimensions of migration and immigration: (1) movement of people and (2) the crossing of interstate or intergroup boundaries. It implies that seemingly the most innocuous forms of cross-boundary movements of people – such as recreational tourism – may engender exaggerated threats to the security of nations, provinces, neighborhoods, or individuals. This inclusive definition is largely consistent with the use of the term *migration* by the United Nations (United Nations 2001; see the Sources and Definitions section). Inclusiveness is also important conceptually and methodologically, as I will show further in this chapter.

The second part of the term *immigration phobia* encompasses threat perception or, simply put, fear. But the notion of phobia is broader than the notions of threat and fear. It relates to the core theoretical arguments in this volume and therefore deserves special attention. *Webster's Third New International Dictionary of the English Language* defines *phobia* as "an *exaggerated* and often disabling fear usually *inexplicable to the subject*, having occasionally a logical but usually an illogical or symbolic object, and serving to protect the ego against anxiety arising from unexpressed aggressive impulses [italics added]."

It is the emphasis on exaggeration and inexplicability of perceived threat that makes *phobia* a particularly appropriate word to describe the phenomenon under investigation in this study. In a sense, this term implies that uncertainty about the causes of real-world developments and exaggeration of their implications are precisely the perceptual mechanisms that make people threatened – whether these developments actually warrant caution or not. The description of the central phenomenon as immigration phobia implies that attributes of demographic, political, and socioeconomic contexts of migration get systematically filtered through a discrete perceptual logic that makes threat "exaggerated," "disabling," "illogical," and "symbolic" across diverse settings – albeit with varying intensity. This definition also links threat exaggeration with "aggressive impulses" or hostility. These two dimensions of the phobia definition – fear and hostility – are the principal phenomena under investigation in this study with respect to migration. The empirical paradoxes discussed in the preceding text, however, suggest that both are likely to arise, in part, from the discrete logic of exaggeration. The latter then must impact on threat–hostility formation independently of cognitive and emotional valuations associated with "real" interests, symbolic identity, and contact.

Threat, Its Attributive Correlates, and the Logic of Exaggeration

The logic of exaggeration is something that would tie together the situational and contextual attributes of migration that previous studies attempted to correlate with conflict – and that were found significant in some contexts, but not in others. To the extent that the logic of threat is inseparable from the logic of exaggeration, both need to be taken into account to improve our understanding of antimigrant sentiments.

Mathematical notation is helpful at this point to clarify the central question of this study and this volume's potential contribution to the international relations and migration literature. The underlying characteristic of previous attempts to examine migration's impact on proclivity for conflict – as summarized earlier in this chapter – is that systematic cross-national comparisons focused on *attributes* of migration context and *attributes* of conflict. In mathematical shorthand, attempts to test *attributive* theories of migration and conflict may be represented as follows:

$$T_i = f(a_{ij}m_j)$$

In this equation, T_i stands for the intensity of threat perception on the part of the host population i associated with migrants coming from a state or area j (hence, m_j), and a_{ij} represents political, socioeconomic, and cultural attributes or conditions of states or areas i and j. These attributes (a_{ij}) may include, among others, differences in military and economic power between sending and receiving states; availability of resources and job opportunities for host and migrant populations; immigration and emigration rules; and ethnic composition and density of host populations. Finally, m_j stands for the quantitative and qualitative attributes of in-migration, such as the number of incoming migrants, the rate of migration, and the ethnicity and regional background of migrants. Theories of realistic threat, symbolic threat, and contact can be formally represented as distinct interpretations of a_{ij} All of them, as the preceding discussion showed, incorporate m in the form of the size of the migrant (p_j) and incumbent (p_i) populations or their ratio.

Specifically, the realistic-threat argument can then be represented as

$$T_i = f\left(\frac{p_j}{R_i}\right),$$

where $R_i > 0$ stands for resources available to incumbent groups. In short, the scarcer the resources and the larger the scale of migration, the more the incumbents are likely to feel concerned about their security.

The symbolic-threat argument may then be written as

$$T_i = f\left(\frac{G_{ij}\, p_j}{p_i}\right),$$

where ΔG_{ij} represents identity distinctiveness and, by extension, the salience of group markers, including ethnicity and cultural or ideological values. In this way, both the potency of group symbols – their cognitive and emotional appeal – and the balances of ethnic population would interactively influence threat.

The contact hypothesis can be formalized more simply as

$$T_i = f\left(\frac{1}{C_{ij}}\right),$$

where $C_{ij} > 0$ represents the percentage of incumbent population having informal contacts – and thus the acquaintance and friendship potential – with migrants. The p_j/p_i ratio is redundant because contact frequency is likely to be a function of the proportion of incoming migrants. Moreover, to be theoretically consistent, one has to assume that the contact effects are going to be stronger than population ratio effects in and of themselves. It follows that the higher the proportion of migrants and, consequently, the higher the volume of intergroup contact, the lower the perceived threat to security (i.e, the "melting pot" model of immigration acceptance).

The synthetic model of threat perception, based on integration of these three formulas following standard algebra, will then be represented as:

$$T_i = f\left(\frac{G_{ij}\, p_j^2}{p_i\, R_{ij}\, C_{ij}}\right).$$

This transformation illustrates the intrinsic importance of population size (p_j is squared in the synthetic model of threat) in existing mainstream theories of antimigrant hostility. In short, ethnic conflict and prejudice should not arise when the ratio of migrants to incumbents approximates 0 – as, in fact, it does in many host states where antimigrant sentiments are systemic and widespread.

Now, in what way is threat a *function* (*f*) of the specified variables? Given the importance of perceptions, let us examine this equation thinking of f as covering some form of perceptual logic (E) that modifies each variable. One can then transform the synthetic model as

$$T_i = f\left(\frac{G_{ij}\, p_j^2}{p_i\, R_{ij}}\right)\frac{1}{C_{ij}},$$

assuming on the basis of the earlier literature review that real and symbolic threats have a significant perceptual component, whereas contact measures predominantly represent behavioral experience (spending leisure time together with members of out-groups, or not). The logic of threat is essentially irreducible to G_{ij}, p_j, p_i, and R_{ij}. It has to be estimated by identifying measures for EG_{ij}, Ep_j, Ep_i, and ER_{ij}. Another way to get into this logic can be gleaned from Gerstle's (2004) identification of historically persistent drivers of antiimmigrant hostility in the United States as "fear of religious subversion," "fear of political subversion," "fear of economic subversion," and "fear of racial subversion." Viewing them as a set of statements, one observes that fear and subversion are constant, whereas the conceptual "transmission mechanisms" between them – religion, power, economic interest, and race – vary. The actual driver of hostility in each of the four factors is an interaction of attributes (e.g., religion or race) and perceived subversiveness potential (or intent) of an out-group. The preceding formula makes a sharp distinction between the attributive and perceptual components of hostility, while at the same time emphasizing that both affect hostility interactively. The following parts of the chapter will address the logic of E, after first specifying the threat–hostility dimensions of immigration phobia (the dependent variables in this study).

Threat Perception

This concept refers to fear or insecurity or general perception of threat, and it is synonymous with dread, fright, alarm, anxiety, disquiet, angst, and apprehension. The theoretical emphasis is on the *magnitude* of perceived threat or the level of insecurity, in a sense that an individual experiences fear or anxiety about his/her personal, group, or national security. *Security* in this definition refers to physical conditions (absence of action that could physically harm individuals or groups results in forced displacement or dispersal of groups or leads to disintegration or colonization of states). This emphasis has crucial methodological implications. In the field of migration, for example, scholars such as Myron Weiner and Warren Zimmermann have conceptualized threats in more context-specific terms. These specific migration-induced threats include threat of insurrection against the sending state, terrorism threat in the host country, threat of cultural "invasion" of a host society, threat to local jobs, or threat of crime (Zimmermann 1995: 90–1). The security-oriented definition of *threat* in this study would encompass Zimmerman's notion of threat of insurrection and terrorism, but not threat of job competition or cultural invasion. In this regard, the concept of threat in the present study differs from the notions of "realistic group threat" and "symbolic prejudice" (for a cogent comparison, see McLaren 2003: 915–17). Key measures related to these concepts – for example, personal income, risk of unemployment, sense of economic competition with migrants, migration effects on income and job opportunities, or sense of group distinctiveness – are used as independent variables in this study.

By default, terms such as *realistic threat* and *symbolic threat* conflate perceptions of security and perceptions of its putative causes. In this sense, they are double-barreled conceptualizations – and their empirical measures in existing studies are not necessarily measures of threat. For example, the notion of "threat of job competition" commingles perceptions of migration's effects on the job market and the host population's sense of security – something that can be caused by factors other than employment prospects. In contrast, by separating perceptions of socioeconomic, political, and cultural implications of migration from general perceptions of threat (sense of fear or insecurity ultimately related to individual or group fears of physical integrity and survival), the present study allows one to account for individuals in a host society who may perceive migration as having a negative effect on local demographic, or political, or economic conditions, yet who would not necessarily feel more concerned about their personal, group, or national security than others because of that. (And as the opinion data analyses show later in this volume, this happens more often than one would think.) Similarly, the distinction between perceived *magnitude of threat* and its putative context-specific *correlates* would allow one to make an assumption that individuals may perceive migration's political or economic effects as positive, yet nevertheless feel more concerned about security than individuals who do not share these positive perceptions. Methodologically speaking, this definition of threat perception enables one to hold independent variables as clearly exogenous and the dependent variable (threat perception) as clearly endogenous – a critical element enabling meaningful substantive inference in social inquiry (King, Keohane, and Verba 1994).

Lauren McLaren of the University of Oxford, England, provides some powerful evidence suggesting that threat perception originates in something that is separate and distinct from the logic of both self-interest and identity. In a statistical analysis of the Eurobarometer 1997 survey conducted in the EU, McLaren (2003: 922) reported that both economic- and symbolic-threat measures had a highly significant correlation with preferences for expulsion of migrants in all fifteen EU member states and in separate samples from East Germany and Northern Ireland. Realistic threat was measured as perceived immigration impact on education, social services, and employment opportunities. Correlation coefficients ranged from .16 for Greece to .43 in Belgium. Symbolic threat was measured by items about immigration's impact on religion and culture, and correlation coefficients ranged from .16 in Greece to .45 in Belgium. What attracted my attention, however, was the pattern of correlations between these two types of threat and preferences for expulsion by country. They varied mostly in sync. EU member states in which realistic-threat measures correlated with support for expulsion of migrants more strongly than in others were also the states where symbolic-threat measures correlated with support for expulsion more strongly than in others. The more self-interest mattered, the more identity mattered. The less self-interest mattered, the less identity mattered. Methodologically, this phenomenon is termed multicollinearity – a situation when two explanatory variables have a significant relationship with one another. When this happens, one is always prudent to ask whether the phenomenon under investigation is caused by neither of the explanatory variables, but by something else, to which both relate strongly. And in fact, correlation between the effects of realistic threat and symbolic threat on preference for expulsion of immigrants – that I estimated across EU member states (McLaren 2003: 922, Table 3) – was much stronger (Pearson $R = .92$, significant at .001 level) than the relationship between each type of threat and preference for expulsion (maximum Pearson R was .45). At the same time, I found that the relationship between expulsion preferences and either realistic or symbolic threat had nothing to do with the migration share in EU member states' population. The correlation was statistically insignificant – that is, the threat-exclusionism complex related to migration size with the probability no higher than chance ($R = .19$, $p = .506$, and $N = 17$). This tentatively suggests that while economic self-interest and identity affect antimigrant hostility, both are themselves a function of the logic of threat that affects perceptions of real and symbolic competition independently.

In the United States, Huddy and Sears (1995: 133) made a special effort to draw "a clear, sharp theoretical contrast between prejudice and realistic interest theories" of racial and ethnic attitudes. Despite this effort, the authors' analysis of mass survey data revealed that Anglo opposition to bilingual education programs related significantly both to ethnic composition of polling areas and a sense of educational conflict between them and the Latinos (ibid.: 142). The authors' concession of their inability "to clearly separate the determinants of the two approaches" is another indication that prejudicial attitudes – many of them forming through symbolic interactions – and perception of "real threats" to group status are both likely to be anchored in other factors. One of them is the discrete logic of threat.

Conceptualization of threat in this study – isolating perceived physical insecurity from its putative symbolic and realistic correlates – enables one to measure individual expressions of fear or anxiety regardless of what cognitive or emotional factors may give rise to them. In this sense, the definition of threat – or the "Fear narrative" in the words of Roger Petersen (2002) – is also distinct from theoretical accounts that attribute systematic differences in threat assessment to the social status of the perceiver. In other words, the definition of threat as a perception in this project is not contingent on whether threat is self-, mass-, or elite-driven. Everyone can hypothetically exaggerate threat. Nor is relative group size – estimated independently from the groups in question – a necessary condition for threat perception, as implied in game theoretic formulations. Perhaps one of the best exemplars of this approach – Weingast's (1994, quoted in Petersen 2002: 69) "reciprocal vulnerability" game – stipulates approximately equal group size as a necessary condition for situations in which lack of credible commitment to cooperation would make threat the predominant factor in behavioral choice.

Hostility

The accompanying dimension of immigration phobia is intergroup hostility – or proclivity of members of one ethnic group for aggressive responding[5] against another ethnic group. Hostility, in this sense, is synonymous with enmity, ill will, animosity, antagonism, hatred, malice,

[5] While an analogous term exists in clinical psychology and medical research, we use it here in a limited sense to denote aggressive political and social behavior expressed through verbal statements and symbolic and physical acts, or policies. The notion of "responding" – while similar to that of "action," "acts," or "behavior" – emphasizes interactivity and retaliatory logic in the emergence of interethnic tensions and violence.

or "aggressive impulses" in Webster's definition of *phobia*. Defining interethnic hostility as one's proclivity for aggressive responding to acts by members of other ethnic groups implies that (1) interethnic hostility is likely to vary among individuals under similar political and socioeconomic conditions; (2) it is likely to be affected by individual perceptions of these conditions – directly and indirectly through the general sense of threat; (3) it will be revealed when individuals are asked how they are likely to respond to ostensibly threatening activities of the ethnic "others" (in this sense, it encompasses elements of retaliatory logic); and (4) it is not necessarily (and often is not) a rational and proportionate response to actions of other ethnic groups.

Defined as proclivity for aggressive responding, hostility implies support for measures that would force the newcomers to return to their places of origin. Such measures may include border closure; street sweeps in search of illegal migrants; or forced deportation of migrants. At the same time, the concept of hostility is broad enough to account for diverse psychological inputs that may generate such aggressive proclivities. This concept, for example, would encompass two principal cognitive–emotional pathways to interethnic violence identified by Roger Petersen (2002). The first pathway originates in "cognitive" or "instrumental" emotions – principally, resentment, fear, and hatred – whereby "the source of the process is an observable change in status, power, and overall condition." (ibid.: 75). The second source of interethnic violence according to Petersen has to do with "noninstrumental" emotions such as rage – "a path centered on the overwhelming desire to simply lash out" (ibid.: 76). Conceptualization of hostility in the present study would measure variation in individual proclivities for antimigrant action regardless of whether these individuals may be driven by "instrumental" emotions or by "noninstrumental" impulses.

It is important to distinguish between hostility as proclivity for aggressive responding and commonly used but variably defined concepts such as prejudice and intolerance. Similar to these concepts, hostility involves emotional valuation (enmity, animosity). But unlike prejudice, hostility, as defined in this study, is more than and distinct from "antipathy based upon a faulty and inflexible generalization" (Allport 1979 [1954]: 9) or "antipathy accompanied by a faulty generalization" (Pettigrew 1980: 821). Hostility is rather a translation of antipathy and "faulty and inflexible generalization" into ideas for specific action(s) directed against ethnic "others." In fact, Gordon Allport, the author of the classic study on prejudice, drew attention to this distinction between what people feel or think about and how they actually act toward groups they dislike: "Two employers, for example, may dislike Jews to an equal degree. One may keep his feelings to himself and may hire Jews on the same basis as any workers – perhaps because he wants to gain goodwill for his factory or store in the Jewish community. The other may translate his dislike into his employment policy." Allport (1979 [1954]: 14–15) identifies five stages of hostile action that are likely to arise from prejudice, "from the least energetic to the most:" (1) negative language ("antilocution"); (2) avoidance; (3) discrimination; (4) physical attacks; and (5) extermination.

In these terms, the phenomenon under investigation – or the dependent variable – in this study is the intensity of support for translating dislike into policy. Aggressive responding, in my definition, encompasses primarily the third and the fourth "degrees of negative action" as defined by Allport: exclusionist discrimination and physical attack. The first two are still rather passive expressions of antipathy, whereas the fifth is the extreme and final expression of antipathy and thus of less interest in the project that aims at identifying early signals of hostile action. In Allport's conception of prejudice, the proclivity for discrimination and physical attack would themselves be a credible warning of likely extermination and genocide. In relation to these proclivities, "prejudice" in the Allportian sense is one of the hypothetical causal variables.

Similarly, the term *intolerance* does not necessarily imply proclivity or readiness to *initiate* offensive behavior, as does my conceptualization of hostility. As "the lack of an ability to endure" or "exceptional sensitivity" – based on the Webster dictionary definitions – intolerance may overlap partially but not coincide with hostility because an intolerant individual may choose avoidance rather than retaliation as a response to threat. Intolerance could be passive, just as racism or racial appeals may be concealed or "implicit" (Mendelburg 2001), and it refers to a general psychological incapacity to endure any real-world condition, such as presence of out-group members. In other words, hostility may be conceptualized as actively manifested and actualized intolerance. But hostility has other sources as well. The practical implication of these distinctions is that individuals identified as prejudiced or intolerant in prior sociological and psychological research would not necessarily qualify as hostile in this study. In this study, I will use the terms *prejudice* and *intolerance* in reference to negative group stereotypes – treated as explanatory variables exogenous to fear and hostility.[6]

[6] Quillian (1995: 592–3), for example, uses Eurobarometer survey data to construct a prejudice index that commingles perceived group stereotypes and effects of group

Finally, hostility in this study is understood as individual expression of their own proclivities, rather than as valuation of the outsiders' proclivity for violent behavior. In this regard, this research project is distinct from the study of ethnic prejudices in Italy by Sniderman et al. (2000: 151, 178–9). In their study, four out of thirteen survey items that measure "hostility toward immigrants" reflect views of out-groups rather than the proclivities of in-group members. The natives are coded as more antiimmigrant if they see immigrants as prone to crime, not law-abiding, intrusive, and violent. (The remaining nine items all measure either the qualities of migrants that are not related to violence, e.g., honesty; or the impact of immigration, e.g., increased demand for public services.) While the assessment that others are prone to violence could relate to one's own proclivity for aggressive responding, the two measures are not necessarily the same. Not all individuals who see other groups as predisposed to violence would be willing to initiate violence against them preemptively. Conversely, not all the natives who would favor coercive exclusionist policies against migrants would necessarily see them as inherently violent.

The Threat–Hostility Nexus

One way to conceive of fear and hostility is to view them as inward- and outward-oriented aspects of immigration phobia. Fear pertains to perception of outside forces targeting the state, the group, or the individual. Hostility pertains to preferences forming inside the state, the group, or the individual mind for responding to these outside forces. In their dual unity, fear and hostility are the yin and yang of immigration phobia and of threat perception more generally. Fear is about threats that one faces from outsiders. Hostility is about threats one wants outsiders to face in response.

The notion of dual unity between fear and hostility has strong empirical support with appropriate individual-level data in psychological research. Psychoanalysts have traditionally linked fear of extinction with hostility. Schafer (1999) conducted experiments showing that participants who felt more safe and secure than others were more likely to opt for cooperative as opposed to combative policy choices. Examining the attitudes of East German youth toward non-Germans with structural equation models, Watts (1996) found that threat was a more powerful predictor than

activities. In this study, I use narrower, more specific measures that allow me to measure the relationship between perceived effects of migrants separately from intergroup stereotypes, fear, and proclivity for interethnic aggressive action (hostility).

right-wing extremism of political xenophobia. She defined the latter as "the desire or willingness to use public policy to discriminate against foreigners" (Watts 1996: 97) – a definition largely consistent with the conceptualization of hostility in this study. With correlation and variance analysis of public opinion and national security surveys of the Jaffee Center for Strategic Studies at Tel Aviv University and the surveys of the Palestinian Center for Policy and Survey Research in Ramallah from 1986 to 1999, Gordon and Arian (2001) found that "the more threatened people feel, the more incendiary the policy choice is – and vice versa." Israeli respondents, for example, who believed that the Arabs, "in the final analysis," aspired to conquer Israel and kill the Jews were likely to completely oppose the establishment of the Palestinian state (even though the establishment of the Palestinian state is not necessarily a precondition for greater Palestinian violence). From 1986 to 1999, as the number of Israeli respondents who found Arab aspirations threatening decreased from about 75 to 40 percent, the number of respondents supporting the Palestinian state increased from about 20 to over 50 percent (Gordon and Arian 2001: 202).

At the same time, it is important to acknowledge that while fear and hostility are closely related, mass fear does not necessarily lead to mass hostility. Whereas exaggerated fears are found in nearly every case of migration, concomitant hostility rarely gets so intense as to engender organized violence against migrants. In two of the world's areas where interethnic tensions and fears have been most apparent since the end of the Cold War – Africa and the former Soviet Union – violent conflict occurred only in a fraction of interethnic dyads (Fearon and Laitin 1996). Another telling piece of evidence pointing to distance between fear and hostility is the nature of anti-Islamic reactions in the EU after the September 11, 2001 attacks on the World Trade Center and the Pentagon. Despite a surge in public threat perceptions associated with Arab and Muslim populations across the EU member states, no mass racist acts of violence against members of the Muslim communities were recorded in the first month after the attacks – precisely when one would expect acts of "lashing out" and revenge (European Monitoring Center on Racism and Xenophobia 2001).

In this study, I assume that while threat perception is an important correlate of hostility, the degree of association between the two would vary contextually – as it would between threat and its social and psychological antecedents. This formulation differs markedly from Petersen's (2002: 75) argument that the fear–violence linkage can only be tested if "an actual

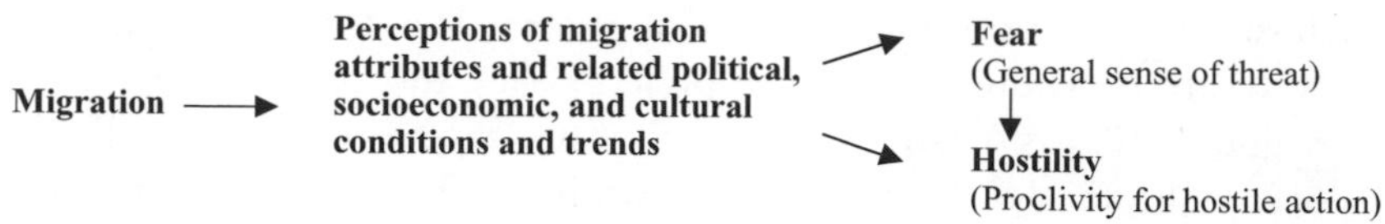

FIGURE 1.1. Two Dimensions of Immigration Phobia.

fear does exist." And "actual fear," as Peterson argues, would in turn require that "individual groups have the mutual ability to inflict physical attacks against each other" (ibid.). From here, Petersen extrapolates that if Group A attacks Group B and Group B is not the one that has the highest ability to inflict physical attacks on Group A, then the attack of A on B must have been caused by something other than threat. However, this framing of the threat–violence linkage underestimates that threat can play this role in multiple ways – for example, by amplifying resentment, hatred, or other emotions.

Given these considerations, the principal question is how perceived attributes of migration and its context – through the perceptual logic of threat exaggeration – would affect individual sense of general fear and individual proclivities for aggressive responding to migration, as outlined in Figure 1.1.

2

The Immigration Security Dilemma

Anarchy, Offensiveness, and "Groupness"

From its origins in ancient political philosophy, the field of international relations has dealt with excessive "securitization" of individual and group behavior that is central to the logic of threat exaggeration. Particular emphasis has been paid to the pervasiveness – if not supreme utility – of fear and mistrust amidst stated intentions for peace. "Who wants peace must prepare for war" has been a policy prescription consistent with political realism since antiquity. In "The Melian Dialogue," Thucydides (1972: 403, 408) articulated the importance of preemptive power enhancement under uncertainty, pointing out that military weakness exposed any society to reckless behavior, slaughter, and enslavement by any hitherto unsubdued state or group of outsiders. In modern political science, this problem has been extensively theorized as the security dilemma. This theoretical perspective has provided parsimonious and nontrivial insights into the logic of interstate behavior underlying World War I (Snyder 1985) and the nuclear arms race during the Cold War (Herz 1966; Jervis 1976, 1978), as well as into the logic of violent interethnic conflict in the post–Cold War era (Collins 2004; Glaser 1997; Kaufman 1996, 2001; Lake and Rothchild 1996; Posen 1993; Roe 1999, 2000; Snyder and Jervis 1999). At its core, the security-dilemma theory in all its variants focuses on perceptual and behavioral implications of anarchy – understood as the lack of central authority and enforceable rules among either states or nonstate actors that may credibly serve to punish rule violators and to compel allies and friends to come to one's assistance. Absence or weakness of central government authority or intragroup authority activates desire for self-preservation and concern for relative power (Jervis 1978). When all individuals or states strive to protect their own security, others grow more apprehensive and the ensuing cycle of mutually reinforcing suspicions leads to less security at a higher cost for all. The original conceptualization of the security dilemma by John Herz (1950: 157) emphasized this linkage between authority strength and the yearning for preemptive self-defense even in the absence of clear and present threats to security: "Whenever such anarchic society has existed – and it has existed in most periods of known history on some level – there has arisen what may be called the security dilemma of men, or groups, or their leaders. Groups or individuals living in such a constellation must be, and usually are, concerned about their security from being attacked, subjected, dominated or annihilated by other groups and individuals. Striving to attain security from such attack, they are driven to acquire more and more power in order to escape the power of others. This, in turn, renders the others more insecure and compels them to prepare for the worst."

In the decades that followed this concept "launch," mainstream definitions of the security dilemma in the field of international relations implicitly or explicitly emphasized the balance of perceived security among individuals, groups, or states and their corresponding behavior. Butterfield (1951: 21) saw "the peculiar characteristic" of international relations as the interaction of fears and counterfears in which worst-case scenarios were likely to turn into self-actualizing tragedies. Jervis (1978: 169) defined the *security dilemma* as a situation whereby "the means by which a state tries to increase its security decrease the security of others." Snyder (1985: 153) went further by positing that the anarchic international environment created incentives for states to *require* the insecurity of others. These and other existing definitions reflect the predominant tendency in the field of International Relations (IR) to model the security dilemma as a behavioral outcome, as reciprocal acquisition of power, as an interactive dynamic, or as the ensuing chain of action–retaliation underlying arms races or ethnic mobilization. The action–reaction, or "spiral" dynamic, has been central to the advancement of the security-dilemma theory and the evaluation of case studies. Schelling (1960: 207) described the perceptual logic of the spiral in a way applicable not only to interstate wars, but also to any situation where individuals or groups may experience reciprocal fears that the other would harm them first in self-defense. An armed burglar and a house occupant who suddenly discovered him may both wish the burglar simply left quietly. But even in that case, "there is danger that he may think I want to shoot, and shoot first. Worse, there is danger that he may think that I think he means to shoot. Or he may think that I think he thinks I want to shoot. And so on."

Most advanced scholarship in IR focused on theoretical challenges posed by the inherent difficulty for any outside analyst to distinguish either *ex ante* or *ex post facto* the offensive versus defensive and security versus predatory motivations of actors – with Wheeler and Booth (1996: 31) aptly observing that when a state accurately perceives threats, it is not in a security dilemma situation. At the same time, a considerable and growing body of research has examined the perceptual logic of this systematic failure to accurately assess threat. What in retrospect one may call the security races among state or ethnic groups – resulting in diminishing security for all – have been linked to the effects of exaggeration of offensive advantages and the scale of power shifts (Snyder 1985: 155, 161–4); "information failures" leading to mutual concealment of motivations by competing groups or states (Lake and Rothchild 1996: 132–3); unsustainability of credible commitments (ibid., 133–7); and increasing acquisition of tangible and especially symbolic sovereignty attributes by ethnic groups (Kaufman 1996: 151; 2001). Glaser (1997) extended the theory by specifying more precisely how increasing one's own security at the expense of others may reduce the state's own relative military capabilities, increase the adversaries' incentives for expansion, and waste money. With respect to interethnic and intersocietal relations, Waever et al. (1993), along with other scholars of the Copenhagen School, suggested that association of identity with survival would also give rise to escalating retaliatory clashes between majority and minority nationalisms within states.

While increasingly sophisticated and persuasive, the existing research principally focuses on conflict and mass violence as dependent variables. The present study diverges from this line of theorizing in IR. The principal dependent variable under investigation is perceptions rather than behavior and their origins more than their implications. It is hostility rather than violent conflict. The perceptual logic examined in this book is that of the origins of hostility before the speculative thought spirals of the I-think-he-thinks-I think-he-may-shoot-me-first kind become widespread in intergroup relations. Instead, this study asks: How does one side in an interaction that could conceivably develop into a self-perpetuating tragedy of preemptive action–retaliation initially come to develop the sense of threat and predisposition for aggressive response to threat? Do people feel threatened for reasons specified in the security-dilemma theory – to what extent, when, and how do anarchy, information failures, credibility, identity distinctiveness, or economic deprivation matter? Does variation in perceived sociopolitical conditions associated with the security dilemma in theory relate significantly to variation in perceived threat and hostility among individuals? Which dimensions of what may be called the perceptual security-dilemma complex are most significant predictors of interethnic suspicions, fears, and hostility? I use the security dilemma as a searchlight – in a Popperian sense – and direct the beam at migration. In doing so, I hope not only to illuminate the logic of antimigrant alarmism and hostility, but also to explore the potency of the theoretical searchlight. In the coming chapters, I will examine these questions in detail and formulate specific propositions testable with mass survey data.

Meanwhile, it must be noted that this study focuses on the perceptual correlates of threat assessment. The security dilemma's assumption that decline of government authority ("emerging anarchy") would engender concerns about security – self-perpetuating fears and suspicions breeding hostility and conflict – becomes a testable empirical question. Central to the realist perspective on the security dilemma, this assumption has been challenged by scholars espousing the constructivist view of world politics – with Alexander Wendt (1992: 407) famously arguing that "anarchy is what states make of it" and that, consequently, "security dilemmas are not given by anarchy or nature."[1] However, looking retrospectively at the origins of the concept that he pioneered, Herz (2003: 412–13) emphasized that the security dilemma was not something exclusively stemming from power realities and anarchy as an "innate psychological condition," but that it was first and foremost a "sociopolitical" phenomenon. This study therefore starts with the assumption that actual or anticipated shifts in ethnic balance would not automatically harden into security-dilemma situations even in near anarchical environments. The book investigates with opinion survey data why individual fears of ethnic "other" newcomers may differ widely in the same fear-producing environments. This focus on the origins of perceptions advances the line of inquiry implicit in the words of caution by Snyder and Jervis (1999: 24) that the security dilemma is "a social situation with social and perceptual causes, not simply a fact of nature. None of the elements that fuels the security dilemma – neither anarchy, nor offensive advantages, nor expectations that others will defect – can be taken for granted as unproblematic givens." But if the security dilemma is flexible, if it is not "simply part of the furniture of inter-state affairs" as Butfoy (1997: 35) puts it, what would explain

[1] And, as Glaser (1997: 198) points out, Wendt's alternative prescription for state behavior under socially constructed anarchy is "essentially the signaling behavior envisioned by realists who emphasize the role of the security dilemma." The argument thus becomes circular.

variation in suspicion, mistrust, alarmism, and support for preventive mobilization across states, groups, or individuals?

The emphasis on the origins and variability of individual threat perceptions in this volume contributes precisely to the advancement of our understanding of the intersubjective and sociopolitical dimensions of the security dilemma that are consistent with Herz's original definition of the concept cited earlier in this chapter. The logic of threat perception in this definition is the logic of threat exaggeration that transcends variation in political and socioeconomic environment, yet that remains sensitive to it and grounded in it. It is the logic of "what if" or "what might be" and how it is linked to the observed "what is." It is also, in this sense, an emotional logic, with nervous tension arising from conflicting impulses that come with visualizing the multiple "what ifs" and their implications. It is the logic of anxiety that feeds on contradictory impulses built into the "what ifs" of life.[2] And it is a socially grounded speculative logic. It implies that distant or even nonexistent threats are likely to appear credible to "men, groups, or their leaders" whenever they find themselves in a "constellation" with outsiders yet without central authority that could enforce contracts. In other words, to understand how and why hypothetical or speculative threats may become credible is to understand how threats become exaggerated or overblown. The security dilemma therefore explains why threats blown out of seemingly rational proportion would nevertheless have solid basis in social reality. Similarly, the logic of retaliation to overrated threats under the security dilemma is the logic of exaggerated hostility, disproportionate to the social phenomena that may cause it. The refocusing of the emphasis in the analysis of the security dilemma from behavioral outcomes (e.g., arms races and ethnic mobilization) to perceptual outcomes (e.g., threat and hostility) makes it possible to investigate whether interethnic perceptions and attitudes are likely to be grounded in the social logic of the security dilemma and to model these valuations. In other words, the security dilemma should explain not

[2] This conceptualization challenges the assertion by Petersen (2002: 68) that in social research – drawing predominantly on the security-dilemma theories of international relations – accounts of "the Fear narrative" "never directly refer to any microlevel mechanisms at all, let alone emotions." Whereas the Emotion narrative – to use Petersen's formulation – may be indeed rare in conceptualizations of threat in IR, the Uncertainty narrative – richly developed in the literature – is, in essence, the Emotion narrative that examines both behavioral microfoundations and implications of Anxiety underlying threat assessment (whether this is expressed in common prose or in the symbolic language of game theory).

only ethnic wars, but interethnic hostility – long before the knives are sharpened and the guns are loaded.

How does immigration phobia fit into this picture? The short answer is: surprisingly well. The perceptual logic of immigration phobia – at least in theory – is strikingly consistent with the perceptual logic of the interethnic security dilemma (although the action–retaliation logic differs substantially, as will be discussed later in this book). As Posen (1993: 103) reminds us, the interethnic security dilemma refers to obsession with relative power "when proximate groups of people suddenly find themselves newly responsible for their own security." But by what process would groups "suddenly find themselves newly responsible" in such situations? All studies of the security dilemma reviewed by this author refer in this respect to the weakening of central government authority – with the collapse of communism in the former Yugoslavia and the Soviet Union presenting classic examples. In other words, ethnic dyads remain the same, while authority weakens. Migration is another process by which groups of people are likely to "suddenly find themselves newly responsible" for their security. While government authority remains the same, the number of ethnic dyads changes through the influx of newcomers – or at least signals to incumbent groups that it may change in the future. Governments may be strong, but they may not necessarily know how to deal with the migrants, contributing to uncertainty and concern about security among the host populations. Viewed through the lenses of the security dilemma, migration – as cross-border movement of ethnically heterogeneous populations – is a process that makes different groups potentially insecure not because government authority suddenly declines, but because these groups become suddenly proximate. Moreover, because any influx of migrants may be ascribed to government failure, host populations are likely to develop a suspicion that their government becomes weaker, even though the opposite may be the case. The governments then face an immigration policy dilemma in very much the same way they face the arms race dilemma. The appearance of being soft on immigration is likely to undermine domestic support for the government. But pursuing a tough restrictionist policy may result in economic costs, and it may criminalize immigration – exacerbating exactly the problems that need to be resolved.

In this sense, the security dilemma directly addresses the central theoretical puzzle of the present study – consistent and paradoxical overrating of the threat that underlies immigration phobia, even when migration generates economic benefits for host societies. The security dilemma also directly addresses the dual unity of threat perception and hostile response.

One of the theory's tenets is that under uncertainty individuals become insecure and prone to manipulative political messages. This context would therefore increasingly prime them for preemptive retaliation against a suspected adversary. Thus, by threatening to change the ethnic makeup of states or parts of states – however illusory the threat – migration conjures up the specter of interethnic security dilemma. The arrival of a new ethnic group into any society explicitly or implicitly triggers the question: "Is it a threat? How much of a threat? Will the threat grow or diminish over time?" (Posen 1993: 103).

Four dimensions of this logic are paramount: a sense of anarchy (decline of central authority and, hence, government capacity to settle intergroup conflicts in the face of shifting ethnic population balances); uncertainty whether the intentions of out-groups are defensive or offensive; a sense of the other group's distinctiveness and cohesiveness, or "groupness"; and a sense of one's group's or state's economic vulnerability. The stronger these perceptions, the harder they would drive threat exaggeration and chronic mistrust typical of immigration phobia – even in cases where desire for cooperation is shared by different groups.

First, the very fact of migration (especially illegal migration across state borders) could be perceived as a symptom of declining state sovereignty and impotency of government sanctions or regulatory rules. If migration becomes associated with anarchy in this fashion, it is likely to be treated with suspicion. By threatening the majority position of "incumbent" ethnic groups, migration would make these groups more likely to view competition for power as key to their security. In this sense, perceptions of government weakness would make host communities more vulnerable to the intrusion of outsiders, while the very arrival of outsiders would signal government weakness. Thus, concern about government capacity is likely to feed on concern about ethnic balance, and vice versa, engendering escalating threat perception. Second, there is a shadow of uncertainty about the intention of migrants. Ethnic incumbents could rarely, if ever, trust guarantees that even a small trickle of newcomers is not the proverbial thin end of the wedge, that marginal migration today is not a migration's equivalent of a nuclear chain reaction ten years from now – for example, that temporary migrant laborers are not going to settle down, that they are not going to attract their friends and relatives, and that the latter may not one day claim political power and sovereignty. In this sense, "offensive" intentions of migrants are hard to distinguish from "defensive" ones – no matter what actual intentions are and how strongly they are articulated. This uncertainty also amplifies histories of territorial claims and records of offensive military activity by migrant groups or sending states in receiving societies. Third, migration brings into contact distinct populations, activating the sense of group differences and the proclivity to ascribe "groupness" to outsiders. While engendering and reinforcing prejudices, negative stereotypes, and the sense that outsiders are undesirable, these perceptions would also furnish the incentives for political entrepreneurs to actively use and manipulate ethnic mythologies and emotionally charged cultural symbols in the struggle for power. Fourth, migration is likely to cause insecurity through a complex sense of economic vulnerability that is discussed separately in Chapter 4.

The immigration security dilemma would not necessarily lead to "dogfights" between the majority host populations and the migrants. Instead, the spiral logic may morph into exclusionist policies with unexpectedly high economic and social costs. As uncertainty about migration consequences rises, governments have the incentives to impose restrictionist policies and treat migration as a security issue. Migrants would then be likely to respond by devising evasive strategies both to enter host states and to gain a foothold in their economies. This would translate into higher rates of illegal migration and clandestine human trafficking increasingly linked to organized crime. Episodic news about these developments would make host populations feel that increasingly restrictive measures had been justified and need to be intensified, turning the negative consequences of immigration into self-fulfilling prophecies in a vicious circle of mutual suspicions.

Finally, this is more than an application of an existing theory to a new problem area; it is a move beyond the pattern of sophisticated theoretical work on the security dilemma backed up by interpretative case studies in most of which mass violence had already occurred (e.g., contributions to Walter and Snyder [1999] by Doyle [1999], Figueiredo and Weingast [1999], Jones [1999], Kaufmann [1999], Laitin [1999], and Woodward [1999], and separate studies by Collins [1998], Lischer [1999], and Roe [2000]). The present analysis of immigration phobia is done with the hope of advancing our understanding of the security dilemma implications with systematic analysis of large-N, individual-level data prior to violence.

"Emerging" Anarchy: Migration as a Sign of State Weakness

Migration (especially illegal migration across state borders) is often perceived as a sign of declining state sovereignty. The very fact that ethnic "others" are capable to cross state borders and are hard to control once inside the host state sets the stage for increasing concerns of the host populations about security. The weakening of central government authority – while most evident in failing states after the demise of colonial and communist rule (Esty et al. 1998) – has been associated more broadly with the interactivity between "transnationalism" and "subgroupism" at the global level (Rosenau 1997: 48). Migration epitomizes both transnationalism and subgroupism by increasing the number and prominence of subdivisions among populations of states whose borders the migrants cross. With the proportion of noncitizens now ranging from 5 to 25 percent in most industrialized countries and reaching more than 50 percent in the oil-producing countries of the Persian Gulf, Myron Weiner notes that at the global level migration creates "nations without borders" (Weiner 1996: 128). One recent study of immigration and ethnic relations in the EU linked the rise in "explosive public conflicts and deep rifts among political elites" over migration and state identity with simultaneous "threats of globalization from without and pluralization from within" (Koopmans and Statham 2000: 1).

The sense of emergent anarchy has two aspects that would arguably drive immigration phobia. The first aspect is perceived capacity of government institutions representing the host populations – and therefore the "incumbent" ethnic group or groups – to prevent, mitigate, or settle intergroup disputes. The weaker this perceived capacity, the greater the likelihood that the incumbent groups will feel uncertain and fearful for their future. Drawing on the security-dilemma logic, the stronger the sense of anarchy, the stronger the likelihood that security will be the primary concern of individuals and groups. An increase in migration – the more sudden and sizeable – would therefore give rise to feelings among incumbent groups that their "political organizations do not care" about them (Posen 1993: 104). At the same time, the perceptual logic of the emergent anarchy under the security dilemma also suggests that migration rates per se may not necessarily relate directly to immigration phobia. If migration continues at any pace at the time when central government authority weakens – and the perception that "political organizations don't care" increases – exaggerated threat perceptions are likely to emerge. This may result not necessarily from the weakening or collapse of nation-state governments, as in the case of the former Soviet Union, but also from delegation of state sovereignty to international institutions on issues such as border crossing, as in the cases of the EU, the North Atlantic Free Trade Agreement (NAFTA), and Mercosur member states. Following

Herber Blumer's (1958) study of race prejudice, it is important to recognize that incumbent ethnic groups facing in-migration are likely to feel especially vulnerable if no reassurance is forthcoming that the government agencies are capable enough to deal with arising challenges. The sense of emergent anarchy thus underlies the sense of threat to group position. This is because the arrival of outsiders in states with weak central authority would threaten the host population's "feeling of proprietary claim to certain areas of privilege and advantage" (Blumer 1958: 4). Blumer therefore argued that this feeling would be crucial to the formation of interracial fear and hostility. He stressed that vulnerability about one's group position would be particularly acute when one anticipates that the outsiders are likely to be "transgressing the boundary line of group exclusiveness" (ibid.). Migrants by their very nature represent precisely such a transgressionary outside claim to insiders' "areas of privilege and advantage." The appearance of migrants would therefore increase the host population's need for reassurance that their privileged claims within their state are protected. This basic need cannot be satisfied if host populations believe their political leaders and institutions do not care about them. The perception of government incapacity is therefore likely to be especially conducive to immigration phobia if migrants are perceived as someone who could undermine or overextend a host government's capacity directly, especially through illegitimate claims on public resources, corruption, fraud, illicit trade, or illegal takeover of local property. These perceptions, in turn, are likely to be reinforced in social contexts characterized by government inefficiency or corruption prior to the arrival of migrants. Finally, Petersen's (2002) findings show that there is a potent emotional "transmission belt" between the sense of emergent anarchy and aggressive responding to out-groups. Finding that "resentment" explained most cases of ethnic targeting in the mass violent conflicts in Central and Eastern Europe during the twentieth century, Petersen defined *resentment* as an emotional response to the prospect that under anarchy social hierarchies may shift in favor of others. Resentment, in Petersen's (2002: 56) view, is about "the belief that one's group is in an unjust position" and that the situation can be improved through violence against the presumably most vulnerable group highest up in the "ethnic status hierarchy." Thus, Petersen traced most interethnic violence in Eastern Europe to situations where a more powerful ethnic group lost its privileged position in the pecking order to a less powerful group and opted to reverse the perceived injustice by force. To this, the present study would add that when defined in this manner resentment is also about the whole gamut of other emotions – anxiety, apprehension, worry, and tension – that relate directly to the sense of emerging anarchy and uncertainty about the future under weak "rules of the game."

Apprehension that one's government may fail to rise up to the migration challenge opens the door to the second perceptual aspect of emergent anarchy: concern about the impact of migration on intergroup or interethnic balance. A "status quo" group in a migrant-receiving society fearing that the ethnic balance may change in favor of the newcomers – especially once government capacity to protect the status quo group comes into doubt – would parallel concerns of world statesmen about the military balance changing in favor of other states in the absence of a transnational sovereign. This basic logic of political realism may induce some members of the host societies to seek "windows of opportunity" for preemptive retaliation against migrants: "If those with greater advantages expect to remain in that position in superior numbers, then they may see no window of opportunity. However, if they expect their advantage to wane or disappear, then they will have an incentive to solve outstanding issues while they are much stronger than the opposition" (Posen 1993: 110–11). In other words, even if migration is never going to materialize as a clear and present danger to the security of the receiving state, it is perfectly rational for incumbent groups in the host state to at least envision aggressive preemptive measures to stop, constrain, or regulate migration. Classic ethnographic accounts of ethnic transitions in the United States provide rich, colorful descriptions of this type of vulnerability to out-group invasion and preemptive alarmism translating into violent "neighborhood vigilantism" (Rieder 1985; Suttles 1972). Applying this type of "defended neighborhood" logic to the statistical analysis of interracial hate crime in New York, Green, Strolovitch, and Wong (1998) found strong empirical support for a seemingly counterintuitive hypothesis that goes a long way toward explaining the paradox about marginal migration alarmism. The highest rates of antiminority hate crime were found in neighborhoods where incumbent groups – primarily whites – constituted the largest proportion of the population initially, but then experienced a sudden and large influx of ethnic "others." Crime incidence declined after the proportion of newcomers increased. Beyond partially explaining the marginal migration hostility paradox, these findings support empirically the central element of the security dilemma's logic: human proclivity for preemptive retaliation.

One potent illustration of this proclivity – and its grounding in human emotions beyond cold-hearted calculation – was offered to this author during his visit to Northern Ireland in December 1990. The trip was sponsored by the British Foreign Office as part of the International Journalist Fellowship program at the University of Oxford. As a journalist in the former Soviet Union, I participated in this endeavor along with colleagues from Argentina, the United States, the United Kingdom, South Korea, Israel, Greece, and India. We had a tight week-long schedule that included extensive meetings with government officials, law enforcement officers, political party leaders, civic activists, and university professors. The principal message that our hosts appeared to be sending us was that continuing British sovereignty over the province was essential for peaceful resolution of violent sectarian conflict in Northern Ireland. These efforts suffered a setback, however, during one of our last official engagements in the city that is known to its Protestant residents as Londonderry and to its Catholic residents as simply Derry. We had dinner with a group of local "common citizens" – both Catholic and Protestant – with an obvious idea to illustrate to us that ordinary Protestants and Catholics could amicably coexist in everyday social situations, outside the political tensions and pressures. As were other members of our group, I was seated between a local Protestant and a local Catholic, and the three of us quickly broke the ice and started a lively and most innocuous discussion that centered on our jobs, education, and families. For a while, the Foreign Office's plan clearly worked. I no longer cared which of these two men was Protestant and which was Catholic. Carried away by the friendly flow of the conversation, I asked the interlocutor to my right if he had children. Yes, he had one child, came the reply. Before I could discuss the pros and cons of raising an only child (myself being one), the interlocutor to my left turned his head toward us and interrupted our discussion. He proudly declared that he had three children and that because Catholics like him had more children than Protestants like the interlocutor to my right, the day would come when Catholics would form a majority in Northern Ireland and declare independence from Britain. A heated debate on the virtues of family size and on the legitimacy of the British rule in Northern Ireland erupted, with my two interlocutors talking right through me, as if I suddenly disappeared. As they raised their voices, broke into sweat, and turned increasingly red in the face, my fellow journalists stopped their conversations and observed the debate, taking in the fragility of interconfessional accord that we were supposed to witness. Eventually, the passions subsided, but for the rest of the evening I was no longer able to revive the cordial chitchat with which the three of us started the evening. Important for this study, my interlocutors did not discuss or refer to actual demographic data. Rather, the passions driving the debate arose from purely speculative assertions and from uncertainty about the future sovereignty over the province that my Catholic interlocutor linked so intimately and vividly to population trends.

At the cross-national and intergroup level, the more fluid the ethnic population balance and government weakness, the more likely will migration increase the ratio of nationalisms to states – and with it the proneness of violent conflict. Individuals in host societies would grow increasingly fearful that migration would give rise to diverse group intermingling, raising the specter of what Stephen van Evera (1995: 146–7) described as "truncated nations" or "nested minorities" emerging inside the receiving states. These "nested minorities" – also known as *ethnic islands* and *ethnic "fifth columns"* – are defined by van Evera as entrapped "parts of nations within the boundaries of states dominated by other ethnic groups" (ibid.). Again, what matters from the security-dilemma viewpoint is not the actual ascendance of such minorities, but the possibility that migration might engender them one day – no matter how far in the future. This is precisely a social situation that in theory would give rise to interactive group suspicions and tensions – the "spiral dynamic" of intergroup hostility. For example, the Russians in the Far East or the Anglo-Americans in California would face a security dilemma favoring preemptive exclusion of migrants (the Chinese and the Mexicans), because they would find it imprudent not to ascribe to these migrants the intent to establish a "nested minority." And once such a "fifth column" is envisioned – however tentatively – host populations would find it imprudent to discount the prospect that these minorities would seek expansion, stronger ties with the sending states, and increasing political influence within the host state. Nazli Choucri (1974: 121) in a multicountry study of population effects on violent conflict using the Computer-Aided System for Analyzing Conflict (CASCON) found that "if a national border divides a particular segmental community, movement across the border tends to emphasize the commitments to communal unity over those to the nation (as, for example, in the case of the Kurds in Iraq and Iran and the Somalis along the Ethiopia-Kenya-Somalia border)." The important point, however, is not just whether violence ensues, but that the perceptual logic of a nested minority is likely to set in, leading to exaggerated threat assessment. Also, in such contexts migration would give political leaders in the receiving state the incentive to overreact to the threat. Feeling no urge to "empathize with their neighbors," both migrants and host communities would remain "unaware that their own actions can seem threatening" (Posen 1993: 104).

Migration does not necessarily produce "nested minorities." But the security-dilemma logic predicts that migration would engender more intense and more pervasive fears when the emergence of "nested minorities" is a possibility, no matter how remote. Such minorities have, in fact, emerged as a result of migration of Brazilians to Paraguay and Mexicans to the United States, even though the national population ratios are vastly different – approximately 10:1 for Brazil–Paraguay and 1:2 for Mexico–the United States. The important issue is how the boundaries of migration regions are conceptualized – the point emphasized by Horowitz (1985: 177–8), who catalogued the concerns of the Assamese surrounded by Bengalis, the Sikhs surrounded by Hindus, and the Sinhalese surrounded by the Tamils in India: "Majorities within a country become minorities within an international region, depending on how the region is conceived.... When once this is conceded, it becomes obvious that there is a realistic component to group anxiety." While immediately cautioning that the utility of this logic for explaining separatist warfare and ethnic violence is "strictly limited," Horowitz amply documented (1985: 176–7) how fears of "virtual extinction," "eventual extinction," "wiped out [group] individuality," and "depopulation" emerged in perceived nested minority situations. In many of the cases Horowitz examined, status quo ethnic groups exaggerated the number of ethnic strangers and demographic insecurity – similar to exaggeration by Russians of the Chinese presence in the Russian Far East by a factor of ten, as discussed in Chapter 1.

The logic of the security dilemma explains why exaggeration of real-world trends is a crucial element in threat perception. Uncertainties about government capacity "to care" and about ethnic population balance make "preparing for the worst" a sensible psychological coping strategy, if not the only conceivably available strategy. Exaggeration in this regard is important for reassurance, and, hence, perceived threats are exaggerated by default. For example, even a small number of Chinese migrants in the Russian Far East triggers widespread fears of the "yellow tide."

This logic suggests that large population disparities – especially between states neighboring on land – are likely to engender exaggerated threats of invasion inside states with smaller populations. Moreover, the shadow of doubt cast by these disparities may induce individuals to discount real-world military and economic power balances or the condition of bilateral relations. Interestingly enough, for example, the magnitude by which residents of the Russian Far East in my September 2000 survey exaggerated Chinese migrant presence corresponded almost exactly to the tenfold preponderance of China's population over Russia's. Also this logic explains why the preponderance of military power and sealing of borders would not suffice to erase exaggerated fears of "invasion" in cases of population disbalances between migrant-sending and -receiving states. Even with Moscow maintaining massive military power along the Soviet-Chinese border since the 1960s and with Soviet overwhelming nuclear superiority over China, Soviet citizens – including this author as a middle and high school student – harbored elaborately exaggerated fears of Chinese invasion and conquest of Russia. These fears stemmed from a simple fact that we lived next door to the most populous state in the world. From my own experience, I can testify that the "what-if-they-come?" suspicion was a pervasive fear-jerker. A sense of insecurity permeated the ruling Politburo discussions and the popular culture. In one Soviet political joke that widely circulated by word of mouth in the 1970s, President Nixon gets a supercomputer capable of predicting events twenty years ahead. However, even Nixon cannot tell the Soviet leader, Leonid Brezhnev, anything about the future of the USSR. This is not, however, because the computer failed to generate a prediction, but because Nixon could not read it. "It's in Chinese!" Nixon tells an astounded Soviet leader. Another joke visualized events 100 years into the future – and they were consistent with Nixon's computer predictions – armed clashes on the Finnish-Chinese border. These persistent prospective fears intensified in the Russian Far East after the Soviet collapse – even despite the end of ideological rivalry between the world's two largest communist parties and normalization of Sino–Soviet and Sino–Russian relations.

Beyond extracting laughter out of subliminal fears, these political jokes reflect anticipation of what may be called "demographic deprivation," or prospective ethnic succession. The most obvious, "ideal type" situations giving rise to the sense of demographic deprivation would be the ones in which the sending state's population is larger and increasing whereas the receiving state's population is smaller and decreasing. These conditions are particularly salient in the case of Chinese migration across the Sino–Russian border. The sense of demographic deprivation would translate into an even stronger threat exaggeration, if the migrant-sending state has high population density and the receiving state has low population density, especially if density is measured not per unit of all national territory, but per unit of productive territory – for example, per acre of arable land. The abundance of such cases is illustrated by Choucri's (1974: 172–3) study of population and conflict. The study found that high population density directly contributed to violence in internal conflicts in Sri Lanka, Dominican Republic, Indonesia (West Irian), Algeria, and Kenya and in interstate conflicts between the Dominican Republic and Haiti, El Salvadore and Honduras, Guyana and Venezuela, Malaysia and Indonesia, Rwanda and Burundi, and over Egyptian claims to Suez.

Global population dynamics would partially explain why concerns about prospective "demographic deprivation" would arise in the global North regardless of actual migration rates. On the one hand, by 2000, the number of known international migrants was approximately 200 million – just over 3 percent of the entire world population. The United Nations estimated their number at 175 million, and, in addition, the number of refugees reached approximately 15 to 16 million (United Nations Population Division 2001: 139). Moving populations in the late 1990s and early 2000s also included an estimated 0.7 to 2 million women and children trafficked across international borders (International Organization for Migration 2001: 1), 7 million illegal immigrants in the United States (U.S. Department of State 2003: 1), 3 million illegal immigrants in the EU, and 2.7 million illegals in East and South-East Asia (Skeldon 2000: 12).

On the other hand, according to projections of the U.S. Census Bureau (2002: 12), for example, the most developed industrial countries (the United States, Canada, Western Europe, Japan, Australia, New Zealand) and post-Soviet states will most likely continue to go down in population rankings among the eight major world regions, reflecting what appears to be a statistically unstoppable trend from 1950 through 2050. Thus, in 1950 the developed countries had the top ranking, only marginally below China and the Soviet Union, and Eastern Europe ranked fifth. By 2002, the developed world ranked fourth and the former Soviet bloc states ranked seventh. By 2050, the developed world states were projected to drop to sixth place and the former Soviet states to eighth place. The United Nations (2001: 149) projected that by 2050 international migration would account for a 20 percent population increase for the United States, a 16 percent increase for Germany, and a 23 to 27 percent increase for Australia and Canada. These estimates point to likely shifts in the ethnic composition of host societies in the coming decades. However, though the data also suggests that the largest demographic clash – and, hence, the expectation of antimigrant and antiminority alarmism, hostility, and violence – is likely to happen not between the migrants from the global South and the incumbent populations in the most developed states of the North, but between the former and the incumbent populations in the global semiperiphery, such as the post-Soviet states. This would be likely even though the overall migration scale to post-Soviet states is almost certain to be significantly lower in comparison to the developed world between 2005 and 2010. But the security dilemma – through the logic of uncertainty about prospective "demographic deprivation" – would likely alarm residents in the former Soviet and East/Central European countries, because most of them are in the world's top ten with the slowest population growth (Estonia, Latvia, Georgia, Bulgaria, Ukraine, Lithuania, Russian Federation, Hungary, Armenia, Belarus) (United Nations 2001: 72). In fact, the term *slowest growth* is a euphemism in this case, because all of these countries were estimated to post population decline at a rate from 0.45 to 1.1 percent a year from 2000 to 2005. And one would expect preemptive alarmism and hostility to be especially acute in anticipation of migrants from poorer states with the fastest growing populations in 2000–5 (Somalia, Liberia, Afghanistan, Sierra Leone, Eritrea, Niger, Palestinian Territory, Yemen, and Uganda), with average annual increases ranging from 3.24 to 4.17 percent (ibid.).

In more than fifty nation-states from 1990 to 2000, migration was a major factor of demographic change – exceeding or comprising more than one-third of natural population increase or decrease (Tables 2.1 and 2.2). Because the predominant ethnic populations in migrant-sending and -receiving states differ as a rule, the data in this table are strong circumstantial evidence that migration-driven ethnic intermingling is and will likely persist as a major global trend – even though demographic changes are slow and subject to transformation in the process.

Migration within states has also produced massive changes in interethnic settlement patterns worldwide. Migration of an estimated 100 million people from rural to urban areas in China has been the largest migratory process in the world at the turn of the twenty-first century. In the United States, in the first half of the twentieth century, millions of African Americans moved from the South to northern cities. When the Soviet Union collapsed, a "beached diaspora" of 25 million ethnic Russians in the fourteen Soviet-successor states was the legacy of these internal population movements (Laitin 1998; Zevelev 2001).

Finally, uncertainty about prospective "demographic deprivation" would naturally stream from an imperfect reporting system on which the United Nations and other international organizations and national governments have to rely in making demographic projections at the global or regional level. The logic of emergent anarchy dictates that the worst-case scenario should be assumed, if estimates are uncertain. And the prudence of this worst-case logic is confirmed every time the United Nations retroactively revises upward its international migration estimates. Thus,

TABLE 2.1. *Net Migration as Percentage of Natural Population Increase or Decrease, 1990–2000*

Country or Area	Migration as % of Natural Population Change	Country or Area	Migration as % of Natural Population Change
Romania	(−322)	Greece	3,975
Lithuania	−311	Slovenia	(2,691)
Bosnia and Herzegovina	−296	Croatia	1,195
Estonia	(−242)	Austria	451
Georgia	−198	Germany	(356)
Kuwait	−176	Italy	(331)
Moldova	−161	Luxemburg	289
Kazakhstan	−140	China, Hong Kong SAR	251
Albania	−129	Denmark	248
Latvia	(−125)	Sweden	220
Bulgaria	(−108)	Switzerland	209
Samoa	−104	Singapore	161
East Timor	−102	Spain	156
Guyana	−76	Belgium	114
Suriname	−75	Israel	89
Sierra Leone	−61	China, Macau SAR	89
Jamaica	−50	United Kingdom	87
Burundi	−47	Canada	86
Tajikistan	−44	United Arab Emirates	81
Fiji	−44	Cyprus	77
Guam	−40	Australia	77
Eritrea	−38	Afghanistan	72
St. Lucia	−38	Czech Republic	(72)
Trinidad and Tobago	−36	United States	68
Kyrgyzstan	−36	Belarus	(67)
		Netherlands	63
		Norway	61
		Russian Federation	(54)
		Finland	52
		Lebanon	49
		Gambia	49
		Rwanda	45
		Western Sahara	45

Country or Area	Migration as % of Natural Population Change	Country or Area	Migration as % of Natural Population Change
		Ireland	44
		Bahrain	43
		New Zealand	41
		Malta	37
		Qatar	35

Note: Negative percentage values signify that net migration is negative, and positive percentage values signify that net migration is positive. Values in parentheses are for states or areas with prevalence of death rates over birth rates (demographers call this "negative natural population increase"). All other values are for countries or areas where birth rates exceeded death rates. For example, the table shows that in Romania out-migration exceeded natural population growth more than threefold, while the death rates exceeded birth rates. In Lithuania, out-migration also exceeded natural increase more than threefold, yet birth rates exceeded death rates. In Greece, in-migration rates were nearly forty times higher than birth rates, and the latter also exceeded death rates, but predominance of migration over birth rates in Slovenia happened against the background of deaths prevailing over births.

Source: United Nations Population Division, *World Population Prospects: The 2000 Revision, Volume III: Analytical Report*, New York: United Nations, 2001, 147–8.

in the early 2000s, the United Nations' estimates of international migration levels for 1990 stood at 154 million (Osaki 2002: 6), more than 50 percent up from the estimates made in the early 1990s (United Nations Population Fund 1993).

Intent Opaqueness: Why Are Migrants Viewed as Having the "Offensive" Advantage?

While setting the stage for fear-producing uncertainties, breakdown of government authority and population disparity are not the only engines of the security dilemma. "The security dilemma is particularly intense," according to Posen (1993: 104–5), under "conditions that make offensive and defensive capabilities indistinguishable." Whereas indistinguishability of offensive and defensive intent are logical derivatives of international anarchy in the realist theory, it is also likely to affect immigration phobia independently of perceptions of government capacity and ethnic balance. One can draw a clear parallel between the perceptual logic of the arms races and antimigrant hostility. Just as any purportedly defensive weapon can be viewed as offensive, so most of the mundane activities of migrants

TABLE 2.2. *Net Migration as Percentage of Natural Population Increase or Decrease, 2000–2010 (Estimate)*

Country or Area	Migration as % of Natural Population Change, 1990–2000	Country or Area	Migration as % of Natural Population Change, 1990–2000
Georgia	(−4,644)	United Kingdom	(922)
Yugoslavia	(−704)	Bosnia and Herzegovina	596
Moldova	(−309)	Portugal	(300)
Estonia	(−137)	Luxemburg	294
Kazakhstan	−136	Norway	223
Poland	(−131)	Denmark	(217)
Guyana	−97	China, Hong Kong SAR	221
Samoa	−74	Singapore	215
Armenia	−71	Netherlands	201
Suriname	−67	Slovakia	180
Albania	−53	Canada	165
Djibouti	−53	Finland	(164)
Tajikistan	−47	Belgium	(157)
Fiji	−46	East Timor	131
Lesotho	−42	China, Macau SAR	118
St. Lucia	−39	Japan	92
Trinidad and Tobago	−37	Australia	91
Bulgaria	(−35)	United States	87
Jamaica	−35	Greece	(87)
Ukraine	(−30)	Germany	(73)
		Spain	(47)
		Kuwait	46
		Czech Republic	(43)
		Sweden	(42)
		United Arab Emirates	38
		Afghanistan	37
		Sierra Leone	35
		Italy	(34)

Note: Negative percentage values signify that net migration is negative, and positive percentage values signify that net migration is positive. Values in parentheses are for states or areas with prevalence of death rates over birth rates (demographers call this "negative natural population increase"). All other values are for countries or areas where birth rates exceeded death rates.

Source: United Nations Population Division, *World Population Prospects: The 2000 Revision, Volume III: Analytical Report,* New York: United Nations, 2001, 147–8.

such as trading in local street markets may be viewed as prospectively leading to illegal settlement or worse – as a cover-up for contraband trafficking and terrorist networking. It is in this – "visionary" – sense that "defensive" and "offensive" capabilities and intentions of migrants are indistinguishable. It is in this sense that migrant activities are shrouded in fear-producing doubts. Moreover, by its very nature migration is all about acceptance of risk and uncertainty and the willingness to undergo hardship, break the rules, defy social conventions, stay flexible, and live with unpredictability. Can such people be inherently trusted not to go back even on their own best intentions, no matter how vigorously stated and defended? Migrant laborers, for example, may have a firm intent to work legally and leave before their visas expire, but if they fail to make as much money as they expected or if they get new lucrative offers, they may decide to stay longer. Necessity often trumps yearning for home. Explaining a rapidly rising number of Brazilian immigrants in the United States at the turn of the twentieth century, Rodrigo Merheb of the Brazilian Consulate in Chicago said: "A lot of people come here thinking they will just stay for a while. But then they start families and make connections and never go back" (*San Diego Union-Tribune*, August 5, 2002: A8). Relatives of migrants may initially have no intention to follow their kin, but once the "trailblazers" find a way to prolong their stay, their family members may change their minds. According to Merheb, "First one person comes, and then a brother; then a cousin comes and brings a friend" (ibid.). In this sense, social networks – especially around ethnic-based economic niches (e.g., Korean dry cleaners, Chinese vegetable traders) – would actually create structural incentives for self-perpetuating migration. Once these networks reach a certain critical mass, migration would likely become self-perpetuating (Fussell and Massey 2004; Myrdal 1957; Waldinger 1996). Given widespread evidence of this kind, one can see the logic of threat perception arising from Russian folk wisdom expressed in the proverb: "Nothing is more permanent, than what you think is temporary."

This logic of preemptive suspicion connects migration with the security dilemma. Scholars who have developed the security-dilemma theory and its implications for intergroup conflict point precisely to the problem of prospective valuation of intent that underlies alarmism and that is hard to dispel by mere reaffirmation of goodwill: "...the actor's concern is often not that the other side is currently aggressive or that the current situation is threatening but that it may become so in the future as others change their capabilities and intentions. Thus, it is incorrect to argue that security concerns and the security dilemma should disappear if the actors could be certain of others' benign intentions. The fact that others or their successors can change and cannot commit themselves not to, are at the heart of the security dilemma" (Snyder and Jervis 1999: 21). In short, threat is bound to be exaggerated as long as there is uncertainty – doing otherwise would result in overexposure to risk that would run against the basic human survival instinct.

For migrant-receiving populations, this kind of vulnerability is akin to that of a prisoner in a classic prisoner's dilemma game. Admittance of migrants creates the situation in which the host population resembles the prisoner in the game who had already "cooperated" with another prisoner by refusing to testify against her, after the two were arrested, charged with the crime, and put in separate cells without any chance to communicate. In this situation, the cooperator – standing for the host population in our analogy – immediately exposes oneself to the risk that the other prisoner would defect by agreeing to testify against her. Thus, any society that opens the doors to migrants automatically exposes itself to migrants' "defection" – if the latter remain in the country illegally, engage in illicit business activities, and attract more illegal migrants. In terms of game theory, this is the equivalent of host societies perpetually risking to be stuck with a "sucker's payoff" – something that would discourage cooperation and encourage xenophobic alarmism and exclusionist sentiments in migrant-receiving societies. It has been shown that proclivity to defect first is overcome in prisoner's dilemma when players interact repeatedly and when the time horizon is indefinite – that is, when the game consists of an unknowable number of moves (Axelrod 1994). However, the repeated interaction incentive is hard to obtain with respect to migration, because no average resident of host states has the wherewithal to track arrivals, departures, and compliance with local laws of most migrants. The shadow of doubt is perpetually there, as long as any given migrant – regardless of past behavior – has a plausible incentive to break the pattern of cooperative ("defensive") behavior. And hypothetical incentives for breaking with the pattern are easily visualized – be it the proverbial "melting" into the host state, finding a legal loophole to obtain residency permits, or selling one's services to transnational criminal groups. Hence, the reputation for cooperation – inherent in the idea of repeated interactions – is hard to obtain for migrants. Due to these considerations, the perceived risk of migrants' free riding and abusing the host society's cooperation on any given entry is unlikely to be assuaged by law-abiding behavior of migrants in the past. In this sense, interaction between the natives and the migrants would be modeled more accurately as a sum of discrete one-move games, rather than as an iterated game – even though the number of game iterations is unlimited. The same pall of doubt would be cast over the intentions of migrant-sending states. Do they encourage migration to increase their influence or to alleviate their burdens? This may be especially a matter of concern if political decision making in the countries of origin is not transparent. But even if political systems in these countries are open, the natives would still require significant time and physical effort merely to find out what the sending state's policies are and whether these policies may translate – wittingly or unwittingly – into the emergence of ethnic "fifth columns" in the receiving states. Thus, once migration increases, host populations may ascribe a multitude of hostile intentions to sending states. What if the latter promote migration in the hope of increasing their political and business influence within the receiving state? What if this influence will undermine governance and economic development in host states – or even challenge the host state's sovereignty over parts of its territory?

In addition to difficulty in distinguishing the nature of migrant intentions, host populations have little knowledge of the migrants' track record and therefore grounds to question the newcomers' loyalty to the host state. This sentiment is easy to find in any antiimmigrant discourse. In the United States, for example, conservative political commentator Pat Buchanan (2002: 2) has argued that the biggest problem with the late-twentieth-century immigration to the United States is not income, ideology, or religion, but immigrants' prospective disloyalty and unfaithfulness: "... among our millions of foreign-born, a third are here illegally, tens of thousands are loyal to regimes with which we could be at war, and some are trained terrorists sent here to murder Americans." This is an indicative statement. This argument has three elements: (1) many migrants are illegal; (2) many migrants are loyal to hostile governments; and (3) some migrants are terrorists. The statements are arranged in descending order with respect to likelihood, but in ascending order with respect to putative threat. This arrangement casts the most threatening and the least verifiable component of the argument (migrants = terrorists) in the most plausible light. The logic is: If so many migrants (one-third) break the law to enter our country and if so many of them maintain loyalty to our enemies, should one be naïve to think that many of them won't be terrorists? This logic reverses the motto of the nation of immigrant colonists – "*E pluribus unum*" ("out of many, one") – into the logic of overrated antimigrant alarmism: "*E unum pluribus*" ("out of one, many"). If one migrant may be a terrorist, who knows how many more can be terrorists?

After all, so many of them are illegal to begin with, so many have split loyalties. . . .

In fact, I challenge the reader to find any statement claiming migration is a threat to national security anywhere that does not raise either suspicions about the intent of migrants or the consequences of their arrival, intended or unintended. In other words, predominantly economic – and most common – migration can only be construed as a security threat if it is presented as having inestimable, uncertain consequences. In the review of studies on migration and security initiated by the Social Science Research Council (SSRC) in the United States, Gary Gerstle (2004) shows how fear of religious, political, economic, and racial subversion explained periodic antiimmigrant backlashes throughout American history – targeting Germans during World War I, the East Europeans during the "Red Scare" of the early 1920s, and the Japanese after Pearl Harbor. Gerstle's (2004: 105) conclusion that "fears of internal subversion during wartime" lead to "government overreach" is in line with the security-dilemma logic of threat exaggeration. To this we may add that "overreach" would be a consistent security-dilemma response to prospective – and unfathomable or inestimable – threats. It makes sense to "oversecuritize" than to "undersecuritize." Perceived security threats of this kind cast a long shadow in the way that migration is framed, as suggested in the same SSRC study by Tirman (2004: 1–10). The nineteen hijackers who drove passenger planes into the World Trade Center, the Pentagon, and the fields of Pennsylvania on September 11, 2001 cast this shadow of insecurity over more than 31 million foreign nationals who entered the United States in the early 2000s (ibid.: 7). Tirman also demonstrated how the assumption that migrants are likely to have subversive intentions informed America's principal policy responses to 9/11: the Homeland Security Presidential Directive 2, "Combating Terrorism Through Immigration Policies" and the USA Patriot Act (ibid.: 2).

Responding to the findings of the 9/11 Commission – which entered the best-seller list as a paperback book – American legislators representing the majority party in the House of Representatives supported the incorporation of more-restrictive immigration laws in the bill designed to improve intelligence and enhance national security against 9/11-type challengers. Expressly motivating this framing of migration as a security threat was, once again, the "out of one, many" logic of worst-case assumptions. In the words of Representative John Hostetter, an Indiana Republican, who proposed an amendment to the intelligence bill removing judicial constraints on deportation of immigrants who spent less than five years in the United States, "abuse of the immigration system and a lack of immigration enforcement were unwittingly working together to support terrorist activity" (*The New York Times*, October 8, 2004: 23). The phrase "unwittingly working together" says it all about the underlying logic of preemptive insecurity. It is not that every migrant poses a threat, but that some might – and that could be just as frightening. Adding that "we don't want an open door to bad people" Hostetter voiced precisely the same argument as Pat Buchanan did in the statement analyzed in the preceding text: Because any migrant may be a terrorist and because so many migrants come illegally, any measure restricting illegal immigration would be an effective antiterrorist measure. Once this logic is accepted or unwittingly embedded in a political statement, migration can be justifiably interpreted as a perpetual and grave national security threat – unless absolutely all instances of abuse of immigration law are eliminated. That, however, is impossible in the real world.

The shadow of doubt about intentions also coated debates across Europe in the aftermath of 9/11 about security threats posed by migrant imams. The debates became particularly intense after France, Italy, and Britain expelled and arrested more than two dozen Muslim clerics, some directly accused of abetting suicide bombings and serving Osama bin Laden (*The New York Times*, October 18, 2004: A8). These developments propelled political leaders as well as intelligence and law enforcement officials to view migration of all Muslim clerics as a national and international security issue, rather than publicly framing and dealing with activities of a tiny minority of migrant clerics as the local law-enforcement issue. The "out of one, many" logic – drawing perceptually on uncertainty about intent – was revealed in press reports on efforts in Europe to train loyal imams for its growing Muslim populations. Summarizing the level of threat perception, the reports ascribed to these efforts a perfect national security objective: the creation of "an *army* [italics added] of learned, law-abiding, Europeanized imams." This characterization reveals that the perceptual microfoundation of this threat assessment was the desire to reduce uncertainty about behavioral consequences of the prospective army of unlearned, law-breaking, and non-Europeanized imams entering European countries. Responding to the arrests of radical clerics, policy proposals in European capitals reflected precisely this type of preemptive, uncertainty-reducing logic. The interior minister of Spain proposed not only mandatory registration of all clerics and churches by the government, but also the monitoring of sermons by law enforcement officers. The Dutch government proposed "courses on integration" for prospective imams and the British government introduced English-language tests for any aspiring "ministers of religion" (ibid.). The point here is not to argue whether and how such policies may enhance national security across Europe, but to show the "out of one, many" logic at work in the interpretation of migration as a security threat.

In some cases, perceptions of hostile intent galvanize intergroup violence directly. In the Ivory Coast heartland, more than 800 ethnic Dioullas migrants who worked on cocoa plantations for generations were attacked and many were killed by the incumbent ethnic Betes in 2004. While economic motivation played a role in this conflict, it did not explain the timing of the violence outbreak. According to *The New York Times* (May 26, 2004: A3) report quoting local Betes, attacks and killings started after one village chief accused the Dioullas of casting secret spells to drive the Betes away from cocoa-rich lands. The intent–suspicion discourse was pivotal in the chief's call on Betes to mobilize and attack the Dioullas: "Witchcraft was being practiced in the village by foreigners against indigenes. We decided to drive them out" (ibid.).

Alarmist perceptions are anchored in another important element of intent assessment under the security dilemma: the difficulty to distinguish between offensive and defensive capabilities of nation-states. In the standard military context, alarmist assessments would presumably arise directly from this problem in the manner cogently summarized by Ned Lebow (1985: 50): "The less that is known about the qualities of the other side's weapons, the greater the tendency to assign high values to them in order to be on the 'safe side.' ... When worst-case analysis is used by both sides, it means that they will interpret a situation of strategic parity as one of imbalance favoring their adversary." Migration is a vastly different social phenomenon. Most migrants do not come with weapons. Yet, the offensive–defensive dilemma applies to migration, as well. In fact, the worst-case-scenario logic is deeply anchored in the social reality of migration, because ordinary residents in migrant-receiving states have little information about the qualities and capabilities of migrants as a group. Concerns about security would thus arise among host populations not because migrants may really nurture aggressive designs, but because their designs are unknown. Offensive intent is easy to ascribe to migrants, because they, by the very nature of migration, credibly appear to have "offensive" advantages. Because their capabilities – in terms of available financing and connections to social networks outside and within host states – are unknown, the worst should be presumed, if one wants to feel safe. In a sense, any member of a host society fearing that legal traders would turn into illegal migrants would be akin to a gambler who knows that his opponent can end the game without warning and claim both players' money, or most of it, on any winning move. It is plausible to argue that the cost to migrants of breaking the rules of the receiving states is significantly lower than the receiving states' cost of apprehending migrants who break the rules. It is generally less costly for any individual migrant to "melt into" the host country than it is for the host country to totally seal its borders or catch and deport illegal immigrants. (And in case of migration within states, the host population doesn't even have these hypothetical protections.) Besides, strong unilateral measures preventing the movement of people across borders are likely to run against international opprobrium as well as formal and informal sanctions. For these reasons alone, governments would find it hard to credibly threaten migrants and therefore to credibly reassure their populations with any kind of exclusionist policies. But because offering no exclusionist measures would make the government look even weaker, some such measures are likely to be adopted. The resulting suboptimal outcomes – such as increasing border security, but allowing illegal migrants to get jobs once inside the country – would thus be preferred to searching for optimal solutions. As the partial security measures, in turn, fail to reduce in-migration, governments would be again perceived as unable to live up to its tasks and the credibility problem will persist. It is unlikely, however, that the general public would understand the nature of this vicious circle or that political leaders would be willing to risk appearing weak in trying to break out of it. In other words, host populations have good reasons to believe that migrants hold an offensive advantage over host communities and that, in general, offense is more effective than defense. Certain characteristics of migration – such as an illicit nature of a migrant-based economy – would exacerbate this perception of vulnerability even further. The stronger this perception, the more will migration enhance the security dilemma's intensity and antimigrant hostility. The logic of threat perception here is consistent with the logic of "ethnic islands" producing incentives for preventive interethnic war in cases such as the former Yugoslavia (Posen 1993: 108–9) – even though actual antimigrant responses in most cases are nowhere as extreme as ethnic cleansing in the Balkans.

Indistinguishability of offense and defense with respect to migration – feeding suspicions that migrants have an "offensive" advantage over host populations – would also enhance the perceived threat to group position in the migrant-receiving communities. The more offensive advantage is perceived to be available to migrants, the more host populations are likely to feel that their "proprietary claim" have come under threat. This threat perception is likely to be persistent and profound, although not necessarily consciously accounted for most of the time. Blumer (1958: 4) specified this perceptual logic with respect to racial prejudice and social stratification, even though he did not point out the role of intent opaqueness that is clearly embedded in the following statement: "Acts or suspected acts that are interpreted as an attack on the natural superiority of the dominant group, or an intrusion into their sphere of group exclusiveness, or an encroachment on their area of proprietary claim are crucial in arousing and fashioning race prejudice. The acts mean 'getting out of place.'"

This last sentence illustrates the inherent pertinence of this logic to immigration phobia, because "getting out of place" is the defining characteristic, the core identity of migrants – albeit in a different sense than the one implied by Blumer. For at the time when Blumer's classic article was published, "getting out of place" referred to acting "above their station" by minority groups. Yet, the core logic of threat perception applies both to minorities who attempt to rise above their social milieu and to migrants who attempt to rise above their geographic milieu. Both acts involve the crossing of group boundaries. After all, when Rosa Parks insisted on staying in the "Whites only" section of the bus, she de facto migrated and announced her intent to stay in the new location on the bus. And all the White riders on that bus – representing a mini migrant-receiving society – would have a credible threat motivation. If they allowed one Black to migrate, others would be likely to follow suit. The exclusionary "*E unum, pluribus*" was again at play. In this sense, there is a deep underlying similarity between acts of protest by minorities defying segregation and migration across state or group boundaries. A migrant is someone who "got out of place," someone who had set the precedent of social behavior that any member of the receiving society would be wise to find threatening. Migrants have thus a reputation for uncertainty by default. They are perceived as a threat in much the same manner as a car swerving across the lane-dividing line without warning signals uncertainty and the need for caution on the part of other drivers (Schelling 1960). In this sense, "getting out of place" is not just what the migrants do (and therefore something one can perceive as changeable), but who the migrants are. Collectively, therefore, migrants are likely to be perceived as a force of nature that constantly gets out of place. The stronger this feeling among host populations, the stronger incentive they have to discount the stated intentions of migrants and to intrinsically favor get-ready-for-the-worst attitudes. This creates the "wilderness of mirrors" environment in which having exaggerated, preemptive fears would be perfectly rational. In the real world, this perceptual logic would explain why host populations fear destitute and defenseless migrants who are abused by smugglers or who die in cargo compartments of merchant ships and in the desert wilderness – that is, migrants' suffering is interpreted as the determination to get out of place. And given that, one would find it logical to ascribe intent to "overrun" host societies to the "huddled masses" whose true intent is most likely to be fleeing from abject poverty, oppression, lawlessness, war, or all of the above.

Migrant "Groupness" and Relative Power

The security-dilemma logic also implies that the natives would be more likely to feel unduly alarmed about migration the more cohesive and distinct the migrants as a group would seem to be from the host population. "Groupness" in its own right can easily be seen as offensive. For Posen (1993: 106), "A group identity helps the individual members cooperate to achieve their purposes. When humans can readily cooperate, the whole exceeds the sum of its parts, creating a unit stronger relative to those groups with a weaker identity." Thus, the stronger the "'groupness' of the ethnic, religious, cultural, and linguistic collectivities" (ibid.) attributable to migrants, the more the natives would be likely to exaggerate the "offensive" nature of migration.

Microfoundations of "Groupness" Valuations

Research in social psychology suggests that the offensive nature of the others' groupness has powerful cognitive and emotional foundations. It appears to be natural for a member of any group to exaggerate or overrate the "groupness" and, consequently, the "offensiveness" of out-groups. As the grass always seems greener on the other side of the hill, so the proverbial "them" seem to have more "groupness" than the proverbial "us." A distinguished line of research in experimental social psychology established that a sense of "groupness" in its own right – arising from any group marker, no matter how trivial – strongly affects relations among individuals (Brewer 1979; Tajfel and Turner 1986). A perception that "the other" is not merely a randomly encountered individual, but a member of another group, has been shown to be "an essential ingredient" of discrimination. According to these experiments, groupness matters even when "(a) group membership is anonymous; (b) no social interaction, within a group or between groups, ever takes place; (c) there is no previous history of intergroup relationship; and (d) where rewards are to be allocated, there is no instrumental link between an individual's gain and a strategy of ingroup favoritism" (Vaughan, Tajfel, and Williams 1981: 37). This is not to say that membership awareness, social interaction within and between groups, history of intergroup relationship, and the scale of in-group rewards do not matter. They do, and they may enhance or reduce the effect of groupness perceptions. What Tajfel and his colleagues showed, however, was that group markers matter in their own right, even in the absence of these amplifying correlates of groupness. Other experiments in "minimal intergroup situations" established that individuals consistently perceive out-groups as more homogenous than in-groups regardless of actual group homogeneity levels (Turner 1987). In the apt summary of one author, "outgroups are black and white, ingroups are shaded" (Vonk 2002: 157). Intergroup boundaries of any kind – no matter how ephemeral the dividing line – set the stage for "intergroup bias" that is typically revealed through in-group favoritism and out-group discrimination. Acts that one would consider normal if done by in-group members may appear threatening if done by out-group members (Dovidio and Gaetner 1998). The greater the perceived distance between groups, the greater the intergroup hostility. Donald Horowitz (1985: 141–86) applied studies in social psychology and psychoanalysis of group behavior to ethnic conflict in Asia and Africa in the second half of the twentieth century and found systematic evidence tracing interethnic hostility to "dichotomization as a result of juxtaposition and comparison" (ibid.: 182). Survey research in South Africa by Gibson and Gouws (2000) found that strong in-group positive identities were associated with strong out-group negative identities engendering antipathy toward one's political opponents and perceptions that those opponents are threatening.

Perceived group distance and threat perceptions share both cognitive-emotional and rational-analytical foundations. As Lawrence Bobo (1999: 453) noted, summarizing Herbert Blumer's seminal work on prejudice, a sense of group position derives first and foremost from strong "socio-emotional" core elements. The sense of group position is not only a "normative construct," but simultaneously a social and emotional construct. In the following citation, Blumer (1958: 5) explains this notion indirectly, by drawing a clear connection between a group's position within a given social order and group identity grounded in emotional affinities: "Sociologically it is not a mere reflection of the objective relations between racial groups. Rather it stands for 'what ought to be' rather than 'what is.' It is a sense of where the two racial groups *belong*.... In its own way, the sense of group position is a norm and imperative – indeed a very powerful one. It guides, incites, cows, and coerces. It should be borne in mind that this sense of group position stands for and involves a fundamental kind of group affiliation for the members of the dominant racial group."

In a later work, "The Future of the Color Line," Blumer (1965: 322) also clearly formulated two dimensions of the socioemotional logic of perceived group position, stating that "...the color line expresses and sustains the social position of the two groups along two fundamental dimensions – an axis of dominance and subordination, and an axis of inclusion and exclusion."

These two dimensions comprise what Blumer called the *inner citadel of the sense of group position*, the tenacity of which cannot be explained by attribution to material and instrumental needs. Socioemotional logic of perceived group position is especially pertinent in cases of migration. The very act of migrants' arrival into an area populated by a different "incumbent" group simultaneously challenges the latter's sense of dominance and subordination and the sense of inclusion and exclusion. Because migrants by definition lack the history of socialization into the behavioral norms of the host society, their proneness to violate these norms – that is, to disobey the rules and codes upholding the receiving state's political and social hierarchies – implicitly poses a threat to incumbents' "normative construct" of dominance and subordination. What the security-dilemma logic suggests in addition is that host populations would be unwise to discount this type of threat to dominance and the sense of entitlement to exclude outsiders, even if the migrants swear with their lives and the lives of their children to abide by the rules of the receiving state. A more prudent perceptual stance would be to expect the unexpected from the migrants with respect to a host state's social order.

Migration's challenge to the incumbent group's sense of inclusion and exclusion is more obvious and no less salient – after all, it is in the very nature of migrants to change the boundaries of inclusiveness by leaving one in-group (the sending state) and join another (the receiving state). The fact of migrants' arrival therefore immediately signifies the weakness of the incumbents' sense of the right to exclude outsiders. From the security-dilemma standpoint, it is important to add that the issue here is not whether any given host society, on the whole, is going to favor inclusion or exclusion, but that migration lays down conditions under which members of host societies will be smart to fear for their very basic power to include or exclude newcomers. Uncertainty about one's group's very capacity to delineate its boundaries – crucial to the sense of identity – would thus likely generate emotional concerns about survival. In this context, instrumental valuations would appear inappropriate, if not treacherous within a threatened group. For if one's group's sense of threat perception is challenged as overrated, in-group members are likely to feel not only that the challenger is imprudent, but that their core emotions are discounted and dishonored. In this manner, the socioemotional norms of group position and identity would enhance the perceptual logic of the security dilemma, and migrant intentions are likely to be seen as more hostile. This also suggests that threat perception and antimigrant hostility are likely to increase in proportion to feelings that "moving around" is in the very nature of a distinct and cohesive out-group. One obvious example of such a group is the Roma, or Gypsies, which is also an example of a "nation without borders," a social network of "nesting minorities." The rise of antigypsy alarmism and hostility in Europe immediately following the admission to the EU of new member states from Central and Eastern Europe illustrates how this logic underlies immigration phobia. While a marginal minority in new EU member states, the Gypsies triggered at least as intense an antimigrant alarmism as other, significantly more sizeable ethnic groups. A newspaper account of public reactions to EU enlargement in the German village of Deutschneudorf shows the "instinctive," knee-jerk nature of anti-Roma alarmism: "Ask a roomful of Germans in this secluded town on the Czech border what will happen now that the European Union has opened its doors to the east and they answer with a line that could have been lifted from a child's fable: 'The Gypsies will come'" (*The New York Times*, May 5, 2004: A4). The reference to a child's fable suggests that this alarmism is deeply rooted in cultural socialization and the image of Gypsies as a group, for which "moving around" is the central part of their identity. "The townsfolk are convinced that these newly minted Europeans [Gypsies] will reassert their right to move freely within the union by picking up stakes and crossing the German border. They foresee Gypsy caravans, with clanking pots and shoeless children . . ." (ibid.). References to stakes, caravans, clanking pots, and shoeless children represent an image of a group on the move, a perpetually migrating group, and it is precisely this group imagery that is directly related to threat perception in the reports.

Two Dimensions of "Groupness": Cohesiveness and Capacity to Assimilate

Substantively, the sense of outsider "groupness" has two dimensions that tend to be expressed independently of one another. The first is the sense of group distinctiveness, or difference, or distance – regardless of whether outsiders are seen as distinct on positive or negative group characteristics. The second is the sense of an out-group's capacity to overcome the divisions and to assimilate with the in-group. In other words, the more the intergroup boundaries – as in "the color line" – are perceived to be both distinct and impenetrable, the greater the proneness for migration phobia in a host society. The more one perceives outsiders as a distinct group, the more entrenched group stereotypes are regardless of their content (Tajfel 1970).

From the standpoint of group categorization theory, perceptions of group distance on the one hand and assimilability on the other are likely to be influenced by the availability of social settings in which migrants can ostensibly preserve and enhance their "groupness." The availability of compact areas of settlement to migrants is likely to provide such social stimuli. If Chinese migrants in the Russian Far East, for example, had no Chinatowns to melt into, the local Russians would have fewer reasons to suspect the migrants of hostile conspiracies. The migrants would be more visible, and they could be identified and penalized or deported if they violated the host society's rules. Host populations would be more likely to believe that the migrants have the incentives to assimilate into the host society and to play by its rules. However, individuals in host states would also have strong reasons to doubt that migrants would allow themselves to be put in this situation, *especially* if they are physiologically and culturally distinct from the host population. The greater the distinctiveness, the costlier the assimilation to each individual migrant would be. Learning English would be easier for a Spanish speaker than for a Vietnamese speaker, for example. Finding a church to pray in would be easier for a Christian migrant than for a Muslim migrant in the Russian Far East or in rural North Carolina. Ethnic and cultural distinctiveness of migrants, therefore, in and of itself, is likely to engender perceptions of migrant "groupness." Residents in host states may not consciously account for this logic to themselves and to others, but they would be foolish not to feel this way at some level. Especially not after observing elaborate social support networks rapidly emerge in migrant communities. Not surprisingly, for example, 76 percent of respondents in my Primorskii krai opinion survey in 2000 wanted to ban (or never to allow) Chinatowns. At some level, this sentiment may strike one as counterintuitive, seemingly suggesting that the Russians may have preferred to mix with the Chinese and to live next door to them, rather than to live in separate compact communities. Rather, given that most of the same respondents supported restrictions on migration and expressed negative views of Chinese nationals, this view merely reflected fears that if Chinatowns were allowed for any reason – such as economic expediency – they would become ethnic "Trojan horses" and make Russia vulnerable to Beijing's historical claims. Similarly, large segments of the Anglo-Saxon Americans insist on strong incentives for all migrants to learn English and oppose funding for bilingual education. This would explain why such seemingly trivial factoids as American stores selling more salsa or soy sauce than ketchup would contribute to perceived security threats in earnest. In supporting major restrictions on Mexican immigration into the United States, for example, Huntington (2004a; 2004b) cites not increasing ethnic diversity, but increasing groupness of "hispanicized" enclaves within the United States as a social trend threatening America's security. The underlying premise of Huntington's book is that threats to identity inevitably pose threats to security.

This perceptual logic is quintessential in the security-dilemma situations. Just as in armed conflicts, national "groupness" is a military power multiplier and in cases of migration, ethnic "groupness" is a prospective economic and political power multiplier. Looking at the origins of anti-immigrant movements around the world, Weiner (1995: 2) wrote: "In many countries, citizens have become fearful that they are now being invaded not by armies and tanks but by migrants who speak other languages, worship other gods, belong to other cultures." Migration discourses are easily convertible into military discourses. Migrant groups are likened to armies, individual migrants to "invaders" or "infiltrators," and immigration policies to military operations. These perceived vulnerabilities tempt power-seeking individuals to exploit xenophobic ideologies. They also increase popular appeal of genuine xenophobes and racists. In Primorskii krai, xenophobic rhetoric has been deployed extensively in gubernatorial and Russian parliamentary elections since the early 1990s, including far-fetched yet politically potent warnings that Chinese migration might transform the Russian Far East into "Asian Balkans" (Nazdratenko 1999: 20–4). In the EU states, the increased in-migration since the fall of European colonial system and the collapse of communism triggered similar fears of outsider infiltration. Ethnic riots intensified in England since the 1990s, and right-wing xenophobic politicians came to contest regional and national offices in Austria, France, and the Netherlands. Some of these fears in Europe have to do not simply with the arrival of ethnic others, but with wholesale regrouping of identities linked to European integration and population trends. Asked to list major domestic concerns in a large EU-wide survey, one top decision maker in

France wrote: "The demographic problem. Less youth and the emergence of a new and immigrant population. The problem of the integration of the youth into this globalized economy. The homogenization of values with the melting of different European cultures and also the emergence of new cultures due to the population moves. The problem of the multiplicity of religious trends, for example, with Islam" (Spence 1996: 20). This type of assessment suggests that antimigrant alarmism has been fueled and magnified, in part, by the unsettled state of individual and national identity brought by European integration.

The issue of identity has also been central in antiimmigrant rhetoric in the United States. Writing in *The Death of the West*, Buchanan (2002: 3) voices dark forebodings over America changing from "the melting pot" into a "salad bowl" of cultures: "... the immigration tsunami rolling over America is not coming from 'all the races of Europe' [the original phrase used in the formulation of the melting pot image of the United States by writer Israel Zangwill – author]. The largest population transfer in history is coming from all the races of Asia, Africa, and Latin America, and they are not 'melting and reforming.'" It is precisely for this reason, according to Buchanan (ibid.) that "Uncontrolled immigration threatens to deconstruct the nation we grew up in and convert America into a conglomeration of peoples with almost nothing in common – not history, heroes, language, culture, faith, or ancestors." Hence, "Balkanization beckons." This is not so much a statement of traditional ethnic animosity or prejudice, but a statement of insecurity arising from the worst-case projection of putative intentions of migrants – a logic central to the security-dilemma trap in human reasoning.

By the same token, ethnicity is an essential – but not the exclusive – component of the "color line" between the natives and the migrants. It has been frequently noted that migrants who successfully assimilate into host societies later oppose further migration of their own coethnics from their own countries of origin. Survey research of Latino immigrants in the United States established that "as immigrants and their children become more incorporated into American society their attitudes toward immigrants and immigration become more negative" (de la Garza 2004: 109, summarizing studies by de la Garza and DeSipio 1998, Newton 2000). Additionally, de la Garza (2004: 113) reports research findings showing most Latinos agreeing with the Anglos that immigration levels in the United States are too high. In other words, the more the "new kids in town" turn into the "old kids in town," the more they start feeling insecure about the new "new kids in town." Negative perceptions of coethnic immigrants also reveal themselves in the redrawing of perceived group boundaries, as the newcomers who physiologically belong to the same ethnic group as the natives may be redefined as a distinct and separate ethnic group. This has been the case with respect to Russians returning to the Russian Federation from the former Soviet republics: Reports received by this author suggest that in some regions the returning Russians were recategorized as different ethnic groups. Perhaps this recategorization only emphasizes that ethnicity is an important element of group distinctiveness and attitude formation. But it is most likely that the crucial factor is the interaction between ethnic distinctiveness and the old- versus new-kid-in-town distinctiveness. Systematic evidence to this effect comes from a survey of approximately 2,500 Italians in a study by Sniderman et al. (2000). Contrary to the intuitive hypothesis that Italians would hold more negative stereotypes of racially distinct (African) rather than ethnically distinct (East European) immigrants, the authors found that the perceptions of both groups were remarkably similar. The "switch" experiment of that study found that Italians attributed the same problems with approximately the same intensity to both African and East European migrants – to the extent that if a group of Italians talked first about one group and then about the other, a listener would not be able to discern a difference. The revealing result was, in the words of the authors: "If you know how many problems Italians blame on Eastern Europeans, you can tell just as well how many unfavorable characteristics they will ascribe to African immigrants as if you know how many problems they blame on Africans themselves" (ibid.: 52). In statistical terms, this meant that correlation between negative stereotyping and the perceived social problems blamed on an out-group were proximate for Africans and East Europeans. In contrast, this correlation was significantly different if one compared perceptions of immigrant groups (both Africans and East Europeans) against perceptions of Southern Italians among Northern Italians. The logic of prejudice with respect to the "insider" out-groups differed from the logic of prejudice with respect to the newly arriving outsiders. In short, the perceived "outsiderness" matters without regard to ethnicity. In this study, all cases involve ethnically distinct natives and migrants. The main issue, however, is not whether and to what extent ethnic distinctiveness or "outsiderness" matter in their own right (the Italian study suggests they both do interactively), but how the varying *intensity* of perceived group divisions – arising from a combination of ethnicity and "outsiderness" – affects alarmism and support for antimigrant exclusionism.

This discussion also suggests that immigration phobia is grounded in both the rationalist and the symbolic logics of the security dilemma. From the rationalist standpoint, opaqueness of migrants' intent sets the stage for perceptions and responses typical under uncertainty and information failure (Lake and Rothchild 1996). The "newcomer–old-timer" distinction, in fact, is more likely to be grounded in uncertainty about "real threats" than in the symbolism of intergroup biases. From the constructivist (symbolic politics) perspective, by activating juxtaposition and "invidious comparison" (Horowitz 1985: 166) between host populations and newcomers, migration enables "myth-symbol complexes" that may "justify hostility toward the ethnic adversary" (Kaufman 2001: 2). These logics are not mutually exclusive, but rather complementary and interactive within the perceptual framework of the security dilemma. The operative threat-inducing notion under the immigration security dilemma is that of the "arrival of ethnic newcomers" – the "arrival" and "new" speaks to the uncertainty, while "ethnic" speaks to cultural and symbolic distinctiveness. As uncertainty and symbolism reinforce each other, they drive the perception of putatively offensive migrant "groupness."

Conclusion

Immigration phobia in host societies is likely to be more intense, the more acute perceptions of emergent anarchy, the more ambiguous the sense of migrant intentions, and the more distinct and cohesive the perceived "groupness" of migrants. These three correlates of the interethnic security dilemma represent the political and intergroup logic of fear and hostility. They are intrinsically present in any migration context. Albeit with varying intensity, some people in host societies would perceive the very fact of migration as weakening state sovereignty, would harbor suspicions about migrants' intent, and would view even atomized and assimilating migrant communities as distinct, distant, and homogenous entity. The embeddedness of these perceptions in any migration context would explain inevitable exaggeration of fear and antimigrant hostility, even under most benign conditions. Overall, however, perceptions on each of these dimensions of the security dilemma would vary across host populations.

3

The Two Faces of Socioeconomic Impact Perceptions

> If only the neighbor's cow would die or, better still, his house would burn down!
>
> A Ukrainian proverb

> Yes, I'd rather the Chinese not come here. But look around. You'll see that all these Russian factories are idle. Salaries are unpaid. Our back is against the wall. We've got to help these Chinese traders.
>
> Mikhail Vetrik, former director of the "Ussuri" market for Chinese traders in the Russian Far Eastern city of Ussuriisk. Interview with the author, May 1999.

In the previous chapter, I linked immigration phobia to perceptions of anarchy, intent, and group distinctiveness. However, these factors are not the only ones that affect threat perception and hostility. Interacting with the political and intergroup logic of immigration phobia is a substantively different logic of economic valuations. While it is rarely disputed that economic perceptions have an effect on interethnic attitudes and relations, the exact nature of these effects is highly contested. It is, in fact, at the heart of some of the most entrenched debates in the study of international relations and comparative politics. While some scholars have provided case studies showing that economic growth favors acceptance of other ethnic groups by engendering a social climate of optimism and generosity, others have countered with cases in which economic growth accentuates and aggravates ethnic grievances by generating a perception of relative deprivation. Still others have presented evidence that economic trends have little, if any, impact on ethnic-based activism, because the latter is rooted almost exclusively in cultural and political issues, such as sovereignty, competitive status, rights, and dignity of ethnic groups (for a discussion of these arguments, see Esman 1994; Horowitz 1985).

Similar controversies have transpired in studies of the effects of trade (economic incentives) on war (aggressive responding with military force). First, as the liberal argument holds, economic incentives make destruction of trade (and, by extension, aggressive responding) too costly and thus reduce both manifest and hidden resolve for conflict. Second, as some neo-Marxists and neo-realists contend, only equitable or symmetrical economic exchanges enhance security and promote peace, whereas asymmetric exchanges engender grievances, tensions, and insecurity. Hence, at the microlevel, the impact of economic perceptions on hostility would depend on perceptions of relative gains across ethnic groups involved in economic exchanges. Third, according to a related view, the simple fact of contact between states or groups resulting from economic exchanges increases the probability of occasional disputes. As disputes accumulate over time, the argument goes, rivalry and confrontation become more likely. Fourth, on some issues economic and security interests are likely to be unrelated, as actors assess these interests separately or compartmentalize them (for a comprehensive review of these perspectives and empirical research, see Barbieri and Schneider [1999] in the special issue of *Journal of Peace Research*; also see Reuveny 2001: 132–4).

The complexity of economic valuations' effects on migration phobia is also enhanced by the fact that one and the same out-group may simultaneously embody the risks and benefits associated with interests, identity, and security. For instance, European and African Americans in Texas or California may associate Mexican migrants with any combination of the following: (a) cheap labor (economic benefit); (b) increased use of Spanish (challenge to cultural identity); and (c) higher probability of crime (security threat). Similarly, Jewish residents in Jerusalem may associate migrant Arab workers from the West Bank with both economic benefits and terrorist threat. And a Russian resident in the Far East would often see in Chinese cross-border migrants both a source of affordable and previously unavailable goods and a threat of Beijing's claims on Russian territory. Milton Esman suggested a case-by-case approach for discerning how these perceptions interact and which may prevail. Stressing the complexity of factors that mediate between economic interest and interethnic relations, Esman (1994: 233) wrote: "Particular grievances, demands and goals in ethnic conflicts are empirical questions that depend on the strategies and reactions of participants, their internecine struggles, and transnational influences that are not readily predictable." Empirical research using both case studies and large-N statistical analyses has indirectly validated this approach by generating contradictory findings. Data aggregated at the national level suggest that economic conditions have a strong negative impact on ethnic violence in weak states with sizeable minorities. Laitin and Fearon (1999), for example, found that gross national product (GNP) trends from 1960 through 1980 in such states were inversely related to levels of ethnopolitical violence in the 1980s. The overall picture remains complex, however. Comparative research suggests that the effects of economic trends on ethnic-based conflicts are ambiguous. While Gurr (1993) found that in Europe and North America economically privileged groups were the ones more likely to engage in ethnic rebellion, Horowitz (1985) found that in Africa and Southeast Asia economically disadvantaged groups had a higher proclivity for protest. These studies, however, focus predominantly on macro- (structural) attributes of societies and groups in conflict.

In this study, I recast these theoretical and empirical controversies by going to the microlevel of analysis (i.e., individual perceptions) into the relationship between economic valuation, threat assessment, and anti-migrant hostility. The question to ask is whether individuals who view interactions with ethnic others as generating net economic benefits to them and their group are likely to be less threatened by and less hostile toward these ethnic others. Conversely, I am asking if threat perception and hostility would be greater among individuals who view interactions across ethnic lines as generating net economic losses.

Underlying these questions are fundamental theoretical issues about the very nature of economic valuations: Do groups assess their gains and losses relative to gains and losses of other groups (e.g., migrants), or do groups assess their gains and losses relative to that same group's prior circumstances? In other words, what is more important to individuals in an intergroup relationship: difference in gains and losses between groups, change in absolute gains to one's own group relative to a certain point in time, or some combination of these two preferences?

Immigration Phobia and the Logic of Relative Gains: "Cleave and Compare" across Groups

Aside from perceptions of anarchy, intent, and group distinctiveness, immigration phobia is strongly grounded in socioeconomic valuations or in some form of perceived effects of migrant activities on the economic, social, and environmental conditions in the receiving states. In previous research, economic valuations under the security dilemma have been straightforwardly related to the perceptual logic of relative gains. According to Barbara Walter (Walter and Snyder 1999: 4), one of the principal characteristics – and the only economic characteristic – of "fear-producing environments" consistent with the interethnic security dilemma is when "economic resources rapidly change hands" or threaten to rapidly change hands among groups. This is intuitively plausible and perfectly consistent with the zero-sum logic underpinning the security dilemma, especially in the absence of clearly defined and enforceable rules of economic exchange. It is self-evident that migration would cause greater fear in host societies the more it threatens to change the balance of economic power in favor of the newcomers. Just as the perceived impact of migration on ethnic population balance would evoke in host societies the fear of demographic deprivation and demographic status reversal, the perceived impact of migration on the apportionment of economic resources would evoke the fear of economic deprivation and economic status reversal relative to migrants. As Weiner (1995: 2) observed, antimigrant hostility among host populations arises from fears that the newcomers would "take their jobs, occupy their land, live off the welfare system, and threaten their way of life, their environment, and even their polity...."

Sociological Findings

These observations are consistent with previous sociological research in North America that established a correlation between ethnic prejudice and perceptions of ethnic-based economic discrimination and competition in the labor markets (Blalock 1967; Kinloch 1974; Kluegel and Smith 1983; Olsak 1989, 1992; Tienhaara 1974). Survey data analysis also suggests that threat of economic competition and deprivation vis-à-vis migrants makes the host populations' views of their economic conditions also relevant to threat perception. In a study of antiimmigrant attitudes in Europe, Lincoln Quillian (1995: 590) observed: "When dominant ethnic group members perceive their economic circumstances as precarious, they fear they will lose their economic advantages over the subordinate group; when economic circumstances improve, the corresponding reduction in perceived competition decreases group feelings of threat." In Africa and Asia, Horowitz (1985: 175) found that "severe anxiety about threats emanating from other groups" was especially acute among economically "backward groups." In American cities from 1877 to 1914, Olzak (1992) found, violence by predominantly non-Hispanic White incumbents against predominantly African American newcomers related significantly to ethnic job queue, unemployment, and business failures. Thus, a significant body of research suggests that ethnic intermingling is likely to generate conflict if ethnic competition for socioeconomic niches is intense.

The logic of relative gains is broad enough to explain that antipathy and hostility may arise not necessarily from zero-sum competition in one sector, but from perceptions that members of a different ethnic group are on the whole doing better than members of one's own group – especially when economic conditions are generally poor or declining. A corollary perception is that something must be wrong with the political and economic system that allows such differentiation to occur. Groups could then plausibly "conclude that they can improve their welfare only at the expense of others" (Lake and Rothchild 1998: 10) and opt for nationalism, even in the absence of direct economic competition (Azar and Burton 1986; Bookman 1994; Gurr 1970, but see Connor 2001 for a cogent critique). Fears would also arise that members of an economically more successful group (whether this success is gained at one's group's expense or not) would gain superior economic resources for advancing their interests in local government institutions at the expense of others; that this influence would translate into outsiders receiving favorable executive appointments; or that they would increase their influence on the policy decisions through graft. In short, economic gains would purchase political capital that could then be used to change the rules of the game in favor of ethnic "others" (Horowitz 1985: 236–43). In the Russian Far East, for example, one would expect local Russians to develop hostility not because Chinese migrants may arrive there in large numbers, but because they, more than the local Russians, are likely to be the group that succeeds economically and translates this success into political advantages. Hence, at the early stages, antimigrant hostility is likely to relate to perceptions of which group gains more from interactions with one another – or simply by perceptions that migrants gain too much.

Nazli Choucri's (1974: 181) study of forty-five internal conflicts with CASCON dataset illustrates how migrants may find themselves in no-win situations when economic effects of migration are perceived in terms of relative gains. Specifically, Choucri's findings show that obsession with relative gains cancels out the role of migrant skills in valuation of migration impacts – even though intuitively one would assume that host populations should welcome migrants whose skills may be viewed as beneficial to the domestic economy: "If migration is voluntary, the fate of the migrant community depends upon the reaction of the host community. This, in turn, rests largely upon the relative socio-economic status of the two communities. If the migrant community is the less skilled, it will be seen as a drain on the economy, as were the Salvadorenos in Honduras. If the migrants are more skilled, they will be resented for their success, as were the Chinese in Malaya, the Ibo in Nigeria, and the Kikuyu in Kenya."

Yet, because cases in Choucri's study were selected on the dependent variable – CASCON lists only cases where major conflicts occurred, but one cannot tell if the same skill differentials also characterized nonconflict environments – this evidence has only illustrative value. In other words, in some cases host communities may indeed perceive the skill differentials between them and migrants as threatening to economic well-being, with the resulting fears spurring violent responses to migration. However, we cannot infer from this evidence that in most cases individuals would, in fact, assess skill differentials in such terms and that, even if they do, such valuations would lead to antimigrant hostility.

Perceptual Microfoundations

The body of texts produced in the field of international relations – in its own right – provides systematic evidence that valuation of relative gains matters in human conflict and cooperation. This evidence differs from traditional sociological arguments that emphasize envy or status. The principal point concerns the assessment of power – a concept central to the study of international relations and political science in general. In this discipline, it is textbook knowledge that power has no meaning in absolute terms but only makes sense comparatively. Because capacity to make others behave in ways they otherwise would not is central to the notion of power, the capabilities of others must be included in any power assessments by default. In the modern world, for example, a state that does not have nuclear weapons may increase the size of its armed forces by drafting millions of additional servicemen and yet remain incapable of forcing states that have nuclear weapons to do anything they otherwise would not. This does not necessarily imply that more-powerful states would always have more influence in world politics at any given point in time. The principal point here is that whenever a state's influence in international affairs is valuated, its power is assessed relative to other actors. This would apply both to "hard" power such as military capabilities and "soft" power such as credibility of one nation's leaders or the media. In other words, what may be described as *ontology* – or definitional essence – of power would circumscribe the framing of group interactions in terms of relative gains.

In economics, where monetary gains such as income can be measured in both absolute and relative terms, Frank and Sunstein (2001) observed that close to half of respondents in surveys said they would rather earn $100,000 a year while others earned $85,000 than earn $110,000 while others earned $200,000. Asking a similar question, Solnick and Hemenway (1998: 373, 378–81) found that more than half of respondents preferred to earn less in absolute terms, but more relative to others. Posner (2000: 1166–7) explained this preference as inherent in individuals' quest for validation of their status and prospects: "If your boss is paying you a lot less than someone who does similar work, something is wrong." Extensive survey research has also led scholars to conclude that referencing one's income or social status to those of other people – rather than absolute income size – is a powerful determinant of happiness. This is typically inferred from the findings that, on average, as people get richer they do not report getting happier, that people in more prosperous countries are not significantly happier than people in less prosperous ones, and that, at the same time, across countries with varying income levels the higher the person's income status, the happier they generally say they are (Easterlin 1974, but see Diener and Diener 1995, reporting that this pattern does not hold under abject poverty). Explaining patterns of overconsumption in industrialized economies, Hirsch (1976) argued that individual valuation of their place in the social pecking order is quintessential to the pursuit of self-interest. For this reason, the price of goods is likely to be a function of their relative or "positional" value. Goods that are viewed as better than others in their own class – such as waterfront houses with panoramic views or fashionable clothes in short supply – are likely to be more desirable and, hence, command higher prices (see also Frank 1985 on the quest for status as motivation for consumption). However, as Hirsch (1976) explains, the more people pursue and acquire such goods, the less their social utility. In a sense, this is the replication of the security-dilemma logic in the realm of consumer behavior – as more individuals seek valuable status symbols, the status symbols they acquire become less valuable. Just as arms races where each state seeks to enhance its security would reduce the security of all, including the state that was the first to unilaterally increase its military power, consumption races would reduce the value of high-status goods for all, including the individuals that were the first to acquire high-value positional goods.

Psychological experiments also show that even when group distinctions are most trivial – as in the "minimal group situations" discussed in the previous chapter – relative gains are the most consistent consideration behind the individuals' allocation of benefits to in-group and out-group members (Tajfel 1970; Turner and Giles 1981; for comprehensive review of earlier work, see Horowitz 1985: 143–9). The salience of relative gains is particularly striking in experiments featuring seven- and eleven-year-old children. The subjects were divided into Red and Blue groups, and they had no knowledge as to who belonged to which group (Vaughan, Tajfel, and Williams 1981). Statistical analysis of experimental results showed that subjects nonrandomly gave more money to in-groups than to out-groups. In psychological terms, they pursued the strategy of "Maximizing the Difference." Hardly any children tried to maximize joint payoffs, or parity between groups.

All these considerations show that the logic of relative economic gains has powerful social bases and psychological microfoundations. And yet, economic valuations – in contrast to assessments of demographic balance, offensive intent, or out-group distinctiveness – also encompass estimates of absolute gains. The perceptual nature of absolute gains needs to be considered in greater detail to understand how perceived economic consequences of intergroup interactions may affect the sense of fear and antimigrant hostility.

Immigration Phobia and the Logic of Absolute Gains: "Cleave and Compare" over Time

Major research findings indicate, however, that perception of one's group's gains relative to others is not sufficient to explain the impact of economic valuations on threat perception and hostility. To begin with, the emphasis on relative gains discounts valuations by individuals of changes in absolute gains of their in-group over time. Individuals in migrant-receiving societies – in addition to or instead of asking which group gains more from the cross-border movement of people – may also ask a different question, namely: Are we better off after migration began, or were we better off before they started arriving? An election campaign theme – "Are you better off now than you were four years ago?" – sought to tap into precisely this perceptual logic. Why and how would interpretation of economic interactions through the prism of absolute gains affect migration phobia? At least three theoretical positions are worth considering.

First, the idea that perception of absolute economic gains may have a strong and independent effect on interethnic hostility is implicit in the commercial liberal perspective of international political economy.

The theory emphasizes that economic issues differ fundamentally from security issues by allowing for a wider range of positive-sum outcomes. Monetary gains can be quickly redistributed among populations and therefore the balance of economic gains is by definition flexible and adjustable. The demographic balance – due to differential fertility and mortality rates or migration – is not flexible and adjustable in this manner. Populations are significantly harder to reallocate and redistribute than money is. Large-scale forced population transfers such as the slave trade, the settlement of Siberia, the Holocaust, Stalin's mass deportations, Mao's intellectuals-to-the-countryside projects, and ethnic cleansing have been infinitely more traumatic, violent, and logistically challenging than money transfers over the transatlantic cable or the Internet.

In addition, from the standpoint of commercial liberalism, economic interactions create interdependence of tangible interests on a daily basis and cue individuals to care more about absolute gains to them and their group rather than about gains of others. As Robert Gilpin (1998: 281) summarized it, "[T]rade and economic intercourse are a source of peaceful relations among nations because the mutual benefits of trade and expanding interdependence among national economies will tend to foster cooperative relations." Transposing this logic to interpersonal and intergroup relations, we should expect residents of migrant-receiving states to value *absolute* gains to them from migration above the assessment of their gains *relative* to migrants. Perceptions of changes in overall group circumstances would also play a pivotal role in one's sense of "group worth." In an important way, the results of the survey reported by Frank and Sunstein (2001) indicate that small differences in total absolute income may matter to individuals than significantly larger differences between their income and the incomes of others. To remind, respondents were asked to choose between two scenarios: (1) own earnings are $110,000, others make $200,000, and (2) own earnings are $100,000, others make $85,000. Given these options and assuming that relative valuations are decisive, one would expect most respondents to prefer a $10,000 reduction of their own income and a $115,000 reduction of others' income over a $10,000 increase of their own income and a $115,000 increase of others' income. Two additional points must be made, supporting the incorporation of absolute gains perception in measures of economic valuations. For once, even if the arrival of ethnic others engenders group comparison and gives rise to "cleave-and-compare" valuations across groups, it does not necessarily follow that individuals would abandon comparing their current economic situation with the one prior to the others' arrival. Second, rather than engendering passive envy and frustration, negative comparison to others may instead boost one's sense of pride and desire to prove one's individual and group worth – perhaps in a different economic sector. This desire could be a psychological driver of the ethnic labor competition paradox profoundly examined and richly documented by Horowitz (1985: 105–43). Horowitz noted a correlation between ethnic division of labor and ethnic division of business on the one hand and a decrease in economic competition, on the other. He concluded (1985: 113), "The net result of the ethnic division of labor is greatly to reduce the occasions for economic competition and to channel competition within trades and occupations in an intraethnic direction." In other words, rather than driving hostility, relative gains perceptions may also increase incentives for ethnic division of labor and indirectly reduce hostility.

Second, prospect theory (Kahneman and Tversky 1979) implicitly links human behavior to perceived changes in absolute in-group gains over time – independently from valuations of differences in gains across groups. As summarized by Levy (2002: 272), "The central analytical assumption of prospect theory is that people define value relative to a reference point (*reference dependence*) rather than in terms of net assets. . . ." In doing so, "People give more weight to losses from that reference point than to comparable gains (*loss aversion*) . . ." (ibid.). This implies that time is a likely factor in economic valuations, whether the reference point relates to one's own or to others' situations. Both reference dependence and loss aversion should therefore be strong factors in valuations of socioeconomic consequences of migration. The arrival of migrants would mark a salient reference point – with both an intergroup dimension and a time dimension – against which changes in value are likely to be assessed. The value in question is the size of absolute gains to the incumbent group, or host population, assessed against a certain reference point in time. Positive views of migrants are likely to arise if the perceived change in absolute in-group gain is positive, and vice versa. The logic of loss aversion suggests, at the same time, that antimigrant attitudes are likely to be stronger than promigrant attitudes given the same amount of absolute in-group losses and gains.

Third, with respect to perceptual microfoundations, the same experiments in the "minimal intergroup situations" that showed children consistently using the Maximizing the Difference strategy in allocating money, also revealed that the absolute gains strategy labeled Maximizing In-group Payoffs "carried some weight of its own" (Vaughan, Tajfel, and Williams 1981: 41). Other psychological experiments (Rabbie et al. 1989) suggested that social categorization – or individual perceptions of the distinctiveness of group boundaries – is in itself a function of perceived "interdependence of fate," in which interdependence of interests plays a key role. This theoretical approach – referred to in psychological literature as the Behavioral Interaction Model – directly implies that maximization of in-group payoffs would soften the distinctiveness of group boundaries. Therefore, a perception that absolute gains accrue to one's in-group, as a result of intergroup economic exchanges, should be expected to mitigate the competitive logic and, hence, reduce perceived threat and hostility toward the newcomers.

Socioeconomic Impact Perceptions: Combining Absolute and Relative Gains

At first glance, the logics of absolute and relative gains work at cross-purposes. At least classic debates in the discipline of international relations between proponents of interdependence theory and political realism would suggest so. If in their interaction with outsiders, individuals predominantly focused on maximizing the payoff difference across groups, host populations would view migration as a threat to their interests if they believed the migrants could disproportionately benefit at their expense. If individuals in intergroup situations predominantly focused on maximizing in-group payoffs, then host populations would view migration as a threat to their interests only if they believed their own group's fortune was declining. The decline in in-group payoffs could be associated either with overall economic conditions in the receiving state or with the impact of migration. Payoffs to the migrants would be discounted.

Perceptual Interactivity

Psychological experiments in minimal intergroup situations strongly suggest, however, that Maximizing the Difference and Maximizing In-group Payoffs are complementary strategies. In fact, individuals in the real world appear to make choices that would maximize both types of payoffs simultaneously. Experiments have shown that the fusion of these strategies is a better predictor of group discrimination than either strategy in its pure form. Brewer (1979) found that Maximizing the Difference and Maximizing In-group Payoffs were both embedded in in-group bias. In experiments by Vaughan, Tajfel, and Williams (1981: 41), a combination of these two strategies influenced money allocation by children more strongly than any other strategy or a combination thereof. They also found that the Maximizing-the-Difference-plus-Maximizing-In-group-Payoff strategy exceeded the impact of pure Maximizing the Difference strategy by a sizeable and statistically significant margin. For example, subjects were more likely to allocate four coins to the in-group (Red) box and three coins to the out-group (Blue) box than one coin to the Red box and zero coins to the Blue box.

These experimental findings suggest that the perceptual microfoundations of the security dilemma with respect to economic valuations should embrace precisely this interaction between preferences for maximizing group differences and preferences for maximum in-group payoffs. This is a major insight, suggesting that the perceptual logic of the security dilemma may not rest on the assessment of relative gains, as much as it would on the assessment of perceived changes in absolute in-group gains over time. Put simply, *relative* in *relative deprivation* would mean not only relative to other groups, but also relative to the same group over time.

More generally, threat perception and hostility would be a product of what I will term *socioeconomic impact perceptions*. Central to this concept is the assessment of how one's group's economic and social conditions are affected by interactions with members of a different group. This concept integrates absolute and relative gains valuations. Absolute gains perceptions are integrated through individuals estimating the effects of migrants' activities on changes in the overall socioeconomic condition of the host community. Relative gains perceptions are integrated through individuals implicitly contrasting their current socioeconomic situation with how they fared prior to the migrants' arrival. In a sense, through socioeconomic-impact perceptions individuals evaluate whether interethnic exchanges do in fact generate the proverbial "comparative advantage" that is likely to lift all boats. This evaluation is also part and parcel of individuals evaluating their "group worth" in relation both to ethnic newcomers and their own situation prior to the newcomers arrival.

Two principal components of socioeconomic impact perceptions would transcend context-specific issues: (a) the assessment of absolute in-group gains as related – although not necessarily directly or even consciously – to some reference point in time ("cleave-and-compare" over time), and (b) explicit identification of that reference point with the arrival of out-groups (e.g., ethnically distinct migrants). The latter suggests that alarmism and hostility are most likely anchored in valuations of economic conditions in the present or in the immediately observable or immediately relevant past. This supposition strongly – albeit not straightforwardly – resonates with studies of economic voting in the United States and Western Europe.

One of the central debates in this literature is whether voting decisions are shaped more by retrospective or prospective valuations of economic circumstances. Do individuals care more about the past or the future when it comes to economic assessments? Leaving aside the debate on whether prospective voting is "rational" while retrospective voting is "naïve" – something that is outside the focus of the present study – there is a solid empirical consensus in the literature that not only *both* looking forward and looking backward matters in voting decisions, but that the two are inseparable, complementary, and interactive (Fiorina 1981; Lanoue 1994; Lewis-Beck 1986; Lockerbie 1991; Stein 1990; Suzuki and Chappell 1996; Uslaner 1989). Significantly, the same inference can be made from theoretical modeling by rational-choice theorists who insist that only prospective valuations matter. Thus, in his spatial model of election, Anthony Downs (1957) asserts that a rational voter would shape decisions on valuation of competing promises about economic future. However, further on Downs acknowledges that when it comes to specific issues, "the [retrospective – author] records of each party" would be "more important to their decisions than party promises about the future" (ibid., quoted in Uslaner 1989: 496). Similarly, Achen (1996: 199) forcefully argues that for the rational voter "bygones are bygones, and only the future matters." Three sentences later, however, Achen implies that the past matters and that looking back is quintessential for looking forward. This comes through in a seemingly dismissive statement that "the past is useful only for its clues about the future" (ibid.). But, if not in the past, where else would such clues lie and how else would reputations emerge upon which prospective valuations could be based? In a sense, ancient folk wisdom appears to transcend the whole debate with the notion that the best prophet is the one who has the longest memory.

Thus, on balance, the weight of empirical evidence in the literature supports the proposition that policy preferences – including antimigrant exclusionism – are likely to be affected more by valuations of the current and recent economic conditions from which individuals could make plausible extrapolations into the future. In contrast, noneconomic valuations would require less of a track record to make judgments about the future and individuals are more likely to use speculative, forward-looking assessments regarding government capacity to resolve disputes, ethnic balances, and group intent. These valuations – and perhaps to a lesser extent the assessment of military balances (because the latter depend on the capacity of other states that are costly to estimate for the average individual) – need to be projected into the future to arouse fear and hostility.

The economic voting literature also suggests that political decisions of individuals are shaped interactively by the perceptions of both personal and national economic circumstances. On the one hand, studies by Kinder and Kiewiet (1978) and Brody and Sniderman (1977) suggest that voting decisions are typically "sociotropic," that is, they arise from valuations of the national rather than the personal pocketbook. On the other hand, Fiorina (1981) argued that personal economic well-being is also a significant component of voting decisions. Building on Fiorina's idea that most economic valuations are not simple, but "mediated" – or conditioned by perceived responsibility of government officials for both personal and national economic conditions – Stein (1991) found that in voting for governors and U.S. senators Americans took into consideration both their personal financial circumstances and economic conditions in their states. To the extent that migration has fewer immediate effects on individual financial circumstances than, say, government taxation and spending policies, "sociotropic" perceptions are more likely to affect immigration attitudes than "pocketbook" perceptions.

Thus, with respect to the socioeconomic impact of migration, this study focuses on what may be termed as "recently retrospective" or "immediately retrospective" valuations among the native populations of the economic and social issues of primary concern to the receiving societies and communities – be it manufacturing output, agriculture, welfare, education, or crime. In addition, valuation of socioeconomic effects is likely also to be affected by perceptions of government capacity to regulate economic exchanges. These, however, need to be distinguished from direct effects of perceived relative and absolute gains for host societies that have been the main focus of this chapter.

From Socioeconomic Impact to Threat and Hostility: The Nature of the Linkage

This last distinction brings us to the question: What kind of perceptual pathways would link socioeconomic impact valuations with the sense of security threat and especially with antimigrant hostility? In the United States, one study (Citrin et al. 1997: 863) tersely suggested that retrospective economic impact assessments matter because they represent "cognitive links in the hypothesized chain between economic circumstances and opinions about immigration policy." Would these cognitive links also matter when individuals weigh socioeconomic impact against security threats, and why?

Theoretical arguments suggest they would, and perhaps no less decisively, for at least three reasons. First, socioeconomic impact perceptions are likely to affect the logic of group comparison. Summarizing sociological studies, Lawrence Bobo (1999: 452) wrote, "to admit of a strong socioemotional dimension of the sense of group position is by no means to mitigate or deny a central place of collective or racial group interests in the dynamics of prejudice." The term *interest* here refers to tangible economic or status considerations, and the latter are, in many ways, linked to one's group position with respect to distribution of resources in society. Perceived threats to individual and group interests and intergroup hostility would therefore arise in conjunction with the sense of group identity and affect. In this sense, estimation of utility – or ranking of economic preferences – interacts with emotional states of individuals, with emotional images of out-groups. As Allport (1954: 233) put it, "Realistic conflict [i.e., rational conflict of interest] is like a note on an organ. It sets all prejudices that are attuned to it into simultaneous vibration. The listener can scarcely distinguish the pure note from the surrounding jangle." By doing so, socioeconomic impact perceptions can slow down or rev up fears that ostensibly arise under the security dilemma. On the one hand, economic gains from migration signal to the host population that migrants would not necessarily exploit local hospitality. Reputations for cooperative reciprocity get a chance. The stronger the perception of economic gains, the easier it is for the host population to attribute "defensive" (legal cross-border trade) versus "offensive" (illegal settlement and competition for resources) intentions to migrants. Taxes, rents, and bribes would reduce incentives for political leaders to reify the host populations' sense of "groupness." Xenophobic campaigning and antimigrant policies would be less appealing. In contrast, negative economic impact perceptions would suggest that expectations of absolute gains to host populations had been illusory. Feeling exploited, betrayed, more ambivalent about migrant intentions, and free of fear to lose benefits, the host population would become increasingly threatened and emotionally responsive to racist and xenophobic symbolism. In either the positive or the negative sense, the interaction of group comparison and socioeconomic assessments would generate a synergy between the rational and symbolic logics of the security dilemma.

Second, this rational–symbolic synergy is likely to be reinforced by the logic of loss aversion. Taking loss aversion into account would emphasize the importance in threat perception of the initial socioeconomic impact of migration on receiving societies. For this reason, socioeconomic impact valuations are likely to relate to immigration phobia particularly strongly in cases where mass migration is a new phenomenon or where migrants represent a new group distinct from host populations in ethnic or cultural terms. This distinctiveness would make it easier for the host populations to identify the reference point in time against which the economic effects will be assessed. If positive initial impact valuations prevail and endure, the host populations may be expected to be averse to losing whatever initial gains they believed to have obtained. Positive initial impact is therefore likely to constrain proclivity for aggressive response to migrants – although not necessarily fear – because host societies would be averse to losing the gains associated with migration. In this sense, loss aversion will restrain migration phobia. Absence of such positive impact or ambiguity about socioeconomic effects of migration would remove this constraint on aggressive proclivities.

Third, clearly implicit in assessments of in-group gains over time is the sense of group opportunity. This sense of opportunity may not matter when life goes on as usual and opportunities are perceived to be open to group members, but it is likely to come into play strongly when groups sense that their collective opportunities are likely to be blocked. Perception of blocked opportunity may be directly associated with the very fact of migrants' arrival, or it may develop gradually when certain migrant activities get interpreted as constraining incumbent groups' chances. In fact, the arrival of migrants may signal unblocking or opening of certain opportunities – an expectation which subsequent experience and impressions may validate and reinforce, or dispel and reverse. The latter are likely to blend with the perception of betrayed expectations and cue stronger fears and antimigrant hostility than the initial negative impact would.

Nathan Caplan and Jeffrey Paige (1968) established the effects of "blocked opportunity" perceptions on interethnic hostility in a survey of African American participants of major riots in Detroit and Newark. Their study is particularly of note because one of the rival hypotheses the authors considered was relative deprivation and its two principal dimensions: perceptions by African Americans "that the lot of the Negro is improving, but not enough ('the revolution of rising expectations')" and "an implicit comparison with the economic situation of whites" (Caplan and Paige 1968: 14). Perceived lack of group opportunity – through a sense of group exclusion – especially in employment and education, was the strongest predictor of riot participation in the study. Blocked group opportunity was also related to a sense of group pride and potential superiority – suggesting that host populations are likely to link negative socioeconomic impact of migrants with a threat to their group position. Through this concatenation of yearning for gains and for pride, the rational and symbolic foundations of insecurity merge once again in the logic of "blocked opportunities."

Socioeconomic Impact and Immigration Attitudes: Empirical Findings in the United States

Recent studies illustrate the potency of socioeconomic impact perceptions in gauging antimigrant sentiments. In their analysis of the 1992 American National Election Survey (ANES, $N = 2{,}428$) published in *The Journal of Politics*, Citrin et al. (1997) found that respondents who believed that Hispanic and Asian immigration to the United States would not have any negative impact on jobs and taxes were also unlikely to favor restrictions on immigration to the United States. Respondents who believed that Hispanics and Asians would positively contribute to culture in the United States were also among those most likely to oppose immigration restrictions. Citrin and his colleagues also found that retrospective valuations of national economy were a significant predictor of preferences regarding the level of immigration to the United States.[1] The index by which these retrospective valuations were measured consisted of three items, one of which was unemployment – suggesting that sensitivity to economic impact was part of this predictor of attitudes toward levels of immigration.

The significance of the "impact" measures in this study – which capture both absolute and relative gains perception – comes through strongly when one compares interactive effects of different factors cueing the level of immigration preferences. For example, consistent with the labor market competition theory, Citrin and his colleagues found in two probit (regression) models that opposition to immigration was associated significantly with blue-collar workers living in counties with a high level of immigration. However, if the same blue-collar workers believed that immigration would have no negative impact on jobs and taxes, they were no more likely to oppose immigration of foreign nationals to the United States than

[1] *Significant* has a conventional statistical meaning here – a significant relationship is one for which the likelihood that it would happen by chance is 5 percent or less.

other categories of respondents. Also, while evaluation of unemployment trends (as part of national retrospective evaluations) did relate to a level of immigration preferences, the actual employment status of respondents did not. As Citrin, Green, Muste, and Wong (1997: 865) concluded, "[T]he unemployed were no more likely to say that the current level of immigration should be reduced than were respondents with steady jobs." Both groups were sensitive, however, to employment trends and evaluations of job and tax impact of immigrants. These findings imply that while respondents may have been sensitive to the possibility that immigration would endanger their jobs and incomes; the same respondents also recognized that even if migrants compete for jobs with the locals, they might have an overall positive impact on employment and taxation. Perceptions that migrants compete for jobs with the host-country residents are insufficient to cause immigration phobia. These perceptions would be balanced against perceptions of overall socioeconomic impact on migrants. Antimigrant hostility would therefore be likely only if the *balance* of these perceptions were negative. The impact perceptions capture the views of precisely this balance and stand as a proxy for complex interactive effects of relative and absolute gains evaluations.

In their study of 1,262 respondents in a CBS News/*New York Times* poll conducted in June 1993, Espenshade and Hempstead (1996) examined the relationship between attitudes toward immigrants and the level of immigration preferences. The survey question regarding the latter was almost identical to the one in the 1992 ANES studied by Citrin and colleagues.[2] Of the eight measures of attitudes about immigrants in the Espenshade and Hempstead study, three dealt with immigration impact on a host population and five predominantly contained characterization of migrant activities. The three impact measures were based on questions asking whether immigrants were likely to take jobs Americans did not want and whether most recent immigrants contributed to the host country or caused problems. All three were found significantly associated with respondents' feelings about overall levels of immigration. The relationship was straightforward: For example, respondents who believed immigrants sought jobs Americans did not want were also likely to say immigration

2 In 1992, ANES respondents were asked if "the number of immigrants from foreign countries who are permitted to come to the United States to live should be increased, left the same, or decreased." In the 1993 CBS News/*New York Times* poll, respondents were asked if they would like to see the level of immigration to the United States increase, decrease, or stay the same.

level to the United States should increase or stay the same. In contrast, all five "nonimpact" measures failed to register any significant relationship with immigration-level preferences.[3]

These studies suggest that by directly linking one group members' conditions with another group members' activities, the assessment of socioeconomic effects across ethnic lines is likely to be a stronger and more significant predictor of interethnic hostility than perceived intensity of labor market competition (and, hence, relative gains assessments) and than most aggregate measures of macroeconomic conditions, valuation of individual economic circumstances and trends, and individual incomes.[4] In several rigorous studies (Espenshade and Hempstead 1996; Fetzer 2000), even one's own employment situation failed to come out as a statistically significant correlate of antimigrant sentiments. Respondents' incomes, union membership, assessment of the health of the national economy, and satisfaction with one's life's circumstances have not been consistently significant predictors of immigration attitudes either.

While important, these studies do not necessarily indicate that socioeconomic impact perceptions would matter decisively in the formation of interethnic hostility – especially where migration is associated with larger security threats than, say, everyday crime. First, assessments of group threat – including, in particular, threats of violent unrest in host communities and threats to territorial integrity of the receiving states – were not accounted for in these studies. One cannot hold this against the study authors, because they were concerned with different questions in the U.S. context. But this limitation warrants that the findings would not necessarily apply to individuals under threat. Second, attitudes and feelings about the level of immigration – while reflecting on tolerance – are not coterminous with proclivity for aggressive response to migration. For example, an individual favoring a decrease in immigration level may also believe that the best way to stem immigration flow is through nonhostile, noncoercive measures. Such measures do not even have to include tougher immigration laws or tighter border protection. Respondents may believe that economic assistance to the immigrant-sending state would be a better idea. Nevertheless, these studies do highlight a significant relationship between socioeconomic impact perceptions and perceived immigration

[3] These five measures were based on survey questions asking if most recent immigrants were in the United State legally; if they worked as hard as or harder than people born in the United States; if most of them ended up on welfare; if most of them came from Latin America or Asia; and if they would be welcome in respondents' neighborhoods.

[4] For an empirical test combining opinion and aggregate data, see Alexseev (2003).

levels – a relationship that plays an important part in the threat–hostility logic.

Conclusion: The Immigration Security Dilemma Model and Its Indicators

The immigration security dilemma is likely to arise from interactive valuations of absolute (in-group) and relative (intergroup) gains. In viewing their economic situation, individuals are likely to value maximum gains relative to out-groups *along with* maximum gains to their own in-groups. Perceptions of relative gains arise from valuations of individuals' economic situation and from a comparison of the incumbent groups' gains and migrants' gains from economic interactions. A more powerful driver of the logic of the security dilemma, however, is likely to be retrospective *socioeconomic impact perceptions*. The perceptions of impact would arise from individual experiences and impressions concerning changes in the incumbent group gains relative to the arrival of migrants (out-groups). Whereas specific indicators of socioeconomic impact perceptions would vary contextually, they are most likely to encompass migration's impact on income opportunities, domestic industries and agriculture, employment, prices, the environment, and crime rates, among other factors.

The immigration security dilemma is distinct from existing models of antimigrant hostility in five crucial respects: (1) threat is defined exclusively in terms of the security of individuals, groups, and states, and hostility is defined in terms of the support for specific policy responses to threat; (2) two new and distinct variables are included in the model: the sense of government capacity to regulate intergroup relations and of the intentions and loyalties of migrants; (3) measures of "symbolic" conflict emphasize group distinctiveness and "assimilability" rather than negative stereotypes; (4) measures of realistic threat – implicit in economic competition – combine valuation of relative and absolute gains; and (5) indirect effects of causal variables on hostility through threat are controlled.

Limited to direct effects, the immigration security dilemma can be modeled as standard regression equations (graphically illustrated in Figure 3.1):

(a) for threat perception:

$$T_i = a + b_1\text{ANARCHY} + b_2\text{INTENT} + b_3\text{GROUPNESS} + b_4\text{IMPACT} + b_5\text{CONTROLS} + e$$

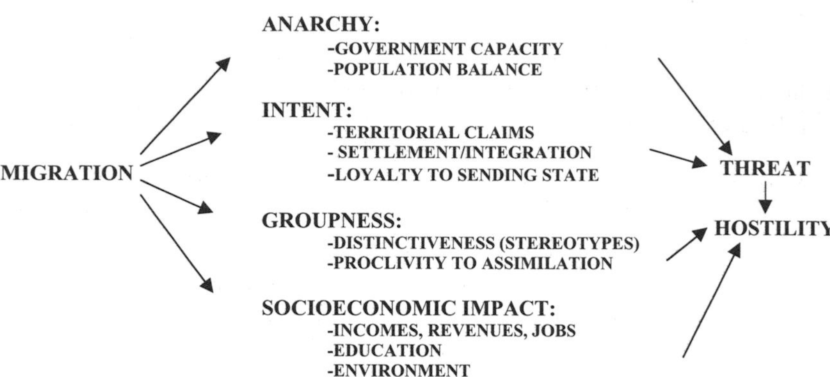

FIGURE 3.1. The Security Dilemma Model of Antimigrant Hostility.

(b) for hostility:

$$
\begin{aligned}
H_i = a &+ b_1\text{ANARCHY} + b_2\text{INTENT} + b_3\text{GROUPNESS} \\
&+ b_4\text{IMPACT} + b_5\text{CONTROLS} \\
&+ b_6\text{INDIRECT EFFECTS } (T_i) + e
\end{aligned}
$$

In these equations, the *b*-values are coefficients corresponding to each independent variable value, *a* is a constant value, and *e* is an error term. INDIRECT EFFECTS (T_i) are estimated for significant predictors of threat (T_i). The direct effects of each predictor are estimated after other predictors have been controlled by inspection of regression coefficients.

While acknowledging broader demographic, political, and socioeconomic contexts in which migration takes place, it is of crucial importance that uncertainty and inability to comprehend these contexts and their implications are part and parcel of the social and perceptual logic of the security dilemma. For estimating alarmism and hostility, therefore, opinion measures are likely to be more proximate and direct predictors – even though it is important to consider them in context. As Snyder and Jervis wrote (1999: 26): "People try to understand their real strategic situation, because they know their fates depend on it, but under uncertainty their ability to analyze these social facts is clouded by cognitive biases and by the manipulation of strategic ideologists who have their own parochial agendas." Table 3.1 lays out hypothetical situational signposts and opinion measures indicative of the immigration security dilemma.

TABLE 3.1. *The Immigration Security Dilemma: Contextual Indicators and Opinion Measures*

Variables	Contextual Indicators	Survey/Interview Questions
Outcome variables:		
Threat (fear)	n/a	Does migration threaten the security of your state, region, county/city/town/village, and you personally? How likely are armed conflicts with the migrant-sending state/group?
Hostility	n/a	What should be our responses to migration regarding border closure, deportation, support for paramilitary antimigrant groups, and support for antiimmigrant politicians/parties?
Explanatory variables:		
"Emergent Anarchy"	Nonpayment to military, police, border guards Proliferation of private "armies" Government failure to pay salaries and provide services Failure of central and provincial governments to divide Jurisdictions, intense center–periphery disputes Intensifying activities of regional separatist movements Endemic corruption Mortality exceeding fertility in host states Outmigration of host population Sending state has larger population than host state Migrant-receiving areas less densely populated than migrant-sending areas	How capable is the government to resolve/prevent interethnic (intergroup) conflict? How capable is the government to protect security and vital interests of its citizens? How easily can migrants bribe our government officials to achieve their goals? How large is the proportion of migrants in the local population – now and X number of years in the future? How capable is the government to protect borders? What is the balance of military power between our state and the migrant-sending state – now and X years ahead?

(continued)

TABLE 3.1 *(continued)*

Variables	Contextual Indicators	Survey/Interview Questions
	Long, permeable borders between sending and receiving states Decline of military capabilities relative to the sending state(s) Economic decline relative to the sending state(s)	What is the balance of economic power between our state and the migrant-sending state – now and X years ahead? How isolated is our area from the capital (political center) of our country?
Offensive Intent	Record of military conflict and violence with sending state Border disputes with sending state Record of territorial claims Competition for resources with sending state/populations Economic, political, and environmental "push" and "pull" factors give incentives for immigration	Do migrants and/or sending-state governments believe that a host state is historically their territory (may they claim it)? Do migrants intend to settle permanently and bring in family members, friends, etc. to increase their group's presence in the host state? How loyal are the migrants to the government of their country of origin?
Groupness	Racial, ethnic, linguistic, cultural, religious distinctions between host and migrant populations Formal and informal institutions promoting group identity and cohesiveness among migrants	Which of the following characteristics are typical of (a) group X (host population) and (b) group Y (migrants): e.g., industriousness, honesty, greed, laziness, etc. How likely are migrants to assimilate (become like us)? How do you feel about you or your family members marrying members of the migrant group?

Economic Impact/Vulnerability	Economic decline/growth Negative economic effects of migration (e.g., low-quality imports, environmental damage, resource plundering, asset stripping, etc.) Positive economic effects (e.g., investment, joint ventures, trade, job opportunities)	Who gains more from migration: us or the migrants? How does migration affect local industry, agriculture, prices, jobs, budget revenues, environment, crime, etc.? What proportion of the host population benefits economically from migration?
Control variables:		
Group Position (Sensitivity to majority-minority status reversal/ minority group size	n/a	Our area will no longer be truly ours if the proportion of group X (migrants) in the local population reaches how much? (followed by options, e.g., 1/10, 1/3, 1/2, etc.) Has migration reached its limits?
Ideology	Percent electoral support for antiimmigrant parties and/or politicians	Measures of trust in parties articulating antiimmigrant positions Where should the borders of our state lie? (measures sensitivity to territorial expansion/contraction of host state)
Education Religion Occupation	Percent of population college educated Percent actively professing dominant group religion Percent unemployed Percent workforce exposed to job competition	Level of education, college eduction Religious preferences of respondents Occupational status of respondents
Gender/Age ("Young male factor")	Percentage males under age thirty in host population	Same among survey respondents

The four principal dimensions of the immigration security dilemma are likely to be enhanced by other factors. These are entered as controls in the model. They include individual sensitivity to overcrowding (Averill 1973; Cohen, Glass, and Philips 1979; Hall 1962; Kelly and Galle 1984; Proshansky 1984) and to majority–minority status reversal (Prislin, Limbert, and Bauer 2000); ideological preferences expressed as group boundaries (Hanson 1996) or support for political issues and parties (Citrin, Reingold, and Green 1990; Thalhammer et al. 2001), including alienation from politics and mistrust of all parties (Bobo 1999; Bobo and Hutchings 1996; Blumer 1958; Caplan and Paige 1968); college education typically linked to tolerance (Chandler and Tsai 2001; Jackman 1978, 1981, but see Jackman and Muha 1984); and standard sociological indicators such as personal income, occupation, gender, and urban or rural residency.

Whereas this study focuses on emergent threat perceptions among host societies, the security-dilemma theory implies that certain situational signposts and opinion measures are likely to predict the rise of retaliatory suspicion and mistrust among migrant populations in response to exclusionist or restrictive policies. Do migrants see any of such policies as threatening the security of their group? Would they be more willing to pay higher prices to smugglers or go into hiding? Would such policies make them more or less likely to return home? In other words, do migrants hate or trust the natives "in return" if they believe the natives hate or trust them? Future research may focus on these and similar measures, although obtaining this data would require extensive and carefully sampled surveys among elusive migrant populations and analysis would require sophisticated longitudinal tests – a substantial, yet potentially rewarding challenge.

4

In the Shadow of the "Asian Balkans"

Anti-Chinese Alarmism and Hostility in the Russian Far East

> One day we will wake up and half the population here will be slit-eyed....
>
> A Vladivostok cab driver talking with the author, May 1999

> If you do not take practical steps to advance the Far East soon, after a few decades, the Russian population will be speaking Japanese, Chinese, and Korean.
>
> Vladimir Putin, Russian president, speaking to residents of Blagoveshchensk, a city bordering China across the Amur River, July 2000

On August 14, 2002, a striking front-page photomontage greeted the readers of Russia's mainstream daily newspaper, *Gazeta*. It showed the Russian president, Vladimir Putin, wearing a benevolent, mellow smile and a Chairman Mao–style blue uniform. The optimism-exuding president, accompanied by his prime minister, was holding a tense, frightened baby on his knees. The child looked distinctly Asian, presumably Chinese. This was not an April Fools' Day joke, a last-minute manipulation by a hacker, or an editorial prank. This was an illustration of a serious front-page story in a serious, politically well-connected Russian newspaper. The story was titled: "Every Other Person in Russia Will Be a Huatsiao [Chinese migrant]." It presented a detailed summary of expert assessments commissioned by Russia's upper house of parliament, the Federation Council. The study concluded that by 2050 the Chinese would become Russia's second largest ethnic group.[1]

[1] The photo was published on the *Gazeta* Web site (http://www.gazeta.ru) and it can be viewed at the author's home pages at San Diego State University (http://www-rohan.sdsu.edu/~alexseev).

I used the opening quotations and the description of the Putin photomontage to introduce the argument that Chinese migration into the Russian Far East after the collapse of the Soviet Union is a critical case study of immigration phobia and the security dilemma. Antimigrant alarmism and hostility – viewing Chinese migration as if it were a demographic tsunami ready to crash into the Russian Far East without warning – became a major social and political force in the Russian provinces bordering on China, from Irkutsk on Lake Baikal to Vladivostok on the Pacific. The alarmism persists at the time of writing, even though the scale of migration since the early 1990s has remained marginal when measured as the percentage of the local Russian population. But while Chinese traders, tourists, laborers, investors, students, athletes, poachers, and gangsters failed to form sizeable Chinese communities in the region, they were crisscrossing the border that had been shut for more than half a century. Starting in the early 1990s, the Chinese migrants arrived into the far-flung provinces of Russia at a time when Russia experienced the collapse of government authority; the "parade of sovereignties" by its constituent units; the breakdown of the largest centrally planned economy in the world; the reversal of the 140-year trend of natural population growth; and rampant organized crime. Migration occurred between states with a long record of conflict and mistrust. It juxtaposed culturally distant groups representing two of Eurasia's largest military powers, against the background of ethnonationalist legacies, a rough frontier culture, and pervasive social alienation in the Russian Far East. At the same time, by the year 2000 threats of Siberian and Far Eastern separatism evaporated into political insignificance; the economy remained functional, and the chronic shortages of the Soviet era became the thing of the past; the ethnic "face" of border regions remained decisively Slavic; the border remained open and visa-free; tourist exchanges persisted; criminal violence failed to translate into mass communal violence; Russia–China relations improved, and most of the border demarcation disputes were resolved; no mass protests or violence against Chinese migrants took place; and joint businesses and cultural exchanges between the Russian and the Chinese border provinces proliferated. A tenuous equilibrium between threats and hopes – between the drivers and constraints of the interethnic security dilemma – emerged in the Russian Far East. By conditioning a wide variation of attitudes toward the Chinese newcomers, this equilibrium makes the Russian Far East an ideal case for examining the interaction of the social and perceptual logics of the interethnic security dilemma arising from cross-border migration. My analysis focuses on Primorskii krai (Maritime Territory) – the most populous and economically advanced region in the Russian Far East and the one representative of the Chinese border migration and its demographic, political, and socioeconomic contexts.[2]

The "Yellow Peril" Revisited: The Scale of Fear vs. the Scale of Migration

Since the late 1930s, when the Chinese and Korean residents were deported en masse from the Russian Far East, the Soviet government sealed the border with China and restricted the flow of people to officially sanctioned delegations until 1988, when the Soviet Union and China signed the agreement on visa-free cross-border tourism. Following the collapse of the Soviet Union and the demise of the communist security state, thousands of Chinese and Russian citizens took advantage of these changes. It did not take long for the Russian media to define Chinese migration as "the yellow wave" and to warn that this wave threatened Russia's sovereignty over vast territories in Siberia and the Far East. Viktor Larin, director of the Vladivostok Institute of the History, Archeology and Ethnography of the Peoples of the Far East (IHAE) counted more than 150 articles in the Primorskii and Russian press from 1993 to 1995 that voiced these threats while providing no specific data on Chinese migration to substantiate them. The Russian national daily *Izvestiia*, for example, asked "The Chinese in the Far East: Guests or Masters?" Another Russian daily, *Komsomol'skaia Pravda* wondered, "Will Vladivostok Become a Suburb of Kharbin?" A Vladivostok mass market tabloid, *Novosti*, warned "The Chinese Are Unarmed, But Very Dangerous" (Larin (1998: 72).

Government officials from Moscow to Vladivostok consistently articulated the same kind of alarmist sentiments. The most brash and vociferous warnings – accompanied by staged public events such as visits to disputed border areas – came from Yevgenii Nazdratenko, the governor of Primorskii from 1993 to 2001. In a book published during the 1999 gubernatorial election campaign – provocatively entitled "And All of Russia Behind My Back" – Nazdratenko starts with a selection of press articles crediting himself with nearly saving Primorskii krai and the Russian Far East from "Sinification" (*kitaizatsiia*).

[2] Primorskii krai's index of economic development was estimated as the highest for the Russian Far East at 3 (with Kamchatka = 1), followed by Khabarovsk at 2.5 (Miller and Stephanopoulos 1997).

Restated and reworded thousands of times, these fears also emerged in statements by other borderland governors. In July 1999, Governor Viktor Ishaev of Khabarovskii krai – to the west and north of Primorskii – warned of "a peaceful invasion" of the Russian Far East by ethnic Chinese (*Rossiiskaia Gazeta*, July 10, 1999: 4, quoted in Wishnick 2000: 98). And speaking to residents of Blagoveshchensk, a city on the border with China across the Amur River, in July 2000, Vladimir Putin said: "If you do not take practical steps to advance the Far East soon, after a few decades, the Russian population will be speaking Japanese, Chinese, and Korean."

Widely divergent and consistently inflated estimates of the number of Chinese migrants settling down in Primorskii krai and in the Russian Far East permeated the media and government discourses. In 1993 and 1994, the Primorskii and Russian press reported that up to 150,000 illegal immigrants were settling in Primorskii krai as part of the 400,000 to two million Chinese migrants who had "infiltrated" the Russian Far East (Larin 1998: 72, 74–5). One article reprinted in governor Nazdratenko's 1999 book claimed – without any basis in fact – that "in the spring of 1993 every third passer-by in Vladivostok was Chinese."

While political leaders and the media disseminated these estimates, other government agencies conducted investigations and collected statistical data on the actual scale of Chinese migration. The interior ministry's administration for Primorskii krai in 1994 carried out systematic sweeps of streets, factories, markets, shops, and farms and reported that the number of Chinese nationals in the Maritime Territory was approximately 12,000 – or nearly twenty times fewer than the estimates for Vladivostok by governor Nazdratenko. Moreover, according to the Pacific Regional Directorate of the Russian Border Service, Sedykh, that same year 17,845 Chinese nationals entered Primorskii krai and 10,587 of them returned to China. Of the 6,872 who stayed over illegally, 2,531 were deported – reducing the interior department assessment threefold. And according to Viktor Plotnikov, head of the foreign citizens department at the internal affairs administration of Primorskii, only up to 2,000 Chinese nationals remained in Primorskii krai at the end of the winter of 1995 (Larin 1998: 76).[3]

[3] Similar exaggeration took place in other Far Eastern regions. In the Amur oblast, according to *Izvestiia* (March 16, 1995), Governor V. Diachenko said that in 1994 local authorities registered 4,000 violations of visa and passport rules, 1,500 of which were by Chinese nationals. At the same time, however, the published government statistics indicate that only 459 Chinese nationals were charged with visa and passport violations in the oblast that year (Larin 1998: 77).

TABLE 4.1. *Chinese Nationals Registered on Arrival in Primorskii Krai, 1994–2002*

	The Chinese in Primorskii			Sanctions Against Violators		
	Total Arrivals	Tourists[a]	Failed to Return	Administrative Penalties	Deportation Orders	Forced Deportation
1994	40,000	18,500	14,400	9,500	2,700	1,500
1995	35,000	18,500	11,200	12,300	6,600	4,500
1996	35,500	21,000	1,065	8,250	3,700	1,900
1997	52,000	39,000	468	8,250	4,000	2,100
1998	73,000	61,000	292	8,250	3,200	1,190
1999	80,287	n.d.[b]	400	n.d.	n.d.	2,825
January–June 2000	41,355[c]	n.d.	n.d.	n.d.	n.d.	1,850[d]
2002	105,000	79,000	negligible	negligible	negligible	negligible

[a] The overwhelming majority of these visitors came as part of a visa-free tourist group exchange allowed by the Russian immigration law. After 2002, most were issued two-week tourist visas.
[b] Whereas no data were provided, Lt.-Col. Plotnikov (see *Sources*) indicated that migration trends remained the same as in 1998, showing approximately the same proportion of administrative penalties, deportation orders, and forced deportation.
[c] This would put the annual number of Chinese nationals who arrived in Primorskii at about 80,000 to 90,000, according to Lt.-Col. Plotnikov.
[d] Projection based on migration service data reported by Yegorchev.
Source: Otdel viz i razreshenii Primorskogo kraia (OVIR), *Spravka*, Lt.-Col. Viktor M. Plotnikov, deputy head of the department, Vladivostok, June 2, 1999 and August 17, 2000. The data for 2002 are reported in Dmitrii Chernov, "Kitatiskaia bolezn' Dal'nego Vostoka: Diaspora zhivet po svoim zakonam." [The Chinese Disease of the Russian Far East. The Diaspora Lives According to Its Own Laws]. *Vremia novostei* (February 19, 2003): 6, at http://dlib.eastview.com; data on deportations in 1999 and 2000 by chief of Primorskii krai's Migration Service, Sergei Pushkarev, quoted in I. Yegorchev, "Nemnogo Istorii," *Sovetskii Sakhalin* (October 21, 2000), at http://dlib.eastview.com.

From 1999 to 2001, I investigated the scale of Chinese migration during five visits to Primorskii krai. I conducted visual observations in Vladivostok, Ussuriisk, Nakhodka, and Pogranichnyi; interviewed Primorskii government officials, scholars, and journalists; and examined press reports and statistical data. Documents that I obtained from the Visa and Registration Department (OVIR) indicated that the number of illegally overstaying visitors plummeted following the introduction by law enforcement agencies, starting in 1994, of tighter visa controls and spot checks in the streets, markets, and in the workplace (Operation Foreigner). These trends, summarized in Table 4.1 continued to the time of this writing in late 2004. By 1999, only 0.4 percent of registered visitors remained illegally in the krai.

A July 1999 internal report on migration and sedentarization (*osedanie*) of foreign nationals in Primorskii by the head of the Pacific regional administration of the federal border service (TORU) corroborated the OVIR data giving the number of attempted entries on forged passports as declining from 230 in 1996 to 120 in 1997 and 107 in 1998 (Tarasenko 1999: 1, 3, 4). In a memorandum issued upon this author's request in May 1999, TORU stated: "The situation on the border with the People's Republic of China (PRC) in recent years has been stable and predictable. It reflects the mutual aspiration of China and Russia to develop the necessary political conditions for a constructive partnership" (Pogranichnaia Sluzhba 1999). The number of legally employed PRC citizens in Primorskii, provided by the krai Goskomstat branch, was 7,895 in 1994, 8,349 in 1995, 8,292 in 1996, 6,968 in 1997, 7,179 in 1998, and 6,374 in 1999, also suggesting a stable and limited flow (Goskomstat Rossii 1999, 2000a). Reflecting the seasonal nature of migrant labor, the actual number of registered Chinese migrant workers on any given day in Primorskii was most likely lower than these estimates. In Ussuriisk, for example, I visited an enclosed area on the outskirts of the city where one is greeted by a sign, "China Town" (*Kitaiskii gorodok*), in Russian and Chinese on a pagoda-style gate with dragon heads. Designed to house some 1,300 Chinese laborers (Mikhail Vetrik, interview with the author, Ussuriisk, May 26, 1999), China Town was deserted during my visits in May 1999 and in September 2000. On both visits, the front gate was chained shut with empty barracks in variable states of dilapidation and no human activity inside. The main difference was that on the first visit mean-looking watchdogs ran around the empty grounds.[4]

Estimates by the chief of the federal migration service in Primorskii krai, Sergei Pushkarev, indicated that Chinese migrants were unlikely to comprise more than 0.3 to 1.1 percent of the local population in 1996–8, and more than 1.4 percent in 2000 (interviews with the author, Vladivostok, May 20, 1999 and August 15, 2000). For Russia's Far East as a whole, Russian scholars Karlusov and Kudin (2002: 81) estimated in May 2002 that the proportion of Chinese visitors (considering most of them return to China) did not exceed 3.3 percent of the Russian population (based on the estimated 250,000 Chinese visitors among 7.2 million Russian population). Finally, Goskomstat's (2003) own count during the

[4] The cover photo at the author's "Russia in Asia" Web page shows one of these dogs at the bottom of the gate (http://www-rohan.sdsu.edu/~alexseev).

census revealed approximately 35,000 Chinese nationals who were in Russia for any reason in 2002.

Despite the availability in the early 1990s of this statistical data from government agencies charged with registration of all Chinese nationals crossing the Russian border, the inflated, alarmist assessments have persisted ever since. The Russian daily *Komsomol'skaia Pravda* estimated in July 1999 that at least 1.5 million Chinese settled down in Russia (*Komsomol'skaia Pravda*, July 15, 1999; http://dlib.eastview.com). In January 2000, Russia's deputy interior minister, Valerii Fedorov, stated that most of about half a million Chinese nationals who arrived in Russia every year remained illegally on Russian territory (*Izvestiia*, January 26, 2000; http://dlib.eastview.com). When minister Vladimir Zorin released Russian census data in December 2002 showing that 390,000 Chinese had entered the country without proper visas (in itself a debatable number due to selection bias and irregularities during the 2002 Russian census), other estimates appeared putting the real number of such illegals at five to thirty times this number. The latter estimate suggested that by late 2002 there could have been as many as 11,700,000 Chinese nationals living in Russia, or 8 percent of the entire population. This unsubstantiated and unbelievable estimate would also make the Chinese the largest non-Russian ethnic group in the Russian Federation and more than twice as numerous as the Tatars. Consistent with the spirit of these exaggerated assessments, in February 2003 the Khabarovsk governor, Viktor Ishaev, again warned President Putin of ongoing "Chinese expansion into the Russian Far East" at the meeting of Russia's State Council (*Gossovet*) (Chernov 2003).

The Dilated Eyes of Fear and Hostility in Primorskii Public Opinion

Given that systematic assessments of the scale of Chinese migration in Russia on a year-to-year basis (as in Table 4.1) have not been reported by the Russian media[5] and that alarmist, speculative assessments have been reported consistently, it is understandable why a large segment of the Primorskii public perceived Chinese migration as a security threat, even though only a minuscule proportion of Chinese migrants settled permanently in the area. The data are from the public opinion survey

[5] Occasional media reports, commentary, and interviews do provide partial data on the actual scale of Chinese migration, but these data are intermingled with multiple alarmist assessments. The Russian public does not have a statistical baseline for evaluating the scale of Chinese migration.

designed by this author and conducted in September 2000 by the Center for the Study of Public Opinion at the Vladivostok IHAE of the Russian Academy of Sciences. The survey was based on a probability sample of 1,010 respondents selected randomly from six locations within Primorskii krai. (See the detailed information on the author's Web site: http://www-rohan.sdsu.edu/~alexseev.)

While the survey showed that local Russians overestimated the scale of Chinese presence by the factor of ten (see details in the next section), the intensity of general threat perception varied widely. This variation had a near-normal ("bell-shaped curve") distribution. When asked about threat to Russia as a whole, about 40 percent of respondents said that Chinese migrants posed no or very little threat, although close to one-third of respondents saw this migration as threatening. However, regarding the Far East and Primorskii krai, the largest proportion of respondents believed that Chinese migrants posed a strong or very strong threat (43 and 55 percent, respectively). At the same time, 42 percent of respondents believed that despite a threat to Primorskii krai, Chinese migrants posed no threat whatsoever to them personally.

Primorskii residents also saw the threat of the Chinese takeover as increasing in the future. Most survey respondents believed that military clashes with China over border territories – such as the one over Damanski Island in March 1969 – were unlikely at the time of polling. Looking five to ten and ten to twenty years ahead, however, they saw such military conflicts as more likely than not (Figure 4.1). The shadow of the future was rather dark for Primorskii residents: The more they looked ahead, the more they anticipated hostile military actions by China amidst increasing uncertainty.

Support for aggressive hostile responses to Chinese migration also showed considerable variation but was on some dimensions several times higher than support for racist exclusionism in the Canadian surveys and for xenophobic policies in the EU surveys. In my Primorskii poll, respondents were given seventeen policy options on how to respond to Chinese migration and asked to grade them on a scale of −3 (most hostile) to +3 (most accommodating), with a midpoint of "change nothing" or "do nothing" (at zero). For example, if someone felt the borders should be totally closed they would choose −3, but if they favored totally open borders they would choose +3. Those favoring some intermediate measures would choose scores in between.

Most respondents preferred hostile political and military measures against Chinese migration. About 65 percent of respondents said they

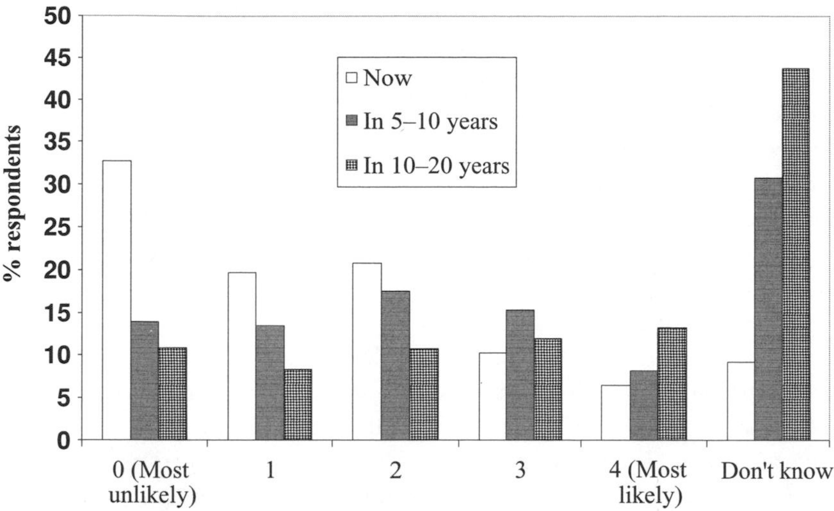

FIGURE 4.1. How Likely Are Armed Border Clashes with China, Similar to Those Over Damanskii Island in 1969? *Note*: Based on the author's Primorskii 2000 survey (N = 1,010).

favored closing the border with China to crossings, including 25 percent who favored complete border closure. Less than 1 percent favored opening the border completely. Approximately 57 percent of respondents said they would support the Cossacks or other voluntary paramilitary groups to stop Chinese migrants. Deportation of illegal Chinese migrants – which in the Primorskii context included the overwhelming majority of Chinese migrant traders and workers – had the support of 89 percent of respondents. A vast majority (78 percent) of those polled supported a ban on Russian residency rights to the Chinese.

Fear that the Chinese would settle in Primorskii also came through on economic issues. While showing less hostility on these issues,[6] 36 percent of respondents still said they favored a ban on Chinese citizens trading in Primorskii krai (compared to 29 percent who opposed such a ban). On Chinese citizens' right to land ownership in Russia, 96 percent of respondents said they opposed it or strongly opposed it. Similarly, 60 percent of respondents wanted to ban Chinese migrant labor, the latter being associated with extended presence of Chinese citizens in Primorskii and

[6] For example, only 27 percent of respondents favored raising taxes and duties on goods imported from China (compared to 36 percent who opposed such raises).

hence, proclivity for permanent settlement in Russia.[7] A substantial proportion of respondents also opposed the legitimization of ethnic Chinese communities within Primorskii: 48 percent of respondents wanted to ban or never allow Chinese-language media, while 76 percent wanted to ban or never allow Chinatowns in Primorskii krai. At the same time, 42 percent of respondents preferred to ban or never allow Russian–Chinese intermarriages – suggesting a rejection of the powerful institution of cultural integration of migrants and the notion of Russian society as an ethnic and cultural "melting pot."

These findings run against widespread antiimmigration discourses exemplified by Huntington (2004) and Buchanan (2002) and charge that migrants threaten national identity and security when they turn out to be reluctant to assimilate. The Primorskii 2000 findings indicate that preemptive alarmism about "swamping" is likely to translate into the reluctance of host societies to incorporate migrants – later on, migrants' difficulties with assimilation would be, in part, a self-fulfilling prophecy of the initial opposition to assimilation within host communities. This preemptive alarmism interpretation – as opposed to a cultural-difference explanation – also gains from the finding that regulated cultural exchanges with China had the approval of most Primor'e residents in the survey (71 percent). About 56 percent of respondents supported the idea of setting up Chinese cultural centers in the area, and 62 percent of respondents favored increasing Chinese-language instruction in the local schools. The security dilemma arising from uncertainty over Chinese intent to settle in Primorskii would explain why the local public supported Chinese cultural centers and language instruction, while opposing Chinese media and Chinatowns. Predominantly associated with touring artists and exhibits representing the cultures of nations outside Russia, Chinese cultural centers hardly signaled the emergence of Chinese settler communities. Nor did Chinese-language instruction – after all, generations of Russians grew up studying German and English as main foreign languages without seeing a massive influx of German- or English-speaking migrants. Besides, learning Chinese could easily be seen as something that would help Russians going to China more than help the Chinese coming to Russia. In contrast, local Chinese media and Chinatowns clearly signaled permanency, as attributes

[7] At the same time, 64 percent of respondents favored increasing cross-border tourism. Even though statistically tourism is the largest source of Chinese illegal migration in the region, the general notion of tourism as a temporary and regulated activity is not linked with long-term stay and migrant settlement.

of established or settled communities – hence, potential "fifth columns" in the minds of the locals.

The security-dilemma model would also suggest in this respect that preemptive opposition to assimilation is not necessarily going to manifest itself in all contexts with equal intensity because it would be dependent on perceptions of threat arising from putative migrant settlement. The latter would depend a great deal on other factors, such as perceived demographic trends, migrant intentions, and the prevailing images of social identity within a state. Future studies may want to ask whether reluctance to incorporate migrants culturally would depend on how strongly the natives see their society as an interethnic "melting pot" as opposed to a multiethnic "salad bowl" or a monoethnic "fortress." At the same time, Chapter 7 will show that alarmism about cultural integration of migrants has been significant in the EU, too – indicating that some substantial elements of "preventive defense" logic transcend context.

While showing the heightened sense of threat and hostility, the Primorskii 2000 poll also recorded a wide variation in the intensity of responses. This variation is characteristic of the tension between the fears and hopes in the broader political, socioeconomic, and cultural context of the Russian Far East, as noted at the beginning of the chapter. In containing elements of drivers and constraints of the interethnic security dilemma, this context also underlies a variation on the key perceptual measures of emergent anarchy, the offensiveness of migrants' intent, migrants' "groupness," socioeconomic impact, and ideology, to which I now turn.

"Asian Balkans" in the "Wild East": Anticipating Anarchy

The beginning of Chinese migration into the Russian Far East in the early 1990s is distinctly related to two developments that signified the decline of central government authority in Russia. First, Soviet President Mikhail Gorbachev "normalized" relations with China in the late 1980s and concluded a border demarcation treaty with Beijing in 1991 – developments that not only ended decades of strict border policing by the Soviet government going back to the late 1930s, but that were part of the unraveling of the communist rule in Russia and the disintegration of the Soviet Union. Second, the opening of the Russia–China border to visa-free tourism coincided with the "parade of sovereignties" by constituent regions of the Russian Federation, which resulted in a gradual shift of the balance of power toward provincial governments. After 1996, the governors were no longer appointed by the Kremlin, but elected locally. In the late

1990s, especially following Russia's 1998 financial crisis, the increasingly tight alliances between governors and regionally based business tycoons and representatives of the military and security agencies ignited fears of "federal collapse" (Herd 1998; but see Alexseev 1999). Hyperinflation, corruption, and "dollarization" of economic exchange in Russia undermined the central government's capacity to fund military, security, and law enforcement agencies. As Russia's Navy servicemen starved on Russkii Island near Vladivostok, as ammunition depots exploded in Primorskii krai, as heat and water supplies broke down during the –40°F winters, as nuclear submarine repair workers blocked the Trans-Siberian railroad in desperation over chronically unpaid salaries, and as violent crime rates soared in excess even of rapidly rising Russian averages, the sense of anarchy became pervasive. Eight time zones separating Primorskii's from Russia's political center, combined with ageing and unreliable transportation and communications infrastructure encouraged sentiments that some local officials described to me as "neo-feudal." The "frontier" sentiments resurged, giving rise to the sobriquet "the Wild East."[8] One of the Russian hit songs in mid-1990s, "Vladivostok 2000," resonated with mass audiences by painting horrific reality-based images of the city – starting with the lead singer walking the empty streets with a hand grenade in his pocket and a fuse in his hand. The song was written and performed by a Vladivostok-based rock band, *Mumii Trol'* (The Troll of Mummies).

When asked in the Primorskii 2000 survey if the Russian government would be able to prevent ethnic conflicts in their region, about 20 percent of respondents said no, while 17 percent said "maybe, maybe not" and another 17 percent said they did not know what to answer. Not that they could expect significant help from Russia's neighbors. A sense that the external environment was just as anarchic as Russia's own *bespredel* ("limitlessness") was plausible, given that international security institutions in Northeast Asia were nonexistent, that Russia and China had a history of deadly territorial disputes as recently as the late 1960s and early 1970s, and that significant territories formerly under Soviet control were being transferred to China under the 1991 border demarcation treaty. Sensing Russia's growing weakness in East Asia, 25 percent of respondents said Moscow would cede parts of Primorskii krai to China under diplomatic pressure.

While interviewing former vice-governor Vladimir Stegnii in his Vladivostok office (August 15, 2000), I witnessed a succinct illustration

[8] For a multidisciplinary assessment of these conditions, see Thornton and Ziegler (2002).

of the worst-case scenario projection under uncertainty about intentions of states whose military and economic powers grow relative to others and whose ambitions may not be credibly constrained by international institutions. I asked the vice-governor if he believed Chinese migration posed a threat to Russia's security and, if so, why. The first point that Stegnii made without giving it a long thought was this: "At present, our military capabilities are such that, according to one estimate, we can destroy China thirty-three times. But the future of the military balance is uncertain. In the future, the military balance will worsen for us. China has a lot of money that it can spend on the military. We cannot invest at the same rate. Whereas president Putin ordered to strengthen the armed forces, our Pacific Naval Fleet had no resources to stage a traditional show of naval vessels [in the bays around Vladivostok, held annually on Navy Day]." At the main entrance to the Primorskii government headquarters earlier in the day, I indeed saw a photo exhibit of the annual naval show, that Stegnii mentioned in the interview. Images of scantily clad women playing mermaids – rather than warships – dominated the exhibit. The Primorskii public echoed Stegnii's apprehension that Russia's military power was likely to decline relative to China in the future. Whereas 57.5 percent of respondents in the 2000 survey said Russia was stronger militarily than China in 2000, only 25.6 percent of respondents saw Russia retaining military superiority by 2020.

Against this background, demographic trends between Russia and China appeared particularly alarming to the Russians in the Far East – who, unlike Plotnikov, have had no access to statistical data on the actual size of Chinese migration. Most ordinary Russians live with a simple knowledge that their country's least and most sparsely populated regions border on the world's most populous country. In demographic terms, Russia's Far East is like a mouse nesting at an elephant's feet – and the Russians are acutely aware of it. Asian faces in the streets of the Russian Far Eastern cities became a constant reminder of this demographic cohabitation problem. After all, by the early 2000s, only about 2 million Russians in Primorskii krai lived across the border from 38 million Chinese in one neighboring Heilongjiang province alone (Alexseev 2001: 134). China's demographic shadow prompted Russian scholars to exaggerate estimates of Heilongjiang's population – typically lumping it in with the population of the neighboring Jilin province and putting the total at around 70 million (Nosov 1996: 8). In late 2002, approximately 6.7 million Russians lived in the entire territory from Lake Baikal to the Pacific Ocean across one of the world's longest borders from China's 1.2 billion people.

Making the demographic shadow more ominous was a sharp decline in the Russian Far East population in the 1990s, as mortality exceeded fertility and as tens of thousands of locals moved to European Russia in search of a better life. According to one conservative estimate, from 1991 to 1997 the population of the Russian Far East dropped by nearly 9 percent (Kontorovich 2000). Whereas China's overwhelming population advantage has been a persistent factor in the Russian Far East ever since the Russian government established its sovereign power in the region in the mid-nineteenth-century, it is important to note that only during the post-Soviet period did this pressure coincide with a decline of the ethnic Slav population in the region. A January 1996 memorandum (*spravka*) to President Yeltsin's administration written by the then presidential representative in Primorskii krai, Vladimir Ignatenko, suggested that local officials became concerned over long-term prospects of the changing ethnic balance in the region: "As a result of out-migration in 1995, the *krai* has 4,700 fewer Russians, 700 fewer Ukrainians, and 400 fewer Belorussians. At the same time, our population increased through the influx of ethnic Koreans (1,500), Chinese (1,300), Armenians (400), and Azeris (200)" (Ignatenko 1996: 4).

Without massive Soviet-era subsidies from the central government, the economy of the Russian Far East also shrank rapidly in the 1990s. In the meantime, the population and economy of China grew steadily, even in the relatively poor Northeastern provinces. From 1996 to 1997, in the Russian provinces bordering China the population declined by 40,000 and the GDP dropped by 8 percent (representing the general trend for the 1990s), while in the neighboring Chinese provinces of Heilongjiang, Jilin, and Liaoning the population increased by one million and the GDP rose by 13 percent (Baklanov 1999: 3). Russian academics and policy makers have framed the security implications of these trends as China's "demographic pressure" on Russia. Baklanov (ibid.) estimated this pressure as 63,000 Chinese nationals per one Russian along each kilometer of the Sino-Russian border. More threatening in his view is the "population density pressure," measured as 380,000 Chinese per one Russian per kilometer inside a one-kilometer zone along the border. When interviewed by the author (Vladivostok, August 15, 2000), Primorskii's vice-governor Stegnii was concerned that by 2050 China's population growth would deplete the environmental sustainability, or "carrying capacity" of China and thus engender territorial expansion in the quest for water, clean air, arable land, and energy resources.

It is not necessarily the perception of government weakness or demographic trends taken separately, but the combination of the two that has been linked to threatening images of anarchy in the Russian Far East. Stegnii, for example, expressed concerns about the Chinese "demographic pressure" while in the same interview estimating the number of Chinese nationals in Primorskii on any given day to be about 15,000 – or less than half the assessment provided by the migration service chief Pushkarev. Former Yeltsin representative Vladimir Ignatenko thus described the interactive effect on threat assessment of perceived government capacity and ethnic balance: "If we lifted border controls right now, more than half of [Primorskii] krai population would be Chinese. Then Russian sovereignty over the Far East will be out of the window" (interview with the author, Vladivostok, June 1, 1999). Using the same argument, governor Nazdratenko's 1999 election campaign book warned that cross-border Chinese migration would turn the Russian Far East into the "Asian Balkans" (Nazdratenko 1999: 20–4).

Respondents in the Primorskii 2000 survey revealed sweeping concerns that once the Chinese migrants arrive, their numbers will keep swelling like a tidal wave. The modal response – at 46 percent (excluding the "don't knows") saying between 10 and 20 percent of Primorskii population were Chinese – exaggerated the Chinese migration scale by at least ten times. Extrapolating from this exaggerated assessment, most respondents (41 percent) projected the proportion of ethnic Chinese in Primorskii at 20 to 40 percent by 2010. Another 20 percent of respondents projected that the Chinese would make up 40 to 60 percent of Primorskii population, pushing the ethnic balance toward or beyond the tipping point. Moreover, the survey revealed a strong perception that Chinese migration in Russia's southernmost Pacific province was much more likely to increase than to stay the same or decline in the next 20 years. For example, respondents who in 2000 estimated up to 5 percent of the Primorskii population to be Chinese were most likely to believe that from 10 to 20 percent of the krai population would be Chinese by 2010. The same holds for those who said this proportion would reach 10 to 20 percent in 2010, and then rise to anywhere from 20 to 40 percent by 2020.[9] The perception prevailed that Chinese migrants would keep coming like a swelling tidal wave. Figure 4.2 graphically illustrates this prevailing perception.[10]

9 Perceptions of migration scale in 2000 and 2010 and in 2010 and 2020 were strongly related. Zero-order correlation coefficients were exceptionally high for the number of cases as large as 1,010 in the survey – R = .6 and R = .55, respectively.

10 It is important to keep in mind, however, that overall perceptions of the scale of Chinese migration varied widely among the Russian respondents, approximating a bell-shaped curve peaking at the lower end (10–20 percent) of the scale.

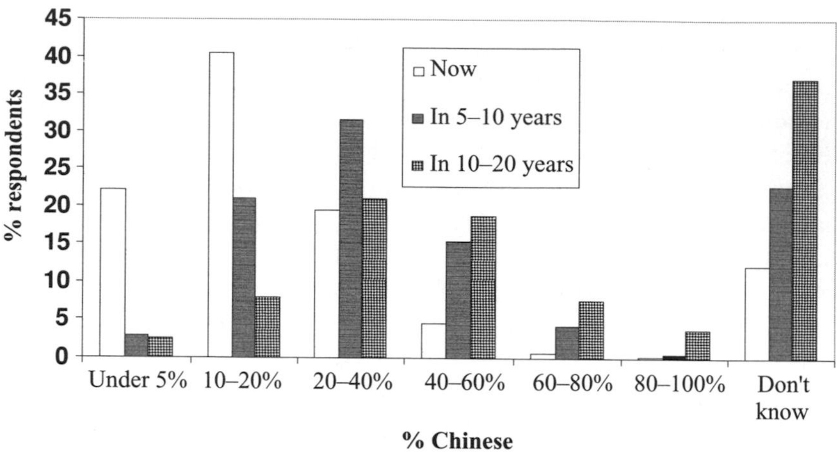

FIGURE 4.2. What Proportion of Primorskii Population Do You Think Is Chinese? *Note*: Based on the author's Primorskii 2000 survey (N = 1,010).

Intent Uncertainty and the "Offensive" Advantage of the Chinese: A Primorskii Perspective

While important in its own right, this combination of perceived weakness of Russian authority and demographic pressure from China also lays down the foundation for an intrinsic credibility problem regarding Chinese intentions – whatever any current state of Russian–Chinese relations, the future would remain uncertain as long as the political, military, economic, and demographic trends make the Russian Far East vulnerable. To reiterate Snyder and Jervis's (1999: 21) argument, this credibility problem vis-à-vis the other's intent is at the heart of the security dilemma. We have a classic situation in which the security dilemma lurks in the shadows of the future even though the Moscow–Beijing relations are benign and improving. Having taken this into account, however, the intensity of the perceived credibility problem would differ among individuals – even when the general conditions are held constant. This variation suggests that while the political, economic, or demographic vulnerabilities underlie the credibility problem, the assessment of the others' intentions has also an independent component – embedded, for example, in the history of interactions; in the interpretation of official pronouncements, media content, and public opinion on "the other side."[11] This section of the chapter

[11] The intent assessment is also likely to be affected by individual characteristics of the perceivers, such as education, personal trajectories, ideology, or social status – something that I consider later as control variables.

focuses precisely on Russian assessment of Chinese intentions taking into account these factors.

In the Russian Far East, Chinese migration since the early 1990s raised major concerns over intentions of both migrants and the Chinese government. In Vladivostok, one hears myth-resembling stories – former vice-governor Stegnii was among those who told me this one – of guest construction workers from China saying, "Eventually, all those things we build will be ours [i.e., Chinese]" (August 15, 2000). Another widespread folk belief shared with the first author on his trips to the Russian Far East from 1999 to 2001 was that the Chinese remember the exact location of the old ginseng patches abandoned by their ancestors and yearn to reclaim possession. Among those from whom I heard this story was Anatolii Tsypliaev, then the first secretary of the Vladivostok communist party committee. Hostile intent is ascribed to the fact that the Chinese use different names for local cities. Vladivostok, for example, is to the Chinese "The City of a Large Sea Cucumber." That the Chinese also use different names for New York or San Francisco doesn't make Vladivostok's association with large sea cucumbers less threatening to local Russians. In the context of the Russian Far East, the use of Chinese city names stands as a proxy for perceived intent to claim Russia's territories. Granted, most local Russians hardly know that the cities currently marked on Russian maps as Vladivostok, Khabarovsk, and Ussuriisk emerged around 600 A.D. as Chinese settlements of Haishenwei, Boli, and Shuaibinfu, respectively (Stephan 1994: 15). However, the Russian Far East residents generally understand that the Chinese lived there before Russia established sovereignty over the region and therefore could conceivably have deep-seated intention to reclaim territories they believe once belonged to them.

These valuations of Chinese intent reflect a history of interactions at the juncture of Russia and China that, in and of itself, engenders a credibility problem independently of political and demographic vulnerabilities. First, the basic source of suspicions about China's intent resides in the legal foundations of Russia's sovereignty over its Far Eastern territories, no matter how solid they may be from the standpoint of international law. The 1860 Treaty of Beijing established the present-day boundary between Russia and China in Primorskii at the time when China was weakened by the war with England and France (1856–8) (Stephan 1994: 18; but see Miasnikov 1996). If Beijing relentlessly pursued the return of Hong Kong, Macao, and Taiwan – which China similarly lost during its "century of humiliation" – why not pursue the return of the southern tier in the present-day Russian Far East? As a preventive measure,

Soviet archeologists and historians in the 1970s cleansed the evidence of Chinese presence in the Russian Far East prior to the mid-nineteenth century. Bohai, Liao, Jin, Yuan, and Qing were renamed Tungus-Korean, Khitan, Jurchen, Mongol, and Manchu. The Soviet central committee ruled in 1972 to change the names of 1,200 places (Stephan 1994: 19).

Still encapsulated in hundreds of changed geographical names and in living memory of the public and political leaders, suspicions about Chinese intent casts a shadow over the 1991 Russia–China border demarcation agreement. As vice-governor Stegnii told me in Vladivostok (August 15, 2000), the treaty amounted to setting a "time bomb" in Russia–China relations. He said, "Today these issues have been decided in a civilized way, but during the next century these decisions could be treated similarly to the way the czarist treaties [with China in the mid-nineteenth century] are treated today. They already talk about fine-tuning demarcation lines using space satellites." Vladimir Ignatenko, meanwhile, complained to me about the "nagging" Chinese demands to verify and reverify the border-line location (August 15, 2000): "They have been so insistent that I got convinced this was not about border demarcation. The border had been mapped with satellites as precisely as one could possibly get. This was manifestation of their deep-seated intent to constantly revise the border and gradually reclaim territories which they believe belong to China."

Precisely because he suspected that Beijing harbored an unswerving commitment to reclaiming old territories, Ignatenko was uneasy about Chinese migration into the Russian Far East. This high-ranking regional official was threatened by migration not because he feared demographic Sinification (he did not believe in the alarmist estimates), but because he feared that gradual depopulation of the Russian Far East would give a pretext to Beijing to redress old territorial grievances. It was the interaction between demographic trends and Chinese intentions that he found most alarming: "In 10–15 years, if China raises demarcation issues and if the population balances changes here and we [Russians] will be leaving the area, the situation here may develop the same way as in Israel. If we leave, there will be a power vacuum" (ibid.) This concern about the "Siberian Israel" scenario stemmed from the same pattern of reasoning as the one articulated by A. Kazannik, the deputy governor of Omsk oblast: "First Chinese migrant, then Chinese cultural center, then Chinese company, then Chinese worker, then Chinese soldier." Representing these perceptions on the part of a significant segment of Russian regional elites, an article in *Pravda-5* (published in late 1997 under the title "The Weakening Fingers in the Nuclear Fist") quoted an unidentified high-ranking Russian official who reported being told this by the late Deng Xiaoping:

"Today you and we must resolve small-scale problems related to our interstate border. After that we shall advance no claims to you, but only till 2010." Observers in Omsk noted that shortly before 2010 the bulk of Russia's Cold War arsenal of intercontinental ballistic missiles would be decomissioned. "So, are we going to see that Chinese soldier here after all?" asked one local analyst, reflecting the lack of trust on behalf of local Russians of China's leaders' commitment to the 1991 border demarcation treaty.

Chinese government intentions being suspect, local Russians in Primorskii and Khabarovskii krais often talk about Chinese maps allegedly showing swaths of Siberia and the Russian Far East as belonging to China. Vice-governor Stegnii also told me he was concerned about these maps, about the general secretiveness of the Chinese communist system, and about the ideological orientation of the Chinese government upon which this system rests: "In China, no one has dismantled Mao's political prescriptions – Mao's portraits have not been taken down in public places. And these prescriptions include Mao's view that 1.5 million hectares of territory stretching from Lake Baikal to the Pacific are China's 'Great Northern Virgin Lands' waiting to be developed some day by and for the Chinese people."

During the gubernatorial elections in Primorskii krai in May 2001, I heard one of the two leading candidates interpret a Chinese communist party's resolution on employment problems as a sign that Beijing had a secret policy of pushing its "surplus population" out to Russia. The Primorskii 2000 survey registered these views. Excluding the "don't knows," almost 82 percent of those polled said the Chinese saw Primorskii krai as historically belonging to China – showing widespread mistrust, albeit of varying intensity, with respect to Chinese intentions (see Map 4.1 for the history of Sino-Russian territorial disputes). As for the actual intentions of the Chinese government with respect to the Russian Far East and migration, they remain opaque. Given the lack of decision transparency in the Chinese system of government, flat-out denial of territorial claims on Russia and benign statements of top Chinese leaders favoring a strategic partnership with Russia are unverifiable. One of the fundamental sources of ambiguity – from which worst-case scenarios are likely to be imputed – is the Constitution of the Communist Party of China. In this fundamental legal document, updated in 2002 at the sixteenth party congress, two adjacent paragraphs outline foreign policy objectives that would appear contradictory from the political vantage point of the Russian Far East (http://www.china.org.cn/english/features/45461.htm). On the one hand, the party constitution pledges adherence to the five

MAP 4.1. Territorial Disputes and the Sino-Soviet Split in the Early 1960s. *Source:* Associated Press Newsfeatures, "Red World Splits Along Chinese Border" (September 23, 1963), black-and-white copy of the color background map, reproduced with permission from the collection of the Library of Congress, Geography and Map Division.

principles of international relations that emphasize "mutual respect for sovereignty and territorial integrity" of all states. On the other hand, the preceding paragraph pledges that the Communist Party of China would relentlessly pursue "the great cause of the reunification of the motherland."

Another dimension of intent assessment concerns the attractiveness of the Russian Far East to Chinese settlers. What may push or pull them into the area? On the one hand, conditions in the Russian Far East – as the czarist and Soviet governments found at massive cost – are inhospitable to the agriculture and manufacturing industries.

Yet, on the other hand, some residents in the Far East point out that while Russians or Ukrainians may find local climatic and economic conditions off-putting, the Chinese would be willing to tolerate them. As Sergei Pushkarev told me in the same interview, "The Chinese don't find Primorskii krai to be 'a region of unstable farming conditions.' They grow everything imaginable here. So if the Russians leave, the Chinese would be glad to settle down in these areas." It is also pointed out that the Chinese, due to their cultural traditions, place higher value on natural resources in the Far East than the Russian residents – especially regarding ginseng, musk deer, bears, frogs, trepang (sea cucumber), sea urchins, and jellyfish. Another view holds that the Chinese are generally tougher, more accustomed to life without modern comforts and more tolerant of adversity. In sum, the local residents may conceivably believe that rough climate and high transportation and energy costs – while driving the Russians out – would not deter Chinese nationals from coming in and colonizing the Russian Far East.

Sociological research into actual Chinese intentions in Russia strongly supports claims that the migrants see Russia as a temporary opportunity and have little desire to "infiltrate" and "colonize" the host state. In a 1999 opinion poll of 430 Chinese migrants who made it from the Far East to Moscow, the Russian China specialist Vil'ia Gel'bras found that only a fraction of Chinese migrants intended to settle down permanently in Russia. Even in Moscow, where living conditions were (and remain) considerably better than in the Russian Far East, only 12 percent of Chinese respondents said they wanted to work permanently in Russia. Only 1.6 percent of Chinese respondents said they would like to become Russian citizens in the future, and only 2.1 percent said they wanted to seek permanent residency status in Russia (Gel'bras 1999: 35). In my own conversations with Chinese traders in Ussuriisk and Vladivostok in 1999 and 2000, most of them told me they came to Primorskii krai to make quick money. When asked about their long-term plans, they said they were saving money to move to Europe, Southern China, Canada, or the United States. None told me they would like to settle down in the Russian Far East. This explains a large number of Chinese currency changers in Chinese markets that I visited throughout the Russian Far East, in Yuzhno-Sakhalinsk, Vladivostok, and Khabarovsk. If anything, these "gray market" currency dealers around the Chinese markets have been proliferating – on my trip to Vladivostok in 2000 and 2001, I observed that these dealers were hiring local young women to stand in the streets outside the markets and aggressively seek people willing to sell dollars for rubles. As one Chinese trader told me in Vladivostok: "As soon as I make any amount of rubles, I change them into dollars. I'm going to save the money and move my family to the United States." This proliferation of currency changers was hardly a sign that Chinese migrants were acquiring a taste for settling down in the Russian Far East. Rather, they were actively seeking to maximize the dollar take so they could get out of Russia faster.

Contrary to these polls and observations, the Russian public – in line with the security-dilemma logic – found it hard to trust Chinese migrants' intentions. The Primorskii 2000 survey suggests that a substantial proportion of Russian residents believed the Chinese indeed were likely to find the Russian Far East attractive. The median intent ascribed to Chinese migrants by the Russians is the opposite of the median intent expressed by Chinese migrants in the 1999 Russian poll. Nearly three-quarters of respondents (other than "don't knows") believed that the Chinese takeover of Primorskii krai was inevitable – implying that the very arrival of Chinese migrants substituted for the intent to take over the Far Eastern territories. Among this cohort of respondents, 56 percent saw this takeover as resulting from the mundane, seemingly benign activities of Chinese nationals, such as work, trade, tourism, and marriages. These benign activities in the respondents' eyes posed a long-term threat to Russia's sovereignty over the Far East. Knowing that once in Primorskii ethnic Chinese could settle down, start families, have children, and bring over friends and relatives, local Russians developed fears that the real intentions of Chinese migrants were offensive – official pledges of friendship and strengthening Russian–Chinese partnership notwithstanding. In other words, a substantial number of respondents saw the Chinese migrants as having an "offensive" advantage over the Russians.

The Offensive Potential of Chinese "Groupness": Stereotypical Distinctions and Assimilability

To estimate the substantive content and intensity of stereotypes of Chinese migrants by the Russians, I used the Primorskii 2000 survey question: "How typical do you find the following qualities among the Russians and the Chinese: hardworking, entrepreneurial, honest, responsible, polite, generous, greedy, sly, aggressive, messy, selfish?" Each of these eleven characteristics represents a separate dimension. For both Russians (in-group valuation) and the Chinese (out-group valuation), attitudes were coded on a scale from zero (not typical) to four (most typical) on each dimension (see Table 4.2).

Whereas the intensity of perceptions varied, as shown in Table 4.2, the Russian respondents generally viewed Chinese migrants as distant, socially undesirable, and reluctant to assimilate. In the survey, respondents were asked to score both groups on qualities perceived to be most typical for each group, on a scale from zero (not typical at all) to four (most typical). Twice as many Primorskii respondents gave the top score to the Chinese than to Russians on "hardworking" and "entrepreneurial." Three times as many respondents said being sly was most typical of the Chinese rather than the Russians. Almost twenty times as many respondents saw the Chinese as not generous compared to the Russians.

To account for variation on the entire zero-to-four scale for all eleven of these character traits and to identify patterns of perceived group similarity and difference, I used factor analysis. This statistical procedure identifies commonalities among respondents on groups of questions that are then recoded as a single variable, or factor. The procedure also reveals how strongly responses on individual questions (factor components) relate to the common factor (see Gorsuch 1983: 3).[12] In the first test, twenty-two variables – eleven items for the Russians and the Chinese – were reduced to six factors. The analysis showed that Primorskii respondents clearly saw the Chinese as systematically distinct from the Russians as a group. To paraphrase Rudyard Kipling, in the mind of Primorskii respondents the Russians were Russians, the Chinese were Chinese. West was West, and East was East.

The question on stereotypes also enabled me to code respondents as to the degree of perceived similarity or difference between the typical characteristics of the Russians and the Chinese as ethnic groups. For each respondent and on each of the eleven characteristics listed in Table 4.2, I computed the difference between scores that each respondent assigned to Russians versus the Chinese (on a zero-to-four scale). These scores measured perceived differences between the two ethnic groups – regardless of which group came out positively and which came out

[12] For a detailed description of the factor analysis, see the author's Web site (http://www-rohan.sdsu.edu/~alexseev).

TABLE 4.2. *Responses to the Primorskii 2000 survey question: "How typical do you find the following qualities among the Russians and the Chinese on a scale from 0 (not typical at all) to 4 (most typical)?"*

	The Russians						The Chinese					
Are they:	0	1	2	3	4	Don't know	0	1	2	3	4	Don't know
Hardworking	1.1	12.2	30.6	33.3	21.2	1.7	0.8	3.2	10	30.6	48	7
Entrepreneurial	1.1	12.6	25.8	31.1	20.7	8.2	0.4	5.5	13	28.9	37	15
Greedy	6.2	18.1	30.4	25	13.8	6	0.8	4.6	17	28.7	29	19.1
Sly	3.9	19.1	29.6	27.9	15.2	3.2	0.5	2.9	14	23.1	50	9.1
Honest	2.3	11.1	31	30.6	17.5	6.3	9.3	25.8	23	12.3	4.6	23.6
Responsible	4.6	21.5	28.9	26.5	13.2	4.8	1.4	9.2	25	25.3	17	21.5
Aggressive	5.8	15.1	33	26.2	14	4.8	1	6.3	13	23.5	38	17.4
Polite	6.1	21.5	34.3	26.2	8.2	2.9	6	18.2	27	23.6	13	10.9
Messy	4.5	23.1	37	23.4	9	2.5	5.7	7.2	10	22.3	46	7.7
Generous	1.1	6.5	13.8	29.3	43.2	4.4	12	27.5	25	7.6	2.3	24.8
Selfish	5.6	18	20.9	22.9	16.8	13.9	1.8	6.8	17	20.2	18	35.4

Note: Based on the author's Primorskii 2000 survey (N = 1,010).

negatively. For example, the response of someone who gave the Russians a "4" and the Chinese a "2" on honesty was coded the same ("2") as the response of someone who gave the Chinese a "4" and the Russians a "2." Factor analysis of these measures showed that respondents fell into three distinct clusters. In the first cluster were those who believed the largest difference between the Russians and the Chinese was on selfishness, messiness, politeness, honesty, and responsibility – concepts related to general norms of social behavior. The second cluster encompassed respondents who saw the biggest dichotomy on negative character traits: aggressive, greedy, and sly, implying hostile intent ascribed to migrants. The third cluster distinguished the Russians and the Chinese on positive traits (entrepreneurial, hardworking, and generous) related primarily to economic behavior. (See http://www-rohan.sdsu.edu/~alexseev for statistical details.)

But – to complete the paraphrased sentence from Kipling – can the twain meet? What were the Russian perceptions about bridging the ethnic divide? The Primorskii 2000 survey generally showed that most local Russians were unwilling to go the distance. After the "don't knows" were excluded, approximately 56 percent of respondents said they opposed their relatives marrying Chinese nationals. With another 40 percent of respondents staying noncommittal on this issue ("marriage is a personal matter for the couples"), only about 5 percent of those who expressed an opinion on this question approved of Russian–Chinese marriages. Earlier surveys conducted by the Center for Public Opinion Research at the IHAE of the Peoples of the Russian Far East show a similar pattern. If anything, they indicate that opposition to Russian–Chinese marriages hardened from the mid- to the late 1990s. In the 1994 IHAE survey in Primorskii krai, about 60 percent of 869 respondents said that marrying a Chinese national would be their relatives' "own business" – expressing a neutral position on the issue. This number dropped to about 40 percent in a 1998 IHAE poll of 522 Primorskii residents and remained approximately the same in my 2000 survey.

Mirroring these attitudes, most Primorskii residents also felt that the Chinese migrants were reluctant to initiate ethnic integration. In the survey, respondents were asked if they believed that the Chinese migrants would be able to assimilate into the Russian society, or "become Russified." On a scale of zero (never assimilate) to four (assimilate fast and easily), 28 percent of those who expressed an opinion chose "0" and 20 percent chose "1" – showing that nearly half of all respondents saw little chance of the Chinese migrants capable of learning the Russian language and behaving like the Russians. About 18 percent of respondents saw the chances of the Chinese assimilating as fifty-fifty (they chose the score of "2"). Another 14 percent believed the Chinese were more likely than not to assimilate (the score of "3"), and 18 percent thought the Chinese could assimilate fast and easily (the score of "4").

Whereas on both ethnic distance and assimilation opinions varied among respondents, the majority of Russians clearly saw Chinese migrants as a distinct and distant group that was generally unlikely to become "Russified." This pattern of responses suggests that perceptions of offensive "groupness" of Chinese migrants deeply permeated Russian society in the Far East and, in doing so, became in themselves a signpost of a security dilemma in the making.

By believing that the distance between the Russians and the Chinese as collectivities was unlikely to narrow, the majority of survey respondents implied that if Chinese migrants were to settle down in the area, they would not play by local Russian rules but instead would start spreading their own way of life. These are precisely the respondents one would expect to fear that the migrants would ask for autonomy and protection from the sending state. Not surprisingly, correlation between opposition to one's relatives marrying Chinese citizens and support for complete closure of the Russian–Chinese border was statistically significant.

Sergei Pushkarev, then in charge of the Russian Federal Migration Service for Primorskii krai, directly linked perceptions of "groupness" and "offensiveness" (interview with the author, Vladivostok, August 15, 2000). Pushkarev made this point by commenting that ethnic Koreans – in contrast to ethnic Chinese – posed a lesser threat to Primorskii krai precisely because they had a tendency to culturally assimilate in Russia (become Russified). To make this case publicly, Pushkarev said he hired an ethnic Korean administrative assistance – "so that I can show all my visitors that here I have a Korean secretary who speaks flawless Russian and acts like a Russian, who is like us." Because Koreans were more prone to assimilation than the Chinese, said Pushkarev, he was lobbying the Russian federal government to adopt laws favoring Korean migrants in the Russian Far East and toughening entry and visitation requirements on ethnic Chinese.

The same views persistently resurfaced in the last 150 years and translated into tangible policy when Korean migrants were allowed to set up Korean villages in Primorskii krai in the late nineteenth century and when the czarist and the Bolshevik governments made entry requirements for Koreans easier than for the Chinese. From the mid-1800s to the late 1920s, the ethnic balance in the Russian Far East changed in favor of Koreans. According to Russian demographic historians, the population of the Far Eastern territories that came under Russian rule by 1860 was somewhere between 20,000 and 25,000. Of these, only 6,700 were Russian citizens (ethnic Russians), 8,100 were Chinese citizens (ethnic Chinese), and 9,200 were multiethnic indigenous peoples without citizenship (Sidorkina 1997: 6, quoted in Tkacheva 2000: 10). In other words, the Chinese comprised between 30 and 40 percent of the local population. Over the next half century, the situation changed significantly. According to the 1926 Soviet census data, the proportion of the Korean population in the Russian Far East was 9.7 percent and that of the Chinese population was 4.2 percent.

Socioeconomic Impact Perceptions: Gains and Vulnerabilities

Positive Impacts

Benign public views of Chinese migration's impact on agriculture, trade, consumer goods, and prices are related to the fact that since the late 1980s Chinese "shuttle" traders in Primorskii eased chronic food and consumer goods shortages endemic to the Soviet centrally planned economy. Later in the 1990s, this trade offset a sharp drop in output of Primorskii's consumer goods producers. Supply from European Russia became too costly as a result of increased electricity and transportation tariffs. While most local residents complain that Chinese goods traded by "shuttlers" (*chelnoki*) are of low quality, many also recognize that these goods have been superior to most Soviet-made consumer products and have come in a wider assortment. In addition, consumers in Primorskii now can buy fresh fruits and vegetables that were unavailable when Chinese nationals were not allowed to trade there. Even a xenophobic-minded chieftain of the Ussury Cossack Army grudgingly admitted to this author that Chinese traders deserve credit for supplying the krai with fresh vegetables (interview with the author, Vladivostok, May 31, 1999). In the Soviet era, even the special officer rations of the Soviet Pacific Fleet provided only dried onions and potatoes as fruit and vegetables. This explains why local residents still see economic miracle in colorful rows of fruits and vegetables at Chinese markets (Yevgenii Plaksen, interview with the author, Vladivostok, May 22, 1999).[13]

[13] Prior to becoming a research fellow with IHAE, Yevgenii Plaksen served as an officer in the Russian Navy in the 1960s and 1970s and was captain of a Soviet Kilo Class submarine.

The virtual collapse of the Soviet-era consumer goods and agricultural industries in Primorskii in the 1990s created positive incentives for cross-border trade with China in two ways. While Chinese shuttle traders filled the gap in Russian domestic supply, Russian employees laid off after sweeping factory closures in the early 1990s seized the opportunity to make a living through cross-border trade. In Vladivostok, Ussuriisk, Artem, and Arsen'ev, according to the krai statistics office, the decline of consumer goods production from 1990 to 1997 averaged 99 percent for shoes, garments, kitchenware, refrigerators, washing machines, and soap, thus increasing the economic incentives for cross-border trade and exchanges. The production of milk, meat, and eggs – Primorskii's key food staples – declined in all of the borderline counties (*raions*) and major cities except one, raising incentives for supply from Chinese traders and growers (Goskomstat 1998: 78, 80–1).

Similarly, a decline in real wages since 1990 made local Russians search for outside sources of income and hunt for best possible bargains discounting quality. Between 1993 and 1997, wages measured in constant 1991 prices decreased on average by 16 percent throughout Primorskii (ibid.: 26). By January 2000, wages in Primorskii amounted to 28 percent of wages paid in 1991, when measured in constant 1991 rubles (Goskomstat 2000a: 28). Cross-border trade provided an escape to local Russians from deteriorating conditions in the old economic sectors. The number of Russians from Primorskii visiting China (with most of these travelers engaging in cross-border trade) exceeded the number of Chinese tourists visiting Primorskii by about ten times from 1992 to 1996 (Larin 1998: 113). This trend largely persisted in late 2000, according to interviews I conducted in Vladivostok markets. The "Chinese markets" sprang up in most of Primorskii's cities. Yevgenii Plaksen of the Vladivostok Institute of History, who conducted opinion surveys at these markets and regularly monitored prices there, reported that prices were on average one-third to one-half lower than those in most shops and department stores in Primorskii's cities (interviews with the author, Vladivostok, May 22, 1999 and August 13, 2000). The head of Russia's Migration Service in Primorskii krai, Sergei Pushkarev, admitted shopping at the Chinese market in Ussuriisk about every two weeks, under pressure from his wife who was attracted by good bargains (interviews with the author, Vladivostok, May 20, 1999 and August 15, 2000).

The city of Ussuriisk, the Chinese trade center during the 1990s, became one of the three major contributors to the city budget, approaching the level of contributions of the two mainstays of local manufacturing:

the sugar factory and the Ussuri Balsam (herb vodka) factory. The Ussuriisk Chinese market continued to flourish at the time of writing in early 2005. It is a telling example of a local government in Primorskii receiving significant economic benefits from cross-border migrant trade. Mikhail Vetrik, former director of the Ussuriisk Chinese trade center, spoke with pride about the expansion of his business from the mid-1990s:

> In 1996 there was a swamp here, and now we have a 20-hectare trading area in its place with five hostels, six halls of residence, loading–unloading facilities, a maintenance service, a passport registration service, a police station, an international telephone exchange, new public restrooms, a new septic system, and Chinese, Korean, and Russian restaurants. We generate 10–11 percent of tax revenues for the city of Ussuriisk (population 160,000), somewhere between $750,000 and $1,000,000 in 1998. We expect to generate at least the same amount of taxes for the city in 1999 and increase that amount in years to come (interview with the author, Ussuriisk, May 26, 1999).

Mikhail Vetrik started the interview accusing the United States of deliberately destroying the Soviet Union and bringing Russia to its knees. He also expressed dislike for ethnic Chinese "infiltration" of the region. However, he concluded this was not the time for aggressive nationalism: "Look around, you'll see that all these Russian factories are idle. Salaries are unpaid. Our back is against the wall. We've got to help these Chinese traders" (ibid.).Vetrik's business success paid off politically in 2000 when he was elected a member of Primorskii krai's Legislature.

The positive economic impact of the Chinese market in Ussuriisk was demonstrated by press reports that city revenues increased threefold as a result of Chinese trade in the late 1990s. The lucrative nature of this trade induced local officials to protect their gains, even if that required bending some rules. Thus, the local customs office blocked the city sanitation department from inspecting the quality of Chinese goods stored at the customs warehouse, fearing a decrease in the customs income (*Zolotoy Rog*, April 1, 1999: 1). Olga Proskuriakova, head of the foreign trade department at the committee for international and regional economic relations of the Primorskii krai government, estimated that cross-border shuttle trade by individuals (both Russian and Chinese nationals) is three times the volume of the officially reported trade between Primorskii krai and China (*Zolotoy Rog*, March 2, 1999: 1).

Hiring Chinese labor has also been associated with economic benefits in Primorskii. According to the chief of the Russian federal migration service for Primorskii krai, Sergei Pushkarev, Russian businesses hired Chinese migrant workers for three main reasons: quality, work discipline, and farming skills. PRC nationals are seen daily at main construction sites in Vladivostok. In May 1999, this author observed them working hard at around 7 P.M. in Vladivostok's central square, renovating the monument in honor of the fighters for Soviet power next to the krai administration headquarters. (Few Russian construction workers are still sober and productive this late in the day.)

Positive perceptions of socioeconomic impact of cross-border exchanges with China are also reflected in the views of Primorskii krai's top government officials. According to Vladimir Ignatenko, who in September 2000 served as the chairman of the committee on regional policy and legality of the krai Duma (legislative assembly), the Chinese benefit Primorskii krai because "tourist business has grown, tourist services – from hotels to cafes and restaurants – have been generating more capital to the extent that it became not all that easy to find hotel vacancies in Vladivostok" (interview with the author, Vladivostok, August 15, 2000). Moreover, Ignatenko said that working in tourist services "forces our people [the Russians] to be more disciplined," improving the local work ethic. "Construction business has also thrived, creating jobs and attracting workforce. We have seen distinct benefits for agriculture: The Chinese have great capacity to work especially when it comes to growing turnips, carrots, tomatoes, and cucumbers. Russians cannot work like that" (ibid.) Brisk sales at colorful Chinese vegetable stands at the Ussuriisk market – reminding this author of Korean vegetable shops in New York – testified in support of this "green finger" image of the Chinese migrants.

Vladimir Stegnii, former vice-governor of Primorskii krai responsible for international economic relations, said that the increase of exchanges with China had led to growing demand for bus and railway services, as well as for shoes, cotton clothes, kitchenware, and souvenirs. "Our sanatoriums and tourist hotels are packed to capacity [the total capacity of these institutions is 30,000 people]," he said in August 2000. "Even the Hyundai Hotel [a large and usually half-empty high-rise hotel in downtown Vladivostok] has become profitable this year; they are slated to turn in a profit of about $5 million, in part thanks to the visit to Vladivostok by Li Peng whose delegation numbering 130 people will stay at the Hyundai Hotel while he is here" (interview with the author, Vladivostok, August 15, 2000).

Negative Impacts

Yet, even these positive assessments have a darker side, according to Sergei Pushkarev, the federal migration service chief for Primorskii. During our interview in August 2000, he took a phone call and after listening briefly yelled angrily into the receiver: "Deport them all!" Then he hung up the phone and said: "You see, my officer just reported they found fifty-seven Chinese tourists building a sewing factory in the town of Slavianka" (interview with the author, August 15, 2000). This brief telephone conversation sums up complex controversies regarding the economic benefits of exchanges with China. Whereas well-regulated tourism is viewed positively, the economic spin-offs of tourism mixed with business have a dual effect. On the one hand, whoever hired Chinese tourists (or whoever issued them tourist invitations) to build a sewing factory in Slavianka was clearly benefiting economically. On the other hand, the same act triggered concerns on the part of the migration service about unregulated flow of Chinese migrant workers into Primorskii – concerns that were not merely about lawlessness, but about security.

Underlying these outward concerns about demographic imbalances and lawlessness, however, are perceptions among the same officials and the general public that economic activities of Chinese migration have had a substantial negative impact on Primorskii. These perceptions went beyond negative assessments of the migrants' direct impact on local job availability, industry, environment, and crime. Fear of migrants has been linked to socioeconomic trends suggesting that migration is a source of relative deprivation, that migrants "exploit" economic exchanges to derive unilateral benefits and leave the local population worse off than before migration began.

Socioeconomic data obtained from the Primorskii government suggests several trends consistent with such concerns. First, investment from China has been sporadic throughout the 1990s and into 2000, signaling low levels of commitment to engaging with the local economy (Table 4.3). The bulk of the investment was in trade and construction, rather than in processing or manufacturing industries. This trend was of particular concern to Vladimir Ignatenko, who had once hoped – while serving as the mayor of the town of Spassk-Dal'nii near the Chinese border – that the opening of the border in 1988 would generate joint Chinese–Russian industrial projects (interview with the author, Vladivostok, August 15, 2000). But investment protocols that he signed, he said, never materialized, and by the mid-1990s the Chinese showed a lack of interest in developing a manufacturing base in Primorskii.

Second, as vice-governor Stegniy pointed out, investment from China had been insignificant, amounting to only about 5 to 6 percent of the $336 million of foreign investment in Primorskii during the first half of 2000. Indeed, around 2000 China ranked distant sixth in terms of

TABLE 4.3. *Chinese Investment in Primorskii Krai*

			Trade and Food Services		Construction and Related Services	
Year	U.S. Dollars (thousands)	Total Rubles (millions)	U.S. Dollars (thousands)	Rubles (millions)	U.S. Dollars (thousands)	Rubles (millions)
1993	1,397		1,259.5		0	
1994	10.1		10.1		0	
1995	417	1,433	22.7	127.3	350	0
1996	95	52	48.5	50.8	0	0.2
1997	48	2,384	18.5	702.4	0	0
1998	15	643.7	15	328	0	0
1999	476.9	6.4	166.8	6.3	136.4	0

Note: The dollar and ruble investments were calculated separately by Goskomstat; they represent different investment flows. Foreign investment that was made in rubles was not included in the estimates in 1993 and 1994.

Source: Goskomstat Rossii, Primorskii kraevoi komitet gosudarstvennoi statistiki [Primorskii krai committee of government statistics], Request No. 19sv-39, August 22, 2000 (data available from the author upon request); Goskomstat Rossii, Primorskii kraevoi komitet gosudarstvennoi statistiki, *Primorskii krai v 1999 godu (statisticheskii yezhegodnik)* [Primorskii krai in 1999, a Statistical Yearbook] Vladivostok, 2000, 153.

foreign investment in Primorskii's economy – generally reflecting the trend for the 1990s. Cumulative hard currency investment from 1991 to 2000, including repaid credits, amounted to $97 million from South Korea, $57.9 million from Japan, $36.9 million from the United States, $29.2 million from Singapore, $18.6 million from Switzerland, and only $6 million from China (Goskomstat Rossii 2000b: 153).

Third, statistical data confirms perceptions that Chinese migrants are disproportionately more interested in trade rather than in investment. While ranking low in terms of investment, China ranked as the number one trading partner of Primorskii krai by the late 1990s. Of the $784 million of Primorskii's foreign trade in 1999, China accounted for $233.6 million (Goskomstat Rossii 2000b: 188), or 30 percent. This imbalance between trade and investment trend was behind Vladimir Ignatenko's negative perception of economic activities of Chinese migrants in Primorskii: "The crux of the matter is that they come here and export valuable raw materials, such as metals and timber, but they bring low-quality consumer goods in exchange to trade at the local markets. As a result, they profit from our exports and they make money here from trade and we end up with their shoddy stuff. They get richer and we get weaker" (interview with the author, Vladivostok, June 2, 1999).

Whereas I found this to be a widespread local sentiment, negative interpretation of Chinese intentions could have similarly been derived if the trade and investment trends were the opposite. Supposing the Chinese businesses and government agencies underwrote large-scale projects in the Russian Far East, one may imagine concerns and alarmism would arise in the same fashion as did the fears of Japanese intentions that were associated with high-volume investment in the United States' industries and real estate in the 1980s. In fact, anyone who read Michael Crichton's best-selling novel *The Rising Sun* would instantly appreciate the depth and intensity of these fears. In fact, in the Russian Far East such fears should be more intense than in the United States. While the Japanese were investing in the world's leading and growing economy, the Chinese were investing in a declining and troubled economy located predominantly in the area covered by permafrost. Because such investment would make little sense in purely economic terms, other ulterior motives – namely, territorial claims – are likely to be inferred from it. In theoretical terms, by implying possession or material stake in an asset, investment is more likely to signal takeover intent than trade. This suggests that it was not specific economic activities of the Chinese that gave rise to alarmism, but rather that in the overall state of alarmism any type of Chinese economic activity stood a good chance to be interpreted as threatening. Otherwise, the officials I interviewed should have told me that the reluctance of the Chinese to invest in Primorskii was a sign that they had little taste for annexing Russian territories.

Fourth, perceptions of relative deprivation are linked to Chinese migrants' involvement in environmentally sensitive, illicit trade. According to Andrei Kopaev, a senior investigator at the "Tigr" department that deals with cross-border smuggling at the State Environmental Committee for Primorskii krai, Chinese smugglers reselling tiger parts provided by Russian poachers can expect to generate around $100,000 each year. Chinese traders who buy illegally harvested ash trees in Primorskii at $40 per cubic meter can resell this timber for $80–100 per cubic foot in China, generating, in Kopaev's estimate, over $1 million a year. The chief of the "Tigr" department, Sergei Zubov, estimates that just in one county of Krasnoarmeiskii, five thousand cubic meters of ash trees were harvested in 1998 with Chinese traders turning up to $70 profit per cubic meter (interview with the author, Vladivostok, May 25, 1999). (During my visit to the border town of Pogranichnyi in late October 1999, I observed that the local railway station was packed to capacity with cargo trains loaded with logs on tracks heading for China.) And with approximately one ton of illegally harvested wild ginseng, Chinese resellers can expect to raise $2 million a year, at the going rate of $2 a gram (ibid.). Overall, Kopaev estimates, about 90 percent of demand for poaching and smuggling is generated from across the Chinese border. The "Tigr" department – funded primarily by the World Wildlife Fund with smaller contributions coming from Exxon and Coca-Cola – intercepts only a portion of this illicit trade. (According to a departmental memo, its workers extracted $219,395 worth of ginseng roots, dried sea cucumbers, timber, and musk deer sex glands during 1998.)[14]

Even discounting the money received by smugglers for items such as fish, frogs, sea cucumbers (trepang), sea urchins, bear parts, musk deer glands, and others, Chinese traders make upward of $3 million per year from smuggling operations (with a similar amount going to Russian poachers and sellers). This rise in illicit trade coincided with the decline in tax revenues collected by the Tax Service of the Russian Federation in Primorskii's largest cities and border districts. In dollar terms, these tax revenues fell from $2 billion in 1997 to $656 million in 1998, reflecting a sharp drop in the ruble-to-dollar exchange rate after the August 1998 currency devaluation (Goskomstat Rossii 1999). Illicit traders increased their financial resources (mostly in ready cash) against the background of declining tax revenues, especially in remote disctricts such as Dal'nerechensk (much of it on paper and in the form of promissory notes). This ready availability of increasing amounts of illegal cash combined with a decline in legally available resources establishes a strong foundation for corruption of government officials in Primorskii. Kopaev and Zubov, based on their experience on the ground, identified the city and district of Ussuriisk as the key transit hub for cross-border smuggling, followed by the Lesozavodskii, Dal'nerechenskii, and Khasanskii districts. Larger traders in these districts, according to Kopaev, pay protection money to police captains who ensure their business is safe from both police raids and

[14] A selection of photographs that I took in the town of Pogranichnyi on the Russian–Chinese border in 2001 and posted on my "Russia in Asia" Web pages at San Diego State University (http://www-rohan.sdsu.edu/~alexseev) shows daily images that fuel anxiety among local Russians about the economic costs of Chinese migration. Among them are images of cheap plastic mannequins piled at the back of the local Chinese market juxtaposed against images of cargo trains loaded with timber (a "strategic raw material") for shipment to China. Photographs from the Ussuriisk market illustrate the positive impacts.

petty criminals. He added, with anger and despondency: "If only these police officers knew for how little they sell their protection" (interview with the author, Vladivostok, May 25, 1999).

Reflecting public anxieties about the Chinese migrants gaining at the expense of the local Russians, the then vice-governor Stegnii said: "No doubt that the Chinese gain more. Compare the border towns of Suifenhe and Grodekovo. Both were deep holes in 1989. I visited Suifenhe in 1989. It had one hotel, called "Intourist," that had bed linens so sullied they were black, with some hair left over from previous guests. In my room there were two glass jars: one with drinking water, the other serving as a toilet. You know how dramatically things changed for the better there. [By 2000, Suifenhe was a bustling trading city, with mirror-glass office buildings, nicely paved streets, and luxury hotels.] But in Grodekovo, nothing changed, except that the restrooms got a bit cleaner" (interview with the author, Vladivostok, August 15, 2000).

These perceptions also correlated with the majority of Primorskii 2000 survey respondents who said that daily routine activities of Chinese migrants – such as trade – were threatening Russian security and sovereignty over the Far East. Among government officials in Primorskii krai, these perceptions were officially expressed in a more sophisticated and more politicized manner in recent years. In the words of the Pacific Border Service chief, General Tarasenko: "[Chinese] tourists pose another threat – while on the territory of the Russian Federation, they are investing the proceeds of their commercial activities into real property, securities, and contraband (smuggling out sea cucumbers, ginseng roots, rare-earth metals, and classified weapon samples). As you realize, such activities of Chinese nationals affect the demographic, economic, military, and other aspects of Russia's national interest in this region. These activities are explicitly aimed at undermining Russia's security" (Tarasenko 1999: 5).

Public Perceptions

In the Primorskii 2000 survey, these controversial perceptions and ambiguities regarding the economic impact of Chinese migrants and cross-border exchanges with China show certain systematic patterns. As shown in Table 4.4, respondents see Chinese migration as predominantly beneficial to agriculture, trade, availability of consumer goods, and the budget. They also see the economic activities of Chinese migrants as helping to reduce prices. On the other hand, the same respondents associate the

TABLE 4.4. *Perceived Socioeconomic Impacts of Chinese Migration in Primorskii krai (September 2000)*

Question: Do the Chinese have negative (−3), positive (+3), or no effect (0) in Primorskii on:	**−3**	**−2**	**−1**	**0**	**1**	**2**	**3**	**Don't know**
Industry	12.5	18.7	16.2	23.2	9.2	6.7	2.2	11
Agriculture	12.5	11.9	12.7	13	17.8	14.7	8.9	8.6
Trade	7.6	7.7	10.3	10.4	25.5	19.8	12.5	5.2
Prices	7.8	5.5	9.7	12	25	21	11.4	5.4
Job availability to Russian citizens	17.6	17.4	19.9	15.3	12.5	7.2	1.8	7.2
Opportunity to make money for Russian citizens	13.1	15.5	18.2	16	14.4	10.4	3.5	7.5
Assortment of available goods	3.3	1.8	6.4	8.4	26	27.3	22.3	3.4
The environment	23.4	17.9	21.9	26.8	1.7	1.2	0.3	5.6
Budget revenues	7.1	10	9.2	25	17.5	8.3	4.3	17
Crime levels	15.4	19	24.8	26	1.3	1.4	2.9	8.6

Note: Based on the author's Primorskii 2000 survey (N = 1,010).

Chinese presence with more harm than good when it comes to local industry, job availability, the environment, and crime.

Factor analysis of items displayed in Table 4.4 revealed significant commonalities among three clusters of responses. The first cluster, or factor, combined perceptions of Chinese migrants' effects on jobs, moneymaking opportunities, and crime. In plain language, this analysis shows that those Russians who thought the Chinese had a negative effect on local employment were the same who thought the Chinese presence reduced Russian incomes and contributed to crime. The second factor revealed commonality among the perceived impacts of migrants on trade, availability of goods, and consumer prices. The third factor identified proximity among Russian perceptions of the Chinese migrant's impact on industry, agriculture, and the environment – quite logically linking the state of the environment with the state of Primorskii's industry and agriculture (both dependent heavily on nonrenewable resource extraction).

The Primorskii 2000 survey suggests that Primorskii residents saw migrant trade activities as benefiting the Chinese more than the Russians. Because most migrants have engaged in trade or business, these responses

TABLE 4.5. *Perceptions of Gains by the Russians and the Chinese from Cross-Border Trade in the Primorskii 2000 Survey*

	Percent of Survey Respondents Saying That:			
Actors/institutions enjoying the gains	**Russians gain a lot**		**Chinese gain a lot**	
"Shuttle" traders (private citizens)	59%	(15%)	74%	(15%)
Private businesses	50%	(26%)	56%	(31%)
Government (budget revenues)	24%	(27%)	45%	(35%)
Smugglers (illicit traders)	73%	(19%)	73%	(22%)

Note: The sum of responses with scores of 3 and 4 on a 0-to-4 scale, as percentage of the total. "Don't know" responses as a percentage of the total are in parentheses.

indicated that Chinese migration was associated with increasing deprivation of Russians relative to the Chinese. The survey asked: "How much income does cross-border trade generate for Russian and Chinese 'shuttle' traders (*chelnoki*), private companies, governments, and smugglers?" Responses, summarized in Table 4.5, show that only Russian smugglers enjoyed "parity" with their Chinese counterparts when it came to perceived economic gains from cross-border exchanges. But this is hardly the kind of parity that would make any host community see migration as something that would help them achieve prosperity, safety, and security. At the same time, these responses show that Primorskii residents varied in their assessment of Russian and Chinese gains. By subtracting the scores assigned (on a zero-to-four scale) to Russian actors or institutions from the scores assigned to the Chinese actors or institutions (Table 4.3), I estimated individual respondents' perceptions of how much these groups gained relative to one another.

One of the best measures of the tension between perceived economic costs and benefits of Chinese migration in Primorskii was this survey item: "In your view, how many people in Primorskii krai benefit from cross-border trade with China now?" Most respondents (close to 37 percent, excluding about 12 percent of the "don't knows") said they believed about one-third of Primorskii's population benefited from – predominantly migrant – trade with China. Approximately 30 percent of respondents stated that this trade benefited less than one-quarter of the local Russian population – a cohort one expects to be the most prone to migration phobia. In other words, nearly 70 percent of the representative sample of Primorskii residents thought that two-thirds of local Russians did not obtain gains from trade with China. Among the remaining respondents,

18 percent said about half of Primorskii residents gained from cross-border trade; 8 percent said two-thirds; and 5 percent said more than three-quarters. These perceptions reflected a general sense of the local public that, on the one hand, interactions with China did improve lives of a sizeable proportion of the local population, but, on the other hand, a lot more local residents were yet to benefit. In this sense, the "extent-of-benefits" measure revealed significant uncertainty embedded in economic valuations of Chinese migration's impact.

Alternative Explanations

The story so far is that conditions in Primorskii krai engendered a wide spectrum of perceptions bearing on fear and hostility toward Chinese migrants. This variation makes it possible to address the crucial question: Were the most threatened and hostile Russians in Primorskii krai also the ones who viewed the Russian government capacity as weak; who believed the proportion of Chinese migrants in Primorskii was higher more than others did; who believed the migrants would abuse local hospitality and would illegally settle down; who saw Beijing as nurturing secret territorial claims; who felt that the Chinese are a distinct and distant – "unassimilable" – ethnic group; who thought migrants gained economically at the expense of the local Russians; and who perceived the migrants' impact on socioeconomic conditions in Primorskii as negative?[15]

However theoretically and intuitively plausible the relationship between these perceptions, one would be unwise to jump to conclusions without controlling for alternative explanations that do not relate directly to the hypotheses based on the security-dilemma logic.

Sensitivity to Minority Group Size and Status Reversal

Whereas suspicions that Chinese migration might pave the way to cultural, economic, and political Sinification of the Russian Far East have been at the heart of threat perception, estimates of migration scale or percentage of migrants in the local population may not necessarily be an accurate indicator of fear. This is because citizens in receiving states may differ as to the political and social significance of shifts in the ethnic balance.

[15] Moreover, statistical procedures allow one to estimate how strong each of these relationships is when others are controlled and thus to answer questions such as this: "Among respondents who overestimate the size of Chinese migration are those who also believe the Russian government capacity to resolve internal conflicts is weak more threatened by migration and more hostile toward migrants?"

In part, this is because they may have different sensitivities to the magnitude of the ethnic balance that would constitute a "tipping point" in their majority group position. As discussed earlier, status reversal sensitivity has its own psychological roots in proclivity for risk acceptance or aversion. What percentage of migrants in the host population would make it impossible for the incumbent ethnic group to continue claiming sovereignty: the monopoly on "the last word" in governing the receiving state or its faction? For example, suppose one respondent in the Primorskii 2000 survey believed the Chinese by 2010 would comprise between 20 and 40 percent of the local population. Suppose further that the same respondent also felt that the proportion of the Chinese in Primorskii would have to exceed 75 percent of the population before Russia could no longer claim Primorskii as its sovereign territory. Suppose another respondent believed the Chinese by 2010 would comprise between 10 and 20 percent of the local population, yet also felt that Russia's sovereignty over Primorskii would be unsustainable if the proportion of Chinese nationals would exceed 10 percent. Which of these respondents is likely to be more hostile to migrants? The straightforward logic of ethnic balancing would suggest the former, whereas the logic of status reversal sensitivity would suggest the latter.

Sensitivity to Chinese migration resulting in political status reversal in Primorskii – in a sense that Russia might lose its Far Eastern territories to China – varied among the survey respondents, with scores distributed, approximately, on a bell-shaped curve. The survey asked: "Given what proportion of Chinese people in the local population would you no longer consider Primorskii krai to be part of Russia?" For about 2 percent of respondents – excluding the "don't knows"[16] – the tipping point was 10 percent Chinese in Primorskii; for 4 percent of respondents, the tipping point was 20 percent Chinese; for 21 percent of respondents, 30 percent; for 43 percent of respondents, 50 percent; and for 24 percent of respondents, 75 percent. The status reversal theory suggests that those 27 percent of respondents who saw the ethnic balance threshold as 30 percent or below were likely to be the ones most threatened by migrants and also the ones favoring the most hostile responses to migration. I included this question in the survey prompted, indirectly, by the former Yeltsin representative to Primorskii krai Vladimir Ignatenko, who told me the region would cease to be part of Russia if the proportion of the Chinese reached about one-third of the local population. Once that happened, he argued,

[16] Approximately 20 percent of respondents said "don't know" in response to this question.

the area would turn into "a Siberian Israel," with ethnic intermingling engendering insecurity, conflict, and violence and with little opportunity to assuage fears on both sides.

Ideology

But what if sensitivity to status reversal and the perceptual drivers of the security dilemma might be captured by respondents' ideological preferences? For example, hostility toward migrants may relate to personal trust in parties that oppose ethnic diversity and emphasize the need for the majority ethnic group to maintain superior political and economic positions relative to other groups, including migrants. Research by Sears (1988) and Kinder and Sears (1996), for example, identified "individualism" as a separate factor affecting interethnic attitudes. To control for ideological identity, I devised two questions asked in the Primorskii 2000 survey.

The first question probed respondents' trust in Russia's political parties represented in the lower house of parliament, the State Duma, that could be associated with distinct ideological positions or with their absence – the latter being a visible social phenomenon in Russia following widespread public disillusionment with communist ideology that used to shape the entire social and political system. Of the 90 percent of respondents who answered the question (the rest said "don't know"), 12.7 percent expressed trust in the pro-Putin *Yedinstvo* ("Unity") block; 3.7 percent said they trusted another centrist block, *Otechestvo* ("Fatherland"); 16.3 percent favored the communists; 3.3 percent favored the liberal *Yabloko* party; 4.4 percent favored a liberal-center "Union of the Right Forces" (*Soiuz pravykh sil*, or SPS); 5.9 percent trusted the ethnonationalist and grossly misnamed Liberal-Democratic Party of Russia (LDPR); and 50.8 percent said they trusted no party at all.

Two opposite ideological dimensions related directly to attitudes on Chinese migration: (a) support for pluralism, including ethnic group diversity, versus (b) support for centralization and uniformity, usually revealed in preferences for the "strong state." The latter also implied support for protecting Russia's territorial integrity against claims of ethnic "others," from Chechnya in the Caucasus to the Chinese border on the Pacific. Representing the polar opposites on this ideological continuum were the prodiversity, politically liberal Yabloko party and the ethnonationalist and statist LDPR. Support for other parties signaled ideological leanings somewhere between these poles. While distinguishing itself from Yabloko by backing Putin's core policies (which included centralization of government authority and war in Chechnya), SPS came out in support of ethnic and political pluralism, including acceptance of migrants. In fact, one of the leading Russian politicians with whom the public associated SPS was Irina Khakamada – a Russian citizen of Japanese origin. For these considerations, SPS was likely to fall between Yabloko and the midpoint of this spectrum. On the opposite side of the midpoint – closer to LDPR – was the Communist Party of the Russian Federation (KPRF) led by Gennadii Zyuganov. Similar to LDPR, the communists vowed to unite "patriotic forces capable of expelling occupiers and traitors" – a hallmark party slogan potentially appealing to anyone in Primorskii who would view the Chinese as prospective "occupiers." Unlike, LDPR, however, the communist party platform did not specifically define "occupiers and traitors" in ethnic terms and stated elsewhere that "we have nothing to do with racism."

I considered those who expressed trust in Unity and Fatherland – both nicknamed a "party of power" for being set up as electoral vehicles by the Kremlin administration and the Moscow mayor, respectively – to fall on the midpoint of the ideological spectrum from Yabloko to LDPR. In their 1999 Duma election platforms, both Unity and Fatherland came through as instrumental movements – campaigning, in a pithy comment by Michael McFaul, Nikolai Petrov, and Andrei Riabov (1999), on a theme that "it's better to be rich and healthy than poor and sick." These experts on the Russian party system also suggested that this instrumental – or nonideological – position reflected "the amorphousness of Russian society, absence of distinct social bases of party support, and lack of distinct and internalized interests among social groups or strata which they could express." Yet, by explicitly affiliating themselves with any mainstream party *at all* the pro-Unity and pro-Fatherland respondents distinguished themselves from trust-no-party respondents on the crucial dimension of political alienation. Even though they also represented ideologically amorphous views, the supporters of the centrist blocks – unlike trust-no-party respondents – nevertheless articulated implicit trust in the electoral system.[17]

The second measure of ideological preferences is derived from the conception of ideology as a "consistent, codified set of criteria for determining the membership and boundaries of a political community" (Hanson 1996:

17 Based on these considerations, I coded responses expressing trust in LDPR as −2; KPRF as −1; Unity and Fatherland as 0; SPS as 1; and *Yabloko* as 2. Trust-no-party responses were coded as missing data along with the "don't know" responses.

10). "Political community" in this case being a nation-state, the Russian Federation. Russia never existed within the same state borders that it inherited after the collapse of the Soviet Union. Visions of where Russia's "true" boundaries should lie diverged significantly among the Russians – a variation also reflected in the Primorskii 2000 survey. I considered respondents who said they were content with Russia's existing post-Soviet borders (37 percent of the total minus the "don't knows") to be less prone to immigration phobia than those who wanted post-Soviet Russia to reemerge within the borders of the former Soviet Union (39 percent) or the Russian Empire – at the time when the latter encompassed Poland and Alaska (6 percent).[18] One would expect sensitivity to territorial gains or losses to especially affect interethnic hostility in situations where borders have been recently established and/or disputed, as has been the case between Russia and China in the Far East.

Education, Occupation, Religion, and the "Young Male" Factor

In the Primorskii 2000 survey, about 43 percent of respondents said they had a high school education or less, 35 percent said they had "secondary specialized" (junior college plus vocational–technical) education, and about 20 percent said they had higher (university) education. Thinking straightforwardly, one might expect antimigrant hostility to relate inversely to education levels, but this is not necessarily plausible in the context of Primorskii krai, or Russia generally. Whereas the 35 percent of respondents with "secondary specialized" education most likely had more years of schooling than high school graduates, their curricula would usually emphasize hands-on training for blue-collar jobs (the ones more likely to be threatened by migrant labor) at the expense of liberal arts education (the kind associated with greater ethnic tolerance). To avoid ambiguity, I simply distinguish between respondents with and without a university/college education.

The survey captured a wide diversity of Primorskii residents' occupations: students (about 5 percent of respondents); industrial workers (17 percent); agricultural workers (5 percent); engineers, technicians, and service sector employees (13 percent); private business operators (4 percent) and employees (11 percent); officers of the armed forces, police, or Federal Security Service (6 percent); retired people (19 percent); housewives and househusbands (6 percent); and intellectuals or "intelligentsia" such as doctors, teachers, and artists (7 percent). Considering Chinese

[18] The "don't knows" comprised 6.7 percent of all respondents.

migrants' excellent farming skills and generally lower levels of education in rural areas of Primorskii krai, one would consider the "yellow peril" sentiments to be the most intense among agricultural workers. For reasons of job competition, one may also place the unemployed in the same camp. Conversely, higher education levels among the intelligentsia, engineers, and students would suggest greater likelihood of promigrant attitudes. To probe whether occupation is likely to relate significantly to threat and hostility, I ran a simple (zero-order) correlation analysis. The test supported the idea that Primorskii agricultural workers would be the most anti-Chinese, but did not show a significant relationship between militant hostility and unemployment. Of the three hypothetical occupations suggested for the promigrant camp, only intelligentsia was significant. So were business owners (apparently, the promise of gains through cooperation outweighed fear of competition) and retired people – suggesting an important role of economic valuations. Retirees in the Russian Far East do not compete with Chinese migrants for jobs and live predominantly on fixed incomes – hence, one would expect them to value lower prices at Chinese markets more so than other occupational groups. All in all, however, for agricultural workers, intelligentsia, business owners, and retired people, occupation seems to be not so much the cause but the mediator of migration attitudes – the causes being captured by education and perceptions of socioeconomic impact of migrants. For these reasons, I excluded occupation from the regression model.

Representing a unique and complex amalgam of social, cognitive, and emotional bases, affiliation with the Russian Orthodox Church in the Russian Far East is likely to affect perceptions of "us-ness" and "otherness" as well as sensitivity to developments challenging political and social order. Self-identification with the Orthodox Church in Russia implies support for a strong centralized state (by traditional historical association of the Orthodox Church with the Russian government), territorial expansion (the Empire), and an idealized concept of ethnically purified "Russianness" – which in Siberia specifically takes on xenophobic overtones (Parthe 1995). In the Primorskii 2000 survey, about 65 percent, excluding the "don't knows," said they were Russian Orthodox Christians, 31 percent said they professed "no religion," and about 3 percent affiliated themselves with other religions.[19]

[19] The "don't knows" represented 4.4 percent of the sample. Other religions included Islam and Judaism. In the statistical analysis that follows, I include a measure distinguishing Orthodox believers from all other respondents in the survey sample.

Of 1,010 survey respondents, about 13 percent were males under thirty years of age – the "young males" cohort associated with emotional volatility and proneness to hostility. However, in the Primorskii survey membership in this cohort did not correlate significantly with threat perception and antimigrant hostility. Inclusion of the "young male" factor in the regression model in preliminary tests did not increase the model's explanatory power.[20]

Piecing Together the Security-Dilemma Matrix: Regression Results for Primorskii 2000

Using a statistical method of hierarchical ordinary least squares (OLS) analysis, we may examine how strongly perceptions of emerging anarchy, offensive intentions, group distinctiveness, deprivation, and socioeconomic impact related to three measures of immigration phobia: (1) the general sense of threat to Russia's and Primorskii krai's security; (2) the threat of armed conflict between Russia and China; and (3) respondents' hostility measured as combined support for antimigrant paramilitary groups and parties. The detailed results are presented in the tables in Appendix A. Here I will summarize and interpret the findings in the context of Chinese migration in the Russian Far East.

General Findings

The statistical analysis of the Primorskii 2000 survey validated the perceptual logic of the interethnic security dilemma in the emergence of antimigrant hostility in the Russian Far East. The tests ruled out the null hypothesis – that is, that the security-dilemma perceptions had at best a random, or chance, relationship with the respondents' sense that Chinese migrants posed a security threat to Russia and Primorskii krai and with respondents' support for militant antimigrant hostility. The security-dilemma model explained approximately 24 percent of variation in general threat perception and in fear of Russia–China armed conflict. The model also explained about 18 percent variation in antimigrant hostility among Primorskii residents. These are significant proportions given a large number of respondents (N = 1,010), diverse interpretations of the nature of the "Chinese threat" by local Russians and high volume of "noise" and

[20] Zero-order correlations between perceived threat to Russia and Primorskii (THRRUPK variable) were .127 (with $p < .001$, one-tailed) for ethnic majority status sensitivity (CHPROP); .130 ($p < .001$) for party trust (PARTY); .078 ($p < .01$) for support for Russian territorial expansion (EXPAND), and .081 ($p < .01$) for Orthodox believers (ORTHRU).

random measurement error in any survey data (see Asher 1983: 39). Statistical probability that threat perception and antimigrant hostility related to the security-dilemma logic by chance alone was less than .001 percent. (See Tables A.1, A.2, and A.3.) Control measures – sensitivity to group status reversal, ideology, education, and religion – had no significant effect on the general sense of threat and threat of armed conflict in the security-dilemma model, even though all of these control measures except education had a significant one-on-one correlation with threat. In other words, all other factors aside, fear of migrants was indeed more intense among those Primorskii residents who were sensitive to the loss of ethnic majority position by the Russians, who trusted LDPR and KPRF, who believed Russia's true borders include Finland and Alaska, and who declared themselves to be Orthodox Christian believers.[21] However, migration phobia had no higher probability than chance to be more intense among status-sensitive, nationalist-communist trusting, imperial-minded, Orthodox believers if they, like other respondents, also had a heightened sense of emerging anarchy, offensive intent of migrants, Russian–Chinese group distinctiveness, and the economic risks of allowing Chinese migrants into Primorskii.

Both measures of threat perception (concern over security in Russia/Primorskii and armed border clashes with China) had a statistically significant relationship with items that represented the conceptual core of the interethnic security dilemma: emerging anarchy, mistrust of migrants' intent, ethnic "groupness," and a sense of economic vulnerability (especially the risks associated with earning a living). In other words, the tests found that insecure individuals in host societies who feel that migrants harbor territorial claims, who provide economic benefits to few local residents, and who believe migration threatens the majority position of their ethnic group are likely to support coercive, and potentially violent, responses to migration.

The linkage between fear and hostility also implies that the tests underestimated the role that the perceptual logic of the security dilemma is likely to play in the emergence of militant antimigrant hostility. Methodologically, this is because predictors that related significantly to threat perception also had *indirect* effects on hostility through threat.[22]

[21] Technically, indirect effects of all independent variables on the outcome variable can be estimated, but here I limit the analysis to statistically significant measures.

[22] Personal income valuation by respondents and their perceptions of Chinese migrants' impact on income opportunities and crime were not significantly correlated. For a more detailed description of economic conditions in Primorskii related to Chinese migration, see Alexseev (2002: 271–3).

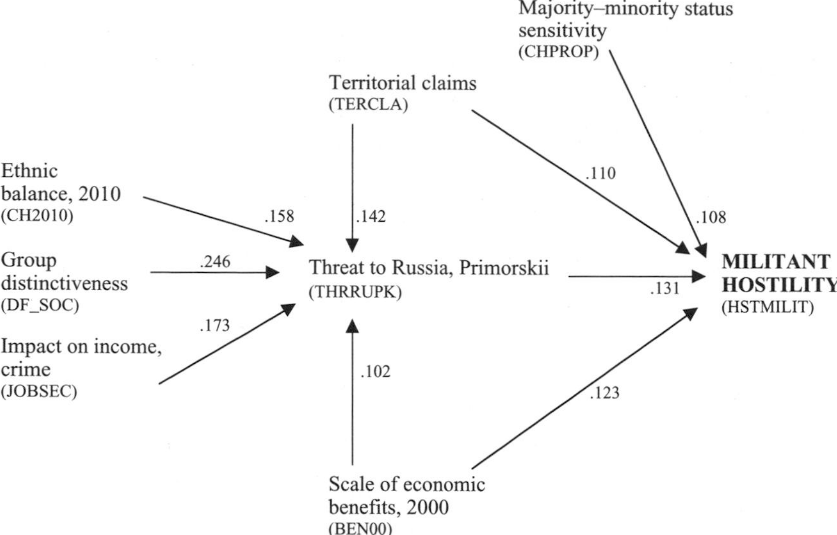

FIGURE 4.3. A Path Model of Antimigrant Hostility in Primorskii krai 2000.

Substantively, this is because threat and hostility are inextricably related, even though triggers of violent behavior in any given context may not appear to be directly associated with the social and perceptual logic of the security dilemma. Figure 4.3 integrates test results by winnowing out statistically insignificant correlates of threat and hostility. In Table 4.6, I summarize the direct and indirect effects on antimigrant hostility of these significant predictors. Two transformations are noteworthy. Valuations of the migrants' impact on income and crime rise to the level of statistical significance in the complete model of hostility. Assessment of the Primorskii population percentage benefiting from Chinese migration becomes the strongest correlate of hostility – exceeding, albeit marginally, general threat perception.

Which predictors of threat and hostility mattered more than others in the statistical analysis? A tally of standardized regression coefficients (Table 4.7) suggests several answers. First, for both measures of threat, valuations of Russian-Chinese group difference were by far the strongest and most significant predictor. However, group differences were not a significant correlate of hostility, even when indirect effects through threat perception were taken into account. Two independent variables – assessment of Chinese territorial claims and of the proportion of Primorskii population benefiting from migrant trade – were the most robust correlates of the

TABLE 4.6. *Direct and Indirect Effects of the Security Dilemma Perceptions on Antimigrant Hostility: Primorski 2000*

	Direct Effect	Indirect Effect	Total Effect
Perceptions of:			
"Anarchy":			
Ethnic balance, 2010 (CH2010)	.079	.021 (.158 × .131)	.100
Offensive intent:			
Territorial claims (TERCLA)	.110	.019 (.142 × .131)	.129
"Groupness":			
Group distinctiveness (DF_SOC)	.065	.032 (.246 × .131)	.097
Deprivation and socioeconomic impact:			
Impact on income, crime (JOBSEC)	.095	.023 (.173 × .131)	.118
Scale of economic benefits, 2000 (BEN00)	.123	.013 (.102 × .131)	.136
Controls:			
Majority–minority status sensitivity	.108	–	.108
Security threat to Russia, Primorskii (THRRUPK)	.131	–	.131

Note: Path coefficients reported in this table are standardized regression coefficients in the complete models of general threat and hostility (for unstandardized coefficients and standard errors, see Tables A.1 and A.3).

threat–hostility complex. Both measures significantly related to all three outcome variables. Assessment of migrants' impact on income opportunities and crime was the only other independent variable that related significantly to at least one measure of threat and to militant anti-Chinese hostility.

While the results generally confirm the security-dilemma interpretation of immigration phobia, they also reveal important nuances and provisos. Five implications of the Primorskii 2000 survey analysis appear to be particularly insightful.

Interstate vs. Interethnic Threat

Primorskii respondents made a meaningful distinction between threat assessment of armed (interstate) conflict versus general security threat perceptions, the latter being associated predominantly with interethnic relations and internal conflict. Estimates of Russian–Chinese ethnic balance by 2010 and intent by the Chinese to claim Russian territories related significantly both to armed conflict and general security threat. Yet, perceptions of central authority strength – a quintessential element in the

TABLE 4.7. *Significant Predictors of Threat and Hostility: Primorskii 2000*

Security Threat to Russia, Primorskii (THRRUPK)		**Armed Conflict Threat, 2010 (ARMC10)**		**Militant Hostility (HSTMILIT)**	
Perceptions of:					
"*Anarchy*":		"*Anarchy*":		"*Anarchy*":	
Ethnic balance, 2010	(.158)**	Ethnic balance, 2010	(.140)***	–	
		Isolation of Primorskii	(.163)**		
		Government capacity	(.102)*		
Offensive intent:		*Offensive intent*:		*Offensive intent*:	
Territorial claims	(.142)**	Territorial claims	(.178)**	Territorial claims	(.129)*
		Intent to settle down	(−.124)*		
"*Groupness*":		"*Groupness*":		"*Groupness*":	
Group difference	(.246)***	Group difference	(.231)***	–	
Deprivation/economic effects:		*Deprivation/economic effects*:		*Deprivation/economic effects*:	
Impact on income/crime	(.173)**	Chinese gains	(−.134)*	Impact on income, crime	(.118)*
Scale of economic benefits	(.102)*	Scale of economic benefits	(.124)*	Scale of economic benefits	(.136)*
Controls:		*Controls*:		*Controls*:	
–		–		Group status sensitivity	(.108)*
				Security threat	(.131)*
Total variation explained:					
Threat to Russia, Primorskii:		*Armed conflict threat*:		*Hostility*:	
24.4% (R^2 = .244)		24.0% (R^2 = .240)		18.2% (R^2 = .182)	

Significance: * = $p < .05$, ** = $p < .01$, *** = $p < .001$ (one-tailed).

Note: Data for the correlates of militant hostility include indirect effects through threat. Coefficients reported in this table are standardized regression coefficients (betas) in the complete models of general threat, armed conflict threat, and hostility (for unstandardized coefficients and standard errors, see Tables A.1, A.2, and A3). These coefficients allow one to compare effect sizes of predictors relative to one another.

security-dilemma logic – related to the assessment of armed interstate conflict threat, but not to the general security threat. Both survey measures of central authority strength came out as statistically significant: (1) valuation of the capacity of government agencies to prevent interethnic conflict (i.e., that domestic institutions are robust) and (2) assessment of Primorskii krai's isolation from central Russia (i.e., perceived strength of political and economic ties with the rest of Russia and chances to get military reinforcement in case of armed conflict with China). Armed conflict threat – more so than general security threat – was linked by survey respondents to alleged Chinese designs on Russian Far Eastern territories.

While this finding was unanticipated, it is generally consistent both with the theory and with migration context. Intuitively, respondents seemed to understand that the strength of central government is more of an issue if Russia comes under attack by an outside power and not so much of an issue in the case of smaller, domestic security challenges, such as unrest or crime. Besides, it is also plausible in the Primorskii context that local residents simply believed the government was too inefficient and corrupt to mobilize resources unless the proverbial push really came to shove in the form of external military invasion. In a decade of post-Soviet transition, Primorskii residents experienced unpaid or underpaid wages; rampant inflation and currency devaluation; police corruption; decay of the Russian military bases and defense industries in the region; and massive power shutdowns in freezing, windswept winters.

Relative Gains vs. Absolute Gains

Another unexpected result was that measures of respondents' sense of relative gains or relative deprivation in the face of Chinese migration – personal income and the assessment of Chinese gains from migrant trade relative to the Russians – had no statistically significant association with threat and antimigrant hostility. The plausible contextual explanation of this finding mirrors the one regarding central authority. Economic decline and hardship following the collapse of the Soviet system of central planning had an overwhelming impact on Primorskii residents. Respondents in the region were perfectly aware that the closure of factories, the abandonment of collective farms, and the de facto bankruptcy of the central government – not the arrival of the Chinese – were the primary reasons why their wages and pensions were unpaid. Whereas comparison of economic gains and losses across groups still matters, these results suggest that valuation of relative gains may not be a potent predictor of interethnic threat under general economic decline that is clearly associated with domestic crises, especially if it precedes the arrival of migrants and may not be attributed to them.[23]

At the same time, the tests lend support to the prospect theory's emphasis on the importance of perceived changes in in-group gains relative to a reference point in time (in this case, the arrival of Chinese migrants). Perceived socioeconomic impact of Chinese migration significantly related to both threat and hostility. Respondents' feelings about migration effects on income opportunities for the local Russians and on crime levels, as well as estimates of the percentage of Primorskii population benefiting from migrant trade with China, explained more variation in militant hostility than blocks of variables related to other dimensions of the security dilemma (see change in Adjusted R^2, Table A3).

These results suggest that focusing on relative gains under the security dilemma may discount valuations by individuals of changes in absolute gains of their in-group over time. Individuals in migrant-receiving societies – as they did in Primorskii krai – instead of asking which group gains more from migration, may also ask: Are we better off or worse off since migration began? Monitoring public responses to this question appeared to be a consistent, unobtrusive measure of threat perception and antimigrant hostility in Primorskii 2000 tests.

Threat vs. Hostility

The tests confirm the linkage between threat perception and hostility posited by the security dilemma. Support for the paramilitaries and antimigrant parties related nonrandomly to the perceived security threat to Russia and Primorskii krai. Perceptions of offensive intent mattered as well. The results also suggest complementarity between the logic of the security dilemma and the logic of prejudice as the sense of group position. The latter adds an important nuance to our understanding of the effects on threat and hostility of ethnic balance estimates. While associating

[23] Bivariate correlations do lend some limited support for the labor market competition hypothesis. Respondents' self-identification as agricultural workers, was significantly – albeit weakly – related to general threat perception ($r = .067, p = .024$) and to militant hostility ($r = .071, p = .014$). About half of Chinese migrants worked in agriculture. However, self-identification of respondents as unemployed did not significantly correlate with either threat or hostility.

increasing Chinese presence in Primorskii with increasing threat to security, the ethnic balance perceptions were not strong enough to connect with support for antimigrant political actors and paramilitaries, such as the Cossacks. However, those respondents who were more sensitive than others to the "tipping effect" of migration on the majority group status of local Russians were nonrandomly more prone to support aggressive anti-Chinese policies and actors, including the paramilitaries. Primorskii survey measures of the tipping point incorporated sensitivity to Russian–Chinese ethnic balance change, while adding sensitivity to majority–minority status change – precisely the type of fear linked to prejudice in research on the role of the perceived group position in ethnic relations. In short, the tests showed that both measures were important: The tipping point perceptions related significantly only to militant hostility, the ethnic balance perceptions related significantly only to threat measures.

Attitudes vs. Attributes

In the tests, the statistically significant measures of threat assessment and antimigrant hostility in Primorskii 2000 were exclusively perceptual. In contrast, respondents' attributes, such as the personal income, age, sex, religion, and education level of respondents, were not significant when assessed against perceptions reflecting the logic of the security dilemma, even though most of them were significantly correlated one-on-one with at least one measure of threat and hostility. In an earlier study (Alexseev 2003), I found that variation in aggregate demographic and macroeconomic conditions across Primorskii krai by city and county (including trade volumes, number of Russian–Chinese joint ventures, population density, or proximity to the border) had indeterminate effects on hostility.

This finding indirectly validates the security-dilemma model of immigration phobia. Assuming fear and hostility are embedded in the logic of threat exaggeration – with overblown estimates of migration size, uncertainty about migrants' intent, ethnic group distinctiveness, and in-group economic losses – one would expect that socioeconomic characteristics of regions or individuals would be less significant. It is intuitive that a sense of clear and present threat is a powerful social equalizer – when a house catches fire, people of defferent education and income levels feel equally motivated to run for their lives. In terms of the house-on-fire analogy (initially suggested in Wolfers 1962: 13–19), the importance of social attributes of its residents would start diminishing before the house goes up in flames, when the residents start exaggerating the probability that it might. Not only clear and present, but anticipated or imagined, threats projected far into the future also turn out to act as powerful perceptual "equalizers." One's education, income, or religion are arguably unlikely to matter decisively even though one's house may never burn, if one starts having fears – however unfounded and inchoate – that the house is increasingly likely to catch fire some day in the future. Again, however, this logic does not suggest that social characteristics of individuals would be uniformly played down in various contexts. Rather, the degree to which they matter would be a function of how closely putative threats ascribed to migration resemble the house-on-fire image (e.g., how intense, profound, and acute they are).

This finding suggests that arguments about rational and symbolic microfoundations of the security dilemma are complementary. Emergent uncertainty about ethnic balances and the intent of ethnic others cues susceptibility to symbolic persuasion, thus creating incentives for xenophobic and racist policy entrepreneurs to sustain and exploit interethnic or antimigrant fears. For its own part, the increasing intensity of symbolic persuasion would inflate the sense of uncertainty and vulnerability. Aggressive responding would become attractive to individuals seeking to release mounting and – more likely than not – exaggerated fears.

A word of caution about this interpretation, however, is also in order. The predominance of attitudes over attributes in the Primorskii survey data does not fly in the face of observations suggesting that specific sociodemographic groups – such as unemployed young males – are more prone to engage in collective violence than other groups. The survey was designed to identify bases of public support for aggressive antimigrant activism – something that would explain the probability of antimigrant behavior but not the social and organizational forms this behavior is likely to take. The analysis simply suggests that whatever the social portrait and the organizational attributes of antimigrant activists, such activists are more likely to emerge and win popular support in societies where migration engenders the sense of the security dilemma.

The Spiral Logic

This study was not designed to investigate the dynamic aspect of the security dilemma, or how attempts by one group to improve its security make other groups less secure, with retaliatory actions spiraling out of control as a consequence. The principal goal of this study was to examine the logic of fear and hostility first among host populations – something that may set the stage for misperceptions and hostile actions and reactions spiraling out of control. It is even more significant therefore that the perceptual logic of the security dilemma, in Primorskii 2000 survey tests, was a significant driver of interethnic fears even prior to the onset of the "spiral" dynamic. In particular, the prospective retaliatory logic – an implicit assumption that the other side cannot be constrained from doing harm unless preempted – played a significant part in respondents' assessments of security threats and in their hostility levels.

Given that this logic was palpable, one can visualize situations when the migrants, too, would misinterpret the host community's intent and react to perceived hostility in ways that they view as self-defense. This self-defense reaction, in turn, may only further aggravate the host population's fears and trigger antimigrant responses. Future research can explore this "spiral" aspect of the security dilemma, possibly with comparisons of opinion data, with focus groups and with longitudinal event–data analysis reflecting the positions of both host societies and migrants.

5

Who's Behind "Fortress Europe"?

Xenophobia and Antimigrant Exclusionism from Dublin to the Danube

Whereas the Russian Far East findings suggest that the perceptual logic of the security dilemma is at the heart of immigration phobia, they come from a one-country probe. Does the perceptual logic of the security dilemma similarly relate to antimigrant hostility and threat perceptions in other countries, where the demographic, geographic, political, and socioeconomic contexts differ significantly from that in the Russian Far East? To address the question, this chapter examines xenophobia and antimigrant hostility at the other end of Eurasia – as reflected in political trends and public opinion in the fifteen member states of the EU. The EU is an excellent test case. On the one hand, differences in context relative to the Russian Far East are massive. The EU has no such neighbor as China and no equivalent of Russia–China demographic imbalance. The EU did not have Russia's problems with center–periphery relations following state collapse. In contrast, the EU context is the one composed of multiple host states, multiple sending states, strong transnational institutions, higher standards of living, and different cultural traditions, to name but a few major factors. And in addition, the nature of migration in the Russian Far East and the EU differed at least in one crucial respect: Most Chinese migrants in the Russian Far East were transients, while most migrants to the EU were settlers. While the Chinese were suspected of harboring intent to take over the Russian Far East, the European migrants expressed the intent to be "taken over" by their new home countries.

On the other hand, the EU has also faced the challenges consistent with the interethnic security dilemma – albeit not as intense as the Russian Far East. The "deepening and broadening" of EU's transnational authority in the 1980s and 1990s – especially with respect to the movement of people – contributed to rising uncertainty about government authority within nation-states. Amidst this uncertainty, European governments had to deal with hundreds of thousands of refugees fleeing war and political instability. Since the 1960s, declining birthrates across Europe and increasing ethnic distinctiveness of migrants from host populations raised concerns that migration would undermine the majority position of incumbent ethnic groups. Arriving from poorer and unstable states, most refugees and migrants also have had strong incentives to risk settling down illegally and to evade host-state law enforcement – hence, one could reasonably ascribe "offensive" intentions to these migrants. On top of that, migration raised concerns about economic and social costs, especially regarding employment and incomes, public education, and crime.

The first part of this chapter examines these trends and antimigrant hostility in the 1990s through the prism of public opinion captured in the EU-wide Eurobarometer polls. The second part of the chapter uses the survey data to probe whether perceptions consistent with the security-dilemma logic within the EU context, in fact, related significantly to fear and antimigrant hostility. The statistical tests are based on the analysis of the Eurobarometer survey "Racism and Xenophobia in Europe" (1997).

Europe on Standby over Migration Fears

In the period that I examine, approximately from 1990 to 2002, immigration phobia and exclusionist sentiments have been at the surface of mainstream politics in the EU member states. A report by the Associated Press on European responses to immigration in May 2002 concluded: "Across the continent, right-wing parties have surged at the polls by exploiting fears of a rising tide of immigrants and refugees – and mainstream politicians are echoing their concerns and their rhetoric." For example, in May 1992, as arguments heated up between Britain and France over illegal migrants using the Channel Tunnel, Iain Duncan Smith, leader of the British Conservative Party, made a much publicized vow that "not one... should be allowed to set foot in Britain" (Associated Press 2002). At the same time, British Prime Minister Tony Blair was in the news with a plan to make aid to Somalia, Sri Lanka, and Turkey contingent on these countries' willingness to take back asylum seekers rejected in Britain. At the 2002 EU summit in Seville, Spain joined Britain in proposing to withhold economic aid to states that failed to stop illegal migrants. While the measure was defeated, the summit did rule to tighten border control – even though the effectiveness of the measure was immediately cast in doubt (Asia Intelligence Wire 2002). In May 2002, Denmark cut down on economic assistance to refugees and enacted laws canceling the right of Danish citizens to automatically bring in spouses from outside the EU; Italy introduced fingerprinting for all non–EU nationals; Britain's Home Office demanded that migrants "make more effort to integrate into British society"; and the president of France called for reducing the review time for asylum cases from the average of about fourteen months to under one month (ibid.). Italian Prime Minister Silvio Berlusconi and the Christian Democrats in the Netherlands (then newly elected as a majority party) joined the chorus of European leaders who – according to the Associated Press report – believed that "to forestall this anti-foreigner surge, they must come up with a tougher joint policy . . . to choke off illegal migration and stop migrants 'asylum shopping' for the most generous host country" (Associated Press 2002). A report on asylum and migration by Human Rights Watch, the International Catholic Migration Committee, and the World Council of Churches accused the European governments of introducing "a barrage of restrictive immigration policies and practices making it increasingly difficult for any migrant or asylum seeker to legally enter their borders" (Human Rights Watch, the International Catholic Migration Committee, and the World Council of Churches 2001). Implementation of these policies included arbitrary detention, racial and ethnic profiling, and police abuse (Asia Intelligence Wire 2002).

European leaders also called for using naval and air power to stem the inflow of migrants. Britain's Tony Blair – according to a leaked memo that conveniently appeared when the Conservative opposition raised the migration specter in May 2002 – proposed using warships to intercept immigrant smuggling boats (Associated Press 2002). Other EU leaders supported this proposal. More controversially, by April 2003 the European Commission and the European Space Agency had drawn up plans to use satellites – including a sophisticated Envisat system developed at the cost of over $2 billion – to monitor refugees outside the EU borders. The plans were unveiled in February 2003 by science minister Lord Sainsbury as part of the Global Monitoring for Environment and Security program. The program envisioned deployment of the new Future Earth Observation Satellite, designed to take detailed pictures from space of objects smaller than ten feet. According to Keith Best, director of the Immigration Advisory Service – a think tank dealing with EU immigration issues – satellite monitoring could make it easier to assist refugees fleeing conflict zones in large numbers, as was the case during the wars in the former Yugoslavia. At the same time, he pointed out, refugee monitoring with satellites would undoubtedly be a tool of antimigrant exclusionism: "My real fear is they could be treated like some nasty cloud from Chernobyl, which would be indicative of the attitude that asylum seekers are some sort of pollutant" (Europe Intelligence Wire 2002).

Precisely such attitudes – while not predominant – were nevertheless held by a sizeable proportion of the European public. In 1997, the Eurobarometer (no. 47.1) poll of 16,154 respondents found high levels of insecurity among host populations about the presence of minorities – the latter mostly emerging as a result of migration. Table 5.1 shows that in thirteen out of seventeen national surveys – comprising fifteen EU member states with separate samples for Northern Ireland/Great Britain and East/West Germany – one-third or more of respondents (excluding the "don't knows") said the presence of these minorities made them insecure. In seven out of seventeen surveys, the number of "minority-threatened" respondents was about one-half or above. For the EU as a whole – after samples from each member state were weighted proportionate to their share of the total EU population – the poll showed that about 44 percent of respondents found minorities threatening. (For descriptive statistics and general survey description, see http://www.rohan-sdsu.edu/~alexseev.) In addition, nearly 33 percent of respondents identified themselves as "quite racist" or "very racist." Reporting on this particular finding, the European Commission analysts noted: "Many of the declared racists were in fact xenophobic, as the 'minorities' who were the target of racist feeling in each country, varied according to its colonial and migration history and the recent arrival of refugees" (Brika, Lemaine, and Jackson 1997: 1).

Hostility levels among the EU public were lower than the general sense of insecurity in the late 1990s, yet still palpable. In the same Eurobarometer survey, about 19 percent of respondents (excluding the "don't knows") agreed that all immigrants, legal or illegal, as well as their children should be sent back to their countries of origin. Whereas significantly lower than support for deportation of Chinese migrants and for antimigrant paramilitaries in Primorskii krai, these numbers did prompt the European Commission analysts to conclude: "[T]his still leaves some 20 percent who agreed with wholesale repatriation, a figure as alarming as the one for the number of respondents who openly described themselves as racist" (Brika, Lemaine, and Jackson 1997: 7). Almost identical results emerged in the Eurobarometer 2000 (no. 53) survey, in which 20 percent of respondents agreed and 65 percent disagreed that all immigrants and their children should be sent back to their countries of origin (Thalhammer, et al. 2001: 56).

TABLE 5.1. *Threat Perception and Antimigrant Hostility in the European Union, 1997*

	Eurobarometer 47.1 (Racism and Xenophobia in Europe) Questions:					
	Minorities cause insecurity			Deport all immigrants and their children		
	Yes (%)	No (%)	N Don't know/N Total	Yes (%)	No (%)	N Don't know/N Total
France	49.2	50.8	96/1,006	20.6	79.4	98/1,006
Belgium	65.1	34.9	105/1,005	27.8	72.2	156/1,085
The Netherlands	35.2	64.8	68/1,020	9.7	90.3	69/1,020
Germany (West)	53.1	46.9	223/1,038	36.5	63.5	221/1,038
Italy	33.1	66.9	67/997	21.5	78.5	86/997
Luxemburg	31.9	68.1	80/597	11.5	88.5	67/597
Denmark	65.1	34.9	75/1,001	16.4	83.6	93/1,001
Ireland	20.6	79.4	226/1,003	8.6	91.4	274/1,003
Great Britain	38.6	61.4	184/1,078	16.1	83.9	172/1,078
Northern Ireland	15.1	84.9	50/301	12.7	87.3	64/301
Greece	70.2	29.8	71/1,010	26.4	73.6	184/1,010
Spain	32.5	67.5	191/1,000	11.4	88.6	150/1,000
Portugal	53.6	46.4	174/1,000	20.6	79.4	200/1,000
Germany (East)	51.9	48.1	247/1,031	31.4	68.7	262/1,031
Finland	26.8	73.2	91/1,011	10.4	89.6	124/1,011
Sweden	24.2	75.8	144/1,000	8.9	91.1	117/1,000
Austria	54.5	45.5	186/1,056	23.9	76.1	245/1,056
EU Total (%)	37.6	47.6	14.8	15.6	67.8	16.6
EU Total	44.2	55.8	2,390/16,154	18.7	81.3	2,682/16,154

Note: Percentages for *yes* and *no* in columns and in the row marked "EU Total" exclude the "don't knows" and "no response" categories. Some totals may exceed 100 percent due to rounding of their components.

How did these fears and hostility relate to migration volume in the EU from 1990 to 2000? Data compiled by the United Nations – including legal migration and refugees who account for most illegal migrants – show that on average net migration into the EU, as a proportion of the receiving country's population, remained low, if not to say minuscule. As shown in Figure 5.1, in most EU member states net migration rates during this period remained less than 0.3 percent of the host state population

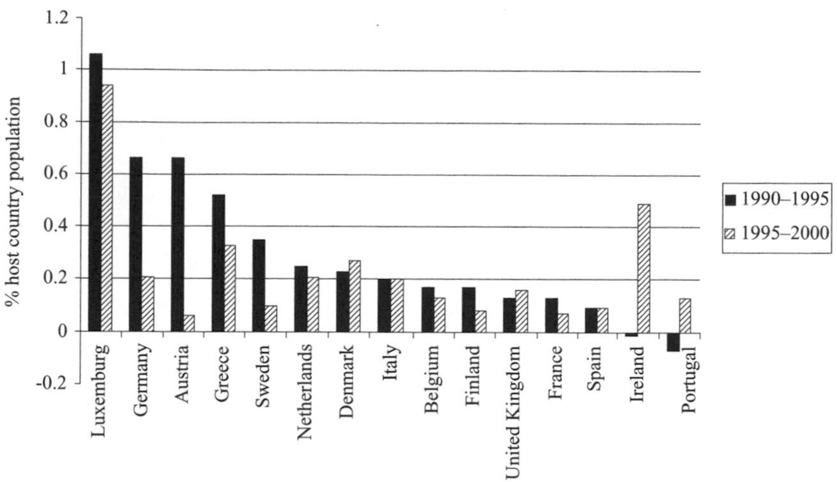

FIGURE 5.1. Net Migration Rates in the EU: Annual Average as Percent of Host Country Population, 1990–2000. *Source:* Population Division of the United Nations Secretariat, World Population Prospects: The 2000 Revision, Volume I: Comprehensive Tables, Sales No.E.01.XIII.8. 2002 (http://www.unpopulation.org).

(i.e., three migrants or fewer per 1,000 local population). The absolute numbers of legal (680,000) and illegal (500,000) migrants produced by the European Commission in 2002 appeared large, but their share in the total EU population was still tiny – 0.18 and 0.13 percent of the host states' population, respectively (Asia Intelligence Wire 2002). At that rate, migration would have to continue apace for thirty years before the proportion of migrant stock would reach about 10 percent of the EU population – but by then, a substantial proportion of the 1990s migrants would die, move, or assimilate. Returning to Figure 5.1, it is also noteworthy that all five EU member states (Luxemburg, Germany, Austria, Greece, and Sweden) in which annual net migration rates from 1990 to 1995 averaged more than three per 1,000 population experienced a substantial drop in migration rates from 1995 to 2000. The rates in Germany – the most populous and politically influential of the five – dropped about threefold, from 6.6 to 2.3 per 1,000 residents. The migration rate in Austria dropped by eleven times.

One realizes how little these changes in migration rates related to immigration phobia across the EU by examining the findings of the Eurobarometer polls in 1997 and 2000 (Thalhammer et al. 2001: 11–13). Specifically, one may consider the four EU members where migration rates declined by about one-half or more between the first and the second half of the 1990s (Germany, Austria, Greece, and Sweden). In Germany and Greece, according to the EU-sponsored report, from 1997 to 2000 more respondents continued to favor repatriation of migrants than Europeans did on average. In Sweden, predominantly accommodating public views of migration showed no significant change. In Austria, support for repatriation decreased, but only marginally – especially against the elevenfold drop in annual migration rates (ibid.).

Few situations signify exaggerated fears better than knee-jerk overreactions to routine, common developments – for example, when someone hiking in the jungle becomes so afraid of poisonous snakes that he or she begins to suspect rapine movement in every tiny crackle in the undergrowth. In the case of the EU, one story that happened in February 2001 stands as an apt metaphor for overblown migration fears: Upon learning that a ship heading for Amsterdam might contain as many as 1,000 asylum seekers from outside the EU, government officials in France, Belgium, and the Netherlands scurried to prevent the vessel from reaching European shores. As it turned out, however, the cause of alarm was an empty coal cargo ship (Hossack 2001). But this type of response is perfectly consistent with the perceptual logic of the security dilemma.

Emergent Anarchy Perceptions

Whereas Western Europe did not experience Soviet-style state disintegration, simultaneous concerns about erosion of nation-state authority, coordination problems at the EU level, and cross-national empowerment of minorities made migration a threatening issue. Concurrent "threats of globalization from without and pluralization from within" have fueled "explosive public conflicts and deep rifts among political elites" over migration and national identity (Koopmans and Statham 2000: 1).

From the standpoint of the security-dilemma logic, several developments associated with simultaneous globalization from without and pluralization from within contributed to exaggerated migration fears. First, the EU by the 1990s evolved into a mostly borderless bloc – hence, a migrant succeeding in getting a foothold in any EU member state could move freely to other EU states. Regardless of how effective the European institutions may be at dealing with this issue, the very notion of borderlessness within the EU would raise uncertainty among any given individual host resident about the strength of their national government authority. Moreover, this uncertainty over central authority concerns the issue associated with the basic function of the state. Whichever way one defines a state, few would disagree with the Weberian notion that the exercise of coercive power *within its borders* is the state's fundamental role. Yet, precisely this role is undermined if the state is unable to exercise coercive power *on its borders* in the first place. To feel secure within such a borderless bloc as the EU – no matter how effective national and transnational institutions may be – any individual would have to trust the capacity of all other member states bordering non–EU countries to control the borders. Obtaining the information that would build such trust, however, is prohibitively costly for any given individual. While few would have the time or the tools to analyze massive bodies of demographic data coming from different countries, a story about a dozen migrants uncovered in a cargo van or about an empty coal ship hauling illegal migrants would be accessible and immediately understandable to millions.

In the EU, the media provide a regular flow of stories that would make residents wary of "borderlessness." Among them would be debates between the EU member states and Turkey (the former accusing the latter of not doing enough to block migrants, the latter accusing the former of not providing adequate assistance in this task); protracted, complicated, and at times volatile discussions of the common EU asylum policies and procedures (or, more commonly, failure to agree on them) (Associated Press 2002); or reports about successes of transnational nongovernmental organizations (NGOs) representing migrants in lobbying the European institutions (Favell and Geddes 2001).

Of course, at the individual level these perceptions of borderlessness would vary, and so would the intensity of concomitant perceptions of central authority strength at the national level. The 1997 Eurobarometer survey (no. 47.1) provided one general measure of perceived national government capacity within the EU. Respondents were asked if they believed that "maintaining order in the country" was one of their state's priority goals "for the next ten or fifteen years." On average, nearly 42 percent of about 16,000 respondents in fifteen EU member states said *yes* – suggesting that concern over the central authority's weakness was widespread, although not predominant.

Against this background – as the perceptual logic of the security dilemma predicts – perceived migration impact on ethnic population balances would be a significant correlate of antimigrant hostility. One of

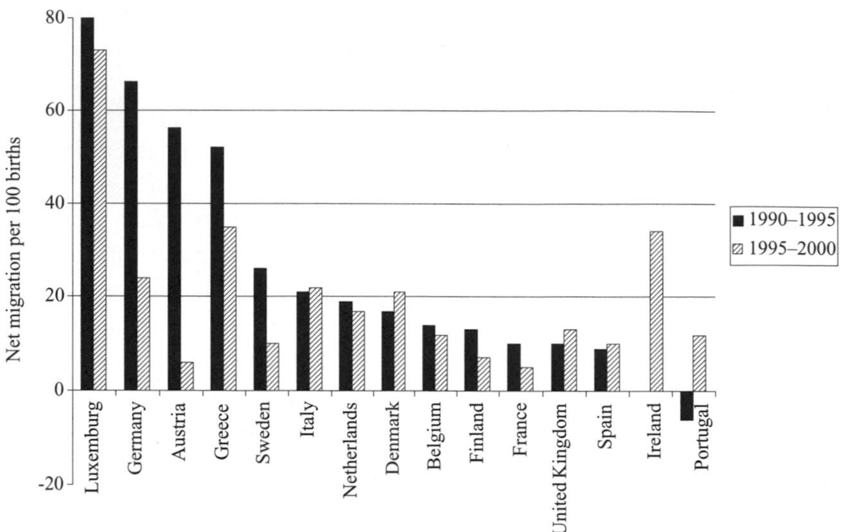

FIGURE 5.2. Net Migration as Percentage of Births in the EU Member States: Average Annual Rates, 1990–2000. *Source*: The United Nations Population Division, Department of Economic and Social Affairs, 2002 (http://www.un.org/esa/population/publications/ittmig2002/locations).

the vivid illustrations of this linkage was provided by intense public controversy on *denatalité* (declining birthrate) at France's Institut National d'Etudes Demographiques in the early 1990s. The debates were sparked by the institute director's study showing that – contrary to conventional wisdom – the fertility rate in France by 1990 returned to the replacement level of 2.1 children per woman (Teitelbaum and Winter 1998: 33–4). The technicalities and the amazing degree of public attention apart, the debates highlighted the linkage between perceptions of population trends and migration phobia – similar to concerns in the Russian Far East about Chinese migrations amidst native population decline. This is how the institute's director of research and editor of its journal, *Population*, Hervé Le Bras, explained the linkage in a Radio Europe 1 interview of May 4, 1990: "This fear of a weak birthrate and population decline has accentuated the fear of the foreigner. For certain politicians, the fact that there was a demographic decline and that some believed this to be so meant we were going to be invaded" (ibid.: 37).

A comparison of fertility and net migration rates in the EU allows for both benign and alarmist interpretations. As shown in Figure 5.2, in none of the EU member states did in-migration rates exceed birthrates, and only in four states (Luxemburg, Germany, Austria, and Greece) did annual net migration rates average over 50 percent of host state births from 1990 to 1995. These trends, however, failed to continue from 1995 to 2000 in three of these four states. In Germany, the average annual number of migrants (after accounting for emigration) dropped from 66 per 100 births in the first half of the 1990s to 24 per 100 births in the second half of the 1990s. In Austria, the migration-to-births rate dropped from 56 to 6 per 100 and in Greece from 52 to 35 per 100. From 1995 to 2000, in no EU member state except Luxemburg did the migration-to-births rate exceed 40 per 100. In most of the EU states, net migration rates were under 20 per 100 throughout the 1990s.

At the same time, migration-to-births rates – more than the proportion of migrants to the total population – make alarmist long-term projections of the ethnic population balance in the EU states plausible. The perceptual "trigger" is the projection of cumulative effects into the future. The more an individual EU resident feels the migration-to-births trends would persist or worsen and the longer one's time horizon, the more alarmist one's views are likely to be. Alarmism intensity would also depend on how perceived birthrates among new migrant minorities compared with perceived birthrates in the host nation. One example of such alarmist birthrate comparison was reported by the mainstream British daily *The Independent* in 1995: "The Asian community has twice the population of under-16-year-olds the white population has. Only 2 percent of the Asian population is over the age of 65, compared with 17 percent of whites. The average British Asian family has about five members, compared with 2.4 among whites." Interestingly, the British national who was quoted in the preceding text also implied in the very next sentence that in the shadow of unfavorable birth trends, host populations may feel threatened even while realizing that birthrate differences will have slow and small effects on the total proportion of ethnic "others" in the host society: "Demographers predict, combining these trends, that the Asian community is set to double from 1.5 percent of the population." Apparently, the British resident quoted here discounted the fact that even if the proportion of the Asian population in Britain doubled, it would still amount to only 3 percent of Britain's population. The interviewee also did not specify how long, in his view, it would take for this doubling of Asian population to occur. The perception seems to be linked, however, to uncertainty and fear that the number of Asian migrants may increase exponentially, bringing on a swelling and unstoppable tidal wave. This view parallels perceptions of Chinese migration in the Russian Far East.

Whereas the Eurobarometer surveys – in contrast to my Primorskii 2000 survey – do not ask respondents to estimate the proportion of migrants in their states' population, the European polls do have a question that captures more-general valuations of migration size: "Speaking generally about people from minority groups in terms of race, religion and culture, do you think there are not many, a lot but not too many, or too many of them living in (OUR COUNTRY)?" The term *minority groups* stands as a proxy for migrant groups, given that minorities have emerged as a result of migration, especially since the era of decolonization. An analysis of responses in Eurobarometer surveys by Lauren McLaren (2003: 919) of Oxford University (United Kingdom) showed, in fact, that the two references – to migrants and minorities – in the European context are typically the same.[1] Given the congruity between these terms, the survey question indirectly suggested that the size of migrant/minority groups might be increasing too fast. In so doing, the question partially probed respondents' sensitivity to group status reversal. In the 1997 Eurobarometer survey on racism and xenophobia, on a scale from one ("not many") to three ("too many"), the mean score was 1.73 with a standard deviation of .69. In other words, EU residents' valuations of ethnic balance trends could be plotted as a classic bell-shaped curve tilted toward "too many."[2]

Of Migrants and the Rules: Suspicions of Offensive Intent

None of the EU member states faces a neighbor across the border that would be to that state what China is to Russia in terms of the history of territorial claims and violent interstate conflict in the last three decades or so. Suspicion of migrants spearheading hostile "fifth columns" that the sending states would use to claim territory is not an issue in the EU.[3] One

[1] For example, in the Eurobarometer 30 (1998) survey, the term *minority groups* was overwhelmingly associated with Indians and Pakistanis in Great Britain, with Arabs and Turks in France, and with Turks in Germany. All of these groups are recent immigrants. Minorities identified on the basis of their religion were also those from recent immigrant groups: Muslims from Pakistan, Turkey, or North Africa; Buddhists from China; and Hindus from India (McLaren 2002). In France, for example, residents commonly refer even to third-generation French citizens of North African origin as immigrants.

[2] 14,573 survey participants answered this question, and 1,581 either chose "don't know" or refused to respond.

[3] Suspicions about territorial claims could conceivably be a factor when the Baltic states join the EU, given a history of territorial disputes between Russia and Estonia and Russia

would therefore expect the overall levels of militant hostility among the EU public to be lower than among the public in the Russian Far East. It is hard to imagine, for example, that support for antimigrant paramilitary units in the EU could be higher than support for repatriation. And public support for wholesale migrant repatriation in the EU was lower in 1997 and 2000 than public support for antimigrant paramilitaries in Primorskii krai in 2000.

Whereas in the EU geopolitical disputes do not factor into offensive-intent perceptions, "softer" socioeconomic issues do. With the closure of large-scale guest worker programs in the 1970s, economic migrants used asylum as a means of improving their lot. "Currently, only illegal channels exist for economic migrants," noted the United Nations High Commissioner for Refugees, Ruud Lubbers, in August 2002 (Asia Intelligence Wire 2002). Except in cases of massive and sudden exodus, such as during the wars in the former Yugoslavia, distinguishing legitimate refugees from economic fortune seekers thus became a thorny issue. The logic of the security dilemma suggests that in such context ascribing offensive intent to migrants becomes feasible regardless of the actual proportion of migrants exploiting the asylum system to their advantage. Just because migrants technically could file bogus asylum claims, just because some of these claims will be accepted, and just because the true intent is frequently unverifiable are enough grounds for suspicion – suspicion that feeds exaggerated fears. One British immigration lawyer, Chris Randall, summarized the effects of these perceptions: "People in Britain have become so indoctrinated that they cannot hear the word 'asylum-seeker' without thinking 'bogus'" (Teitelbaum and Winter 1998: 60). While making the public more receptive to antiimmigrant "indoctrination" alleged by Randall, the security-dilemma logic suggests that uncertainty about intent would give rise to immigration phobia even in the absence of any indoctrination.

This issue of "bogus" asylum seekers relates to broader suspicions that migrants may or may not "play by the rules" of the receiving state. In this sense, the 1997 Eurobarometer survey on racism and xenophobia offers a proxy measure of perceived migrant intent. The poll asked whether respondents believed that "not everybody belonging to these [migration-produced] minority groups" wanted to be a "full member" of the host state's nationality. Essentially, this question asked whether respondents

and Latvia as recently as the early 1990s. In contrast to the Russia–China case, however, past territorial losses were claimed by migrant-receiving states.

suspected that some migrants had no intent to play by the rules of the host states or that they harbored "offensive" intent. In twelve of the seventeen polls across the EU, more than 80 percent of respondents agreed with that statement. The mean score – weighted for the proportion of each state in the EU population – was 1.16 on the 1-to-2 scale, suggesting that about 84 percent of the EU public were uncertain about migrants' willingness or capacity to play by the host states' rules.

The Specter of Non-European "Groupness"

One does not require superhuman powers of observation to note that in the EU area population issues became "politically explosive" in the 1960s, following a rapid increase in the number of non-European (and, hence, non-White and non-Christian) migrants. This increase came partly as a consequence of decolonization and partly – principally in the case of Turkish guest workers in Germany – as a consequence of growing labor demands amidst declining fertility rates. Since the 1950s, Pakistanis and Indians in the United Kingdom, Algerians in France, Turks in Germany, Surinamese in the Netherlands, and Moroccans in Spain – to name just a few of the non-European groups – literally changed the face of Europe. Demographic statistics broadly illustrate these trends. From 1992 to 2000, among the refugees received by the thirty-eight industrialized countries – of which the fifteen members of the EU accounted for about two-thirds – the largest groups came from Iraq, the former Yugoslavia, Bosnia and Herzegovina, Somalia, Sri Lanka, and Afghanistan (United Nations High Commissioner for Refugees 2002: 62).

In the real world, these numbers translated into palpable lifestyle contrasts. A walk through downtown Marseilles, described by Tayler (2000: 59), illustrates how this contrast would permeate the minds and emotions of the native White French residents on a daily basis:

> I set out for a walk across the center of Marseilles, passing the sleek glass-and-granite headquarters of the regional administration and weaving my way between joggers in spandex tights and fashionably dressed young men and women immersed in cell-phone conversations. I turn down the two-lane Rue d'Aix and enter a shadowy defile of soot-encrusted five-story buildings, and all at once I am in a different world. Arab men in djellabahs crowd the sidewalks. Narrow-faced youths with curly black hair, who might be from any district of Tangier or Algiers, cycle between pedestrians, zinging their bells and shouting, "*Attention!*" At the corner, a turbaned old man whining a beggar's chant in Arabic

sits barefoot on a stained sheet of cardboard, his knees drawn up to his shoulders, his palm extended. Tall African women wearing floral scarves and toting bulging plastic bags talk in Wolof and make their way around Berber women with tattooed chins. Side streets weave away into a warren smelling of grilled chicken and harissa – the immigrant nighborhood of Belsunce, which is, from all appearances, as lively and North African as any quarter of the Casbah in Marrakesh.

As migrant flows became increasingly distinct from host populations ethnically and culturally, "the question of the compatibility of non-European, non-Christian, or even nonwhite immigrants . . . had come to prominence" (Teitelbaum and Winter 1998: 56). It was this issue of compatibility that has galvanized firebrand and not-so-firebrand xenophobes on the European political scene from those years to the present. In a memorable tirade, a former classical scholar and Conservative member of the British parliament, Enoch Powell, linked migrant distinctiveness with prospects of violent urban riots: "I am filled with a foreboding. Like the Roman, I seem to see the River Tiber foaming with much blood" (ibid.). Powell was not the only prominent politician to accentuate ethno-cultural differences between the host and migrant populations. In the late 1990s and early 2000s, brash antiimmigrant politicians in Denmark, the Netherlands, Austria, and France won sizeable shares of the vote in national and local elections, even though they stopped far short of winning national majority votes.

Public perceptions of minority distinctiveness and prospects for assimilation into the host societies have differed widely across the EU. The 1997 Eurobarometer survey (no. 47.1) has a perfect question to measure individual valuations of group distinctiveness – specifically tied to assimilation prospects. The poll asked if respondents agreed with the statement: "People belonging to these minority groups are so different, they can never be fully accepted members of (NATIONALITY) society." With country samples weighted to account for each country's share of the EU population, the survey showed that about 62 percent of the EU public who had an opinion about the issue tended to disagree with this statement and 38 percent agreed. Another question measured respondents' acceptance of marriages between respondents' children and members of minority groups. Here the data suggest that the European public was split about evenly on the issue, with 45 percent in favor and 55 percent opposed to such marriages once the scores were similarly weighted for the EU as a whole. Two questions that I did not use in regression analysis revealed that cultural distinctiveness was a factor in acceptance of minorities among a sizeable segment of the EU public. About 21 percent of respondents in 1997 and 22 percent of respondents in 2000 agreed with the notion that minority groups must give up their own culture to be fully accepted by the receiving state. By another measure, Europeans became somewhat less tolerant of minority cultural distinctiveness between 1997 and 2000. The percentage of respondents who agreed that "minority groups must give up such parts of their religion and culture which may be in conflict" with the host country law was fifty in 1997 and fifty-six in 2000 (Thalhammer et al. 2001a: 58).

Socioeconomic Impact: Drain on Public Services or Remedy against Labor Shortages

At Germany's Christian Social Union party congress in June 2002, presidential candidate and opposition alliance leader Edmund Stoiber delivered a fiery speech. Pounding the podium, Stoiber proclaimed that Germany could no longer shoulder the "heavy additional burden of integrating migrants into society" and needed to limit immigration. In blaming immigrants for crime and unemployment, Stoiber joined the chorus of antiimmigration populists who had at the time scored electoral gains in Denmark, the Netherlands, and France (ibid.) This antiimmigrant chorus appealed to classic economic concerns associated with migrant accommodation anywhere in the world. As the rise of political debates around migration issues visibly coincided with the increasing ethnocultural distinctiveness of migrants since 1960s, so many Western European states declared themselves to be zero-immigration countries during the economic downturn of the 1970s (ibid.).

As elsewhere, the actual effects of migration on the economy and social conditions of the EU member states have been complex and contradictory. On the one hand, as Stoiber's argument went, accommodating migrants imposes costs on EU states' public services that, in turn, are supported by some of the highest tax rates among industrialized democracies. Regardless of the actual costs of supporting migrants to individual residents, the very basic – gut-level – realization that migrants do impose some costs lends credibility to speculative and alarmist claims. One example of such claims was provided by Britain's conservative tabloid *Daily Mail* in September 1995. The paper asserted – without providing the basis for the estimate – that each asylum seeker cost 100 pounds sterling per week to "the tax payer... in income support and housing benefits" (Teitelbaum and Winter 1998: 60). The wording left open the possibility that readers may interpret "the taxpayer" as referring to them, rather than to the national treasury. Migrants are also a convenient scapegoat for such economic and social problems as unemployment and crime.

On the other hand, media reports also note that "conflicting with the anti-immigration rhetoric is a stark fact: Europe relies on immigrants to fill not only menial jobs but also positions requiring skills where native manpower is insufficient. Given low birthrates, Europe needs immigrants to keep the ratio of working to retired people high enough so that income taxes can continue to foot the bill for the generous welfare benefits that the right wing accuses illegal immigrants of encroaching upon" (ibid.). In other words, precisely the same demographic trends in the EU that raised concern about ethnic population balance shifting migrants' favor also keyed economic incentives for inviting more immigrants – legal and illegal. In Germany, for example, press reports indicated that without immigration 40 percent of the native population would be over age sixty by 2050, up from 23 percent in 2002. And so, despite Stoiber's fiery antiimmigrant rhetoric and despite the fact that he was leading in the opinion polls over the incumbent Chancellor Schroeder, Germany passed a law in June 2002 designed to attract migrant workers and younger people. The law imposed no ceiling on the number of migrants (ibid.).

As the analysis the of Primorskii 2000 survey in Chapter 5 and in earlier publications (Alexseev 2003) suggests, public perceptions of migrants' socioeconomic impact – and not necessarily the actual magnitude and nature of the impact reflected in aggregate statistics – are significantly linked to migration phobia. In my analysis of the 1997 Eurobarometer poll, I identified six questions capturing a sense of economic deprivation and socioeconomic impact associated with migration in the EU. The first one was valuation of respondents' family income. The second question identified respondents (about 30 percent in the EU weighted total) who said they were unemployed once or more in the previous five years. The third question asked whether respondents' economic situation improved, stayed the same, or worsened during the same five-year period prior to the poll. The modal response was no change, with a mean score of 2.12 on a scale of 1 (got worse) to 3 (improved), suggesting a slight majority of respondents believed their economic conditions got better. These three questions sought to identify respondents who would be more concerned about economic deprivation and competition with migrants, as well as more vulnerable to migration effects on public service financing. These measures would also relate to immigration phobia if respondents assessed economic effects of migration in terms of relative gains between host and migrant populations.

The 1997 Eurobarometer survey also provided multiple measures of direct socioeconomic effects of migrants on host societies – something that would be more salient, the more respondents would be attuned to changes in the host population's (in-group) gains over time. Three survey questions cover socioeconomic issues related to migration and regularly featured in migrant-phobic public discourses – namely, perceptions of ethnic minorities' impact on public welfare system, education, and crime. The distribution of responses to these questions remained about the same between 1997 and 2000. Forty-six percent of respondents in 1997 to 52 percent in 2000 felt the "quality of education suffered" in schools with "too many children from minority groups." The number of respondents who believed minority groups abused the system of social welfare was 48 percent in the 1997 poll and 52 percent in the 2000 poll. Sixty-four percent of respondents in 1997 and 58 percent in 2000 agreed that minorities were more often than average involved in criminality. Another indirect measure of perceived migration effects once again indicated that the majority of Europeans (44 percent in 1997 and 45 percent in 2000) saw migration-induced diversity of races, cultures, and religion as adding to their countries' strengths, although a sizeable minority of respondents (35 and 37 percent, respectively) disagreed.

Controls

Some of the alternative explanations I used in the analysis of the Eurobarometer data closely resemble control variables in the Primorskii 2000 study, while others relate exclusively to the European context. In the 1997 Eurobarometer, an excellent proxy for sensitivity to majority–minority status reversal was the question asking whether respondents agreed that migration had reached its limits. The majority of Europeans (about 65 percent in a weighted survey sample) said *yes*, suggesting that for them migration was at or beyond the "tipping point." Ideological preferences were also likely to matter – the Right by its association with racist exclusionism, the Left by its association with labor unions protecting the interests of workers potentially threatened by migrant workers. In the 1997 Eurobarometer poll, the mean score on a scale from 1 (Left) to 10 (Right) was 5.04, with a standard deviation of 2.11 – showing that the majority of Europeans placed themselves squarely in the political center.

Given that in the EU concern about migration plausibly related to concern about national sovereignty under evolving multinational political institutions, I also took a measure of respondents' pride in their nationality as a potential indicator of immigration phobia. On a scale from 1 (very proud) to 4 (not at all proud), the modal EU-wide response was about 2.

Standard sociodemographic characteristics of respondents included education (number of years), gender, and religion (distinguishing between respondents who identified themselves as Christian and non-Christian or nonbeliever). In addition, to control for concerns about interethnic labor market competition, I identified respondents who said they were manual workers on the assumption that this occupational group was vulnerable to migrant labor competition. Finally, I controlled for migration history of respondents, distinguishing between those who said they had a parent or grandparent from a different nationality (i.e., country of origin) and the rest. Conventional wisdom suggests that residents of the "countries of immigrants" (of which the United States is often cited as the prime example) would be more readily to accept migrants and would be less hostile toward them. Using this question, I probe whether conventional wisdom applies at the individual level.

Eurobarometer 47.1: Regression Analysis and the Findings

Using the Eurobarometer 47.1 dataset (available through the Inter-University Consortium for Political and Social Research, Study No. 2089), I ran multiple regression analyses to test whether insecurity about minority groups and attitudes toward wholesale deportation of all immigrants and their children related nonrandomly to respondents' views about anarchy, intent, groupness, and deprivation. I also controlled for minority size sensitivity, ideology, pride in one's nationality, education, occupation, religion, gender, and immigrant ancestry. The complete list of variables, the wording of survey questions and descriptive statistics are provided at http://www-rohan.sdsu.edu/~alexseev.

I must admit that having prepared the data and having set the commands in the computer program (SPSS 6.0) I felt a mixture of excitement and trepidation – perhaps similar to the one scientists do right before starting a laboratory experiment. In my Russian Far East case, I designed the opinion survey, trained the interviewers, ran pilot surveys and debriefings, interviewed local officials, and, generally, "soaked and poked" in the area for a long time to be confident about my hypotheses. Yet in this case, I was testing whether the same perceptual logic would work in a vastly different political, socioeconomic, cultural, and historical context. The Eurobarometer survey was not specifically designed to test my hypotheses, and it included more than 16,000 respondents. And so I pushed the OK button and ran the tests.

The findings, however, turned out to be remarkably consistent with the security-dilemma predictions and with Primorskii 2000 results. The upshot: different contexts, same logic of antimigrant hostility. Again, multiple regression tests revealed that migration phobia relates significantly to perceptions associated with the interethnic security dilemma. As in Primorskii 2000, the Eurobarometer 1997 tests ruled out the null hypothesis – that is, that the security-dilemma perceptions had at best a random, or chance, relationship with respondents' sense that migrants caused insecurity and with respondents hostility toward migrants. Across the EU, the security-dilemma model explained approximately 25 percent of variation in general sense of insecurity about migration. The model also explained about 19 percent variation in antimigrant hostility (deportation attitudes). These proportions are especially significant, given a much larger number of respondents (N = 16,154) than in the Primorskii 2000 survey – exacerbating even further the perennial "noise" problem and random measurement error inherent in opinion data (Asher 1983: 39). As in Primorskii krai, statistical probability that threat perception and antimigrant hostility in the EU related to the security-dilemma logic by chance alone was less than 0.001 percent. (In particular, see summary statistics for Model 4 in Tables B.1 and B.2.)

The interethnic security-dilemma model explained more variation in support for wholesale deportation of immigrants than the model developed by the EU-commissioned analysts did.[4] The analysts – affiliated with the Institute for Social Research and Analysis (SORA) in Vienna – mostly relied on the "usual suspects" to explain views on repatriation: sex, age, education, employment status, satisfaction with personal situation, retrospective and prospective assessment of personal situation, experience with unemployment, income, immigrant/minority ancestry, belonging to a minority group, ideology on a Left–Right scale, and voting behavior. Only

[4] McLaren (2003) used a model that explained slightly more variation (21 percent) in support for deportation than did the security-dilemma model in this study. However, the principal hypothesis in the study centered around the independent variable – personal friendship with migrants – that was unlikely to be exogenous with respect to exclusionism, because by definition those who supported exclusionism would avoid making friends with minorities.

in three of the seventeen polls comprising the EU sample – in Belgium, France, and Great Britain (excluding Northern Ireland) – did the SORA model explain 15 percent or more variation in repatriation attitudes.[5] In nine surveys out of seventeen, the model explained less than 10 percent variation in attitudes toward repatriation (Thalhammer et al. 2001b: 25, 28, 33).

Overall, statistical analysis of the 1997 Eurobarometer survey replicates the Primorskii 2000 findings – albeit in a different context and with some context-sensitive nuances. Insecure individuals in host societies who feel migrants have offensive intentions, who have negative economic impact, who are too different to assimilate, and who threaten the majority position of ethnic incumbents are the ones who are more likely to support coercive and potentially violent responses to migration. Control variables explained little variation in insecurity about migration (slightly over 1 percent) in addition to the security-dilemma variables. For antimigrant hostility, ideological identification came out as a significant correlate. Respondents who identified themselves with the political Right tended to be somewhat more likely to support deportation. For both threat perception and antimigrant hostility, occupation, religion, and gender showed no statistically significant effects. Education that was significantly related to threat turned out to be an insignificant predictor of hostility. Immigrant ancestry, however, was nonrandomly associated with opposition to deportation. (For complete regression results, see the tables in Appendix B.)

It is also clear from Tables B.1 and B.2 that perceptions of ethnic balance; acceptance of family union with minorities; ethnic group difference; migration's impact on social benefits, education, and crime; minority size sensitivity; pride in one's nationality; and education do have indirect effects on hostility through threat perception. This means, for example, that host populations may support hostile antiimmigrant policies not only because they believe there are too many migrants in the host state, but also because their assessment that migrants are too numerous translates into a general sense of insecurity – and from there into additional support for antimigrant responses. Also, this logic would suggest that being better educated does not necessarily make one more opposed to

[5] The SORA model explained 15 percent of variation in repatriation views in Belgium, 17 percent in France, and 15 percent in Britain. The complete model in this study explained close to 19 percent of variation in deportation attitudes in the EU as a whole.

TABLE 5.2. *Direct and Indirect Effects of the Security-Dilemma Perceptions on Antimigrant Hostility: European Union, 1997*

	Direct Effect	Indirect Effect	Total Effect
Perceptions of:			
"Anarchy":			
Ethnic balance	.068	.006	.074
Government weakness	.022	–	.022
Offensive Intent:			
Intent to integrate	–.096	–	–.096
"Groupness":			
Ethnic group difference	.216	.013	.229
Family union acceptance	.072	.008	.080
Deprivation and Socioeconomic Impact:			
Personal income	.047	–	.047
Life improvement	.029	–	.029
Impact on education	.041	.015	.056
Impact on crime	.038	.012	.050
Impact on social benefits	.025	.013	.038
Controls:			
Insecurity about minorities	.100	–	.100
Pride in one's nationality	–.044	–.003	–.047
Ideology (Left–Right)	–.035	–	–.035
Minority size sensitivity	.035	.011	.046
Immigrant ancestry	.032	–	.032

Note: Path coefficients reported in this table are standardized regression coefficients in the complete models of insecurity and hostility (unstandardized coefficients and standard errors are reported in Appendix B, Tables B.1 and B.2).

antiimmigrant policies – yet better educated respondents would be so opposed because they are likely to feel less threatened by migration overall than respondents with less education. The sums of indirect and direct effects on hostility for statistically significant predictors are estimated in Table 5.2.

Accounting for these indirect effects, Table 5.3 lists the measures found to have significant (nonrandom) relationship with threat perception and antimigrant hostility in the EU in the 1997 survey.

A comparison of the 1997 Eurobarometer and Primorskii 2000 findings suggests that both similarities and differences are embedded in the same perceptual logic of the security dilemma, adjusted for migration context. These results not only identify those measures of perceived anarchy, intent, groupness, and deprivation that are nonrandom and robust

TABLE 5.3. *Significant Predictors of Threat and Hostility: European Union, 1997*

Threat Perception (Insecurity) (EB47V340)		**Hostility (Support for Deportation) (EB47V382)**	
Perceptions of:			
"Anarchy":		*"Anarchy":*	
Ethnic balance	(.062)***	Ethnic balance	(.074)***
		Government weakness	(.022)*
Offensive Intent:		*Offensive Intent:*	
–		Intent to integrate	(−.096)***
"Groupness":		*"Groupness":*	
Group difference	(.125)***	Group difference	(.229)***
Family union acceptance	(.081)***	Family union acceptance	(.080)***
Deprivation/economic effects:		*Deprivation/economic effects:*	
Personal income	(.047)***	Life improvement	(.029)*
Impact on education	(.151)***	Impact on education	(.056)**
Impact on crime	(.121)***	Impact on crime	(.050)**
Impact on social benefits	(.126)***	Impact on social benefits	(.038)***
Controls:		*Controls:*	
Education	(.040)**	Insecurity about minorities	(.100)***
Pride in one's nationality	(−.029)**	Pride in one's nationality	(−.047)***
		Ideology (Left–Right)	(−.035)**
Group status sensitivity	(.114)***	Group status sensitivity	(.046)*
		Immigrant ancestry	(.032)**
Total variation explained:			
Threat perception:		*Hostility:*	
26.3% (R^2 = .263)		18.6% (R^2 = .186)	

Significance: * = $p < .05$, ** = $p < .01$, *** = $p < .001$ (one-tailed).

Note: Coefficients reported in this table are standardized regression coefficients (betas) in the complete models of general threat (insecurity) and hostility (support for deportation) (Appendix B, Tables B.1 and B.2). These coefficients allow one to compare effect sizes of predictors relative to one another. Estimation of the correlates of militant hostility includes indirect effects through threat (calculated in Table 6.2). However, R^2 for hostility does not include indirect effects.

correlates of immigration phobia, but they also identify persistent – and therefore potentially significant – interaction effects among these measures.

Threat vs. Hostility

Same as in the Primorskii study, threat perception in the 1997 Eurobarometer study was among the most statistically significant and strongest predictors of antimigrant hostility – precisely as the security-dilemma logic would predict. In a probability sample of 16,154 EU residents weighted by the share of member states' population in the EU, those who said the emergence of minorities made them insecure were likely to support sending back all immigrants and their children to their countries of origin. A general pattern across the EU upholds this threat–hostility connection – countries with the top five scores on threat have higher support for exclusionism than most others; countries with the bottom five scores on threat have lower support than most others (see Table 5.1). At the same time, some cases suggest that the relationship is not all that straightforward – that is, insecurity does not explain how support for deportation may vary across country dyads. For example, in the Netherlands and Italy and in Belgium and Denmark the 1997 Eurobarometer registered about the same levels of insecurity, but in Italy support for exclusionism was twice as strong as that in the Netherlands and in Belgium almost twice as strong as in Denmark. But then again, these dyadic variations are unsurprising given that other variables related significantly to hostility.

In both Primorskii and the EU, insecurity related nonrandomly to valuations of ethnic balance between the migrants and host populations, group difference between ethnic incumbents and migrants, and socioeconomic effects of migration. In addition, in the 1997 Eurobarometer study insecure respondents were also more likely to have had fewer years of education, less pride in their nationality (citizenship), and higher sensitivity to minority group size than other respondents.

Antimigrant hostility in both Primorskii and EU was significantly associated with measures of migrants' intent, socioeconomic impact, group status (minority size) sensitivity, and threat perception. In addition, the EU 1997 survey analysis revealed that other key elements of the interethnic security-dilemma model – namely, perceptions of anarchy, group distinctiveness, and proneness to relative deprivation – were also significant predictors of hostility. Pride in one's nationality, ideology, and immigrant ancestry also related to hostility nonrandomly, but not as strongly as most of the security-dilemma perceptions.

Overall, the EU tests confirmed the Primorskii findings regarding the significance of ethnic balance, migrant's intent, group difference, and socioeconomic impact perceptions on the threat–hostility perceptual complex. It is also noteworthy that both in Primorskii and in the EU tests the security-dilemma model and control variables explained about one-third less variation in threat perception than they did in support for hostile antimigrant responses. The replication of this general pattern – first identified in the Russian Far East study – across the EU suggests that while the perceptual logic of the security dilemma lays down the foundations of insecurity, the transition from insecurity to intergroup conflict depends on other factors. However, the significant association between threat perception and antimigrant hostility does not necessarily suggest that the logic of the security dilemma becomes less important as intergroup relations become more hostile. In the EU and Primorskii contexts, exaggerated fears abounded but mobilization for mass antimigrant violence was not an issue. However, in contexts where insecurity starts translating into such hostile mobilization, the security dilemma model could plausibly explain more variation in hostility than in threat. The conceptual beauty of the security-dilemma model is that – with contextually and situationally sensitive opinion measures – it not only explains a substantial variation in fear and hostility, but also captures the interactive dynamic between the two.

The Security Dilemma vs. Prejudice as a Sense of Group Position

Similar to the Primorskii study, the Eurobarometer 1997 tests also support the idea that the logic of ethnic balance perceptions under the security dilemma and the logic of prejudice as a sense of group position are complementary. Sensitivity to minority group size reaching an individually envisioned limit (or "tipping point") across the EU was significantly correlated in a separate test with the overall sense of ethnic balance ($R = .436, p < .001$) and significantly related to insecurity about minorities and support for wholesale deportation of migrants when controlled for all other variables in the regression analysis. In both Primorskii and the EU, the insertion of group status sensitivity reduced the effects of perceived ethnic balance on antimigrant hostility.

However, Primorskii and EU studies also revealed differences in the relationship among majority status perceptions, threat, and hostility. In the EU, but not in Primorskii, group status (minority size) sensitivity significantly related to threat. Moreover, in the EU sensitivity to minority size related more significantly and more strongly to threat than to hostility. And unlike in the Primorskii study, accounting for minority size sensitivity in the Eurobarometer analysis did not "undo" the statistical significance of ethnic balance perceptions on antimigrant hostility. These differences, however, are logical, considering that in each study the minority size tipping point perceptions were measured differently. The Primorskii question being more closely related to concerns about the sovereignty of the receiving state over one of its constituent units, it is hardly surprising that the tipping point perceptions subsumed much of the effects of perceived ethnic balance on antimigrant hostility. For a more abstract sense of prospective security threat, however, overall ethnic balance mattered more to respondents. With an emphasis on minority group size reaching individually defined "limits," the EU definition was less specific and not necessarily equated with the loss of political power by host populations – hence, a weaker association with feelings about migration policy, yet a stronger association with a more abstract sense of insecurity.

Attitudes vs. Attributes

In both the Primorskii and the EU studies, sociodemographic attributes of respondents had little relationship to insecurity about migration and antimigrant hostility when controlled for perceptions consistent with the security-dilemma complex. This finding should not be prematurely interpreted as a claim that sociodemographic variables have no impact on antimigrant alarmism and hostility, or that they play no role in making some individuals more susceptible to the security-dilemma logic than others. However, this finding does provide a new interpretation of the flash potential of migration as a political issue, as evidenced in the late 1990s and early 2000s by the meteoric rise to prominence and positions in government of antiimmigrant parties in Europe. The bottom-line inference from this study in this regard is that opinions about migration are highly manipulable – as one would indeed expect opinions to be under the logic of the security dilemma. In short, messages that migration is a national security threat are likely to cut across various sociodemographic groups. Immigration phobia comes through as no respecter of income, class, religion, gender, and even not so much of one's immigrant origins. Whereas these inferences are crude and should only be applied to any specific individual case of immigration phobia with caution, the results of two large bodies of survey data show that for large populations these inferences have a solid empirical basis. These findings would explain why – even in relatively calm, comfortable societies with small levels of migration – xenophobic politicians would always find a sustainable base of popular support. Ensconced in their niches, such politicians can strike out and rapidly expand their support base at times of political crises, mounting economic problems, or rapidly changing migration trends.

Central Authority vs. Ethnic Balance

While in theory, decline, weakness, or collapse of central authority is the fundamental part of the security-dilemma logic, in practice valuations of government weakness related significantly and strongly only to perceptions of armed-conflict threat in Primorskii krai. (Perceived lack of order within EU member states is a significant, but not a strong, predictor of support for deportation.) This is despite the fact that three measures of government capacity in Primorskii krai were used (ability to settle intergroup conflict, ability to overcome geographic isolation, and military capability). It is plausible that a stronger relationship between perceptions of central authority and migration phobia in the EU would have been found if the Eurobarometer surveys included questions about the degree to which European institutions undermined national power. Yet, the overall finding suggested in the Primorskii krai analysis appears to be supported – that in the context of uncertainty about central authority it is not the estimate of government capacity so much as perceptions of the emerging ethnic balances that play a pivotal role. This finding may not square directly with the classic, "interstate" security dilemma projections, but it does conform to the logic of the security-dilemma applied to intergroup conflict.

Central Authority and Socioeconomic Vulnerability

One finding both in Primorskii krai and in the EU offers a plausible explanation as to why perceived government strength did not come out in all tests as a significant correlate of insecurity and antimigrant hostility. In both studies, statistical significance of government capacity measures "faded away" after perceptions of the socioeconomic impact of migration were taken into account (cf. Tables A.1–A.3, B.1, and B.2).[6] This finding – remarkably consistent from Vladivostok to the EU – implies that concern about government weakness had a lot to do with concern about socioeconomic effects of migration. Government capacity to ensure that host populations would benefit from migration was most likely associated with government capacity to control migration and, more broadly, to provide social order. It is therefore plausible, judging from survey analyses, that perceptions of socioeconomic effects of migration are a conduit for perceptions of "anarchy." Indeed, to most ordinary residents in host societies government capacity per se is too abstract a notion. Practical socioeconomic issues (e.g., education, incomes, crime, public services), however, are important yardsticks of government performance to most common people. Once migration starts affecting these issues (which would especially be the case with large numbers of refugees), overall concerns about order in the country and government effectiveness would arise. Yet these concerns about "anarchy" are more likely to link up with

[6] The exception was perceived threat of armed conflict between Russia and China.

fear and antimigrant hostility through perceived socioeconomic effects of migration.

This perceptual logic gets more complicated if one considers that some respondents would realize that too much government regulation – that is, too strong a central authority – may actually reduce economic benefits from migration. In the Russian Far East, these kinds of perceptions would arise if someone compares the abundance of colorful fruits and vegetables in the Chinese markets and opportunities to make money through cross-border trade with empty shelves and stagnant incomes of the Soviet era, when the border was under lock and key. In the EU, one of the rationales for national governments to delegate some of their sovereignty to trans-European institutions was precisely economic growth through less-restricted trade.

However, one way or another, these considerations – mediated by socioeconomic impact valuations – would subdue or muddle the direct effects of feelings about government capacity on threat and hostility.

Offensive Intent and Territorial Claims

It was not altogether surprising that assessment of new minorities' intention to integrate did not significantly relate to insecurity in the 1997 Eurobarometer survey. This finding contrasts with the Primorskii 2000 results, which revealed a strong and highly significant relationship between concern that migrants harbor territorial claims and fear of migration. The nature of the "offensive" intent clearly explains the difference. In the EU – unlike in the Russian Far East – most non-EU migrants came from many states, none of which measure up to China's size, population, and economic power. The migrant-sending states outside the EU also lacked credible power to claim any of the EU members' territory even if they wished to do so – especially given that most EU states were also members of the North Atlantic Treaty Organization's (NATO's) transatlantic system of collective security. But one measure of intent available in the Eurobarometer survey (intent to integrate into the host states) overlapped conceptually with one of the intent measures in Primorskii (intent to settle permanently). These measures revealed some consistency in explaining – or rather, failing to explain – migration phobia in Primorskii and in the EU. Just as fears about migration in Primorskii did not relate significantly to concerns that Chinese migrants had the intent to settle down permanently in the area, fears of migrants in the EU did not relate significantly to perceived intent of migrants to integrate (or not to integrate) into the EU member states (Tables A.1 and B.1).

The Nature of Intent Offensiveness

Two findings – one in Primorskii and one in the EU – contradicted the initial hypotheses, raising the question about the nature of perceptions about migrants' intent. What exactly about intent is perceived as offensive? In the Primorskii 2000 survey, I expected that respondents who believed the Chinese harbored intentions to settle down permanently would be more threatened by these migrants. For a general sense of threat and for hostility, as it turned out, this perception was not statistically significant. For fear of Russia–China border wars, however, valuations of Chinese intent to settle was a significant correlate – but not in the way I anticipated. Respondents who did *not* feel the Chinese harbored an intent to stay illegally in Russia turned out to be more fearful of armed conflict with China. The explanation for this is context-sensitive: Respondents who believed the Chinese would settle permanently also believed this type of "peaceful infiltration" would make border clashes unnecessary. The Chinese, they believed, would establish control over the Russian territory gradually, by displacing the Russian population through migration.

In the EU, perceived intent of new minorities (i.e., recent migrants) to integrate into host societies was supposed to be associated with acceptance of migrants. Yet, in the EU 1997 surveys, respondents who believed new minorities intended to integrate into host states were significantly more likely to support wholesale deportation of migrants. This result squares better with the logic of the security dilemma (host populations fear the emergence of "ethnic islands" or "truncated minorities" in their midst) than with the straightforward essentialist/group distance logic (the more they become like us, the more we like them).[7]

The sum of the Primorskii and the EU results on this issue is that – absent concerns about armed interstate conflict – migrants are likely to appear more threatening when they make genuine and well-intentioned efforts to integrate into the host states rather than when they maintain their separate communities and ways of life. Indirectly, these findings support the argument of the ethnic competition theory that desegregated minorities are more threatening than segregated minorities (Olzak 1992). The logic of the security dilemma strongly suggests – and

[7] I am grateful to Balasz Zseleniy, a fellow at the John W. Kluge Center at the Library of Congress and the U.S. Holocaust Museum, who studies the history of Nazification of German minorities in Eastern Europe prior to World War II, for pointing out to me that the same logic applied to attitudes toward Jews in Germany at the time in a sense that "dissimilating Jews" were found to be less threatening. The Nazi policy of identifying, isolating, and exterminating the Jews was consistent with this logic.

the EU and Primorskii data failed to falsify this claim – that even overtly well-intentioned efforts by migrants to integrate into the host states are likely to be misinterpreted as trends leading to the entrenchment of potentially hostile ethnic "fifth columns" in host societies. In part, this can be explained by fears that migrants would only integrate into the host states to the extent that would benefit them, but not benefit the host societies. However absurd such a belief – it is hard to imagine how migrants can benefit unilaterally from becoming more socially and economically interdependent with the receiving communities – it is perfectly logical the more one views migration through the lens of the interethnic security dilemma. This is one of the nontrivial and counterintuitive contributions of the present study.

Relative and Absolute Gains

The same as in the Primorskii krai, perceptions of overall socioeconomic effects of migration on host populations came out in the EU study as far more significant correlates of threat and hostility than respondents' susceptibility to deprivation through competition with migrants. EU residents who experienced unemployment, had lower incomes than others, or believed their life situation had been deteriorating were nowhere near as likely to feel insecure about migration or to support deportation of migrants as residents who believed the arrival of minorities strained the system of social benefits, harmed education, or contributed to crime. Two measures of susceptibility to economic deprivation in the EU – personal income and assessment of changes in one's life situation – were significant, but marginal, correlates of hostility. As in the Primorskii survey, socioeconomic impact valuations in the EU study related more significantly and strongly to fear than to hostility. This difference, even though not as pronounced once indirect effects of socioeconomic valuations on hostility through threat perception are considered, is intriguing. One plausible explanation is that statistically estimated indirect effects do not capture the emotional intensity of the real-world effects of insecurity on hostility. Thus, while socioeconomic consideration plays a visible and commonsensical part in the emergence of insecurity about migration, such valuations lack the emotional charge that insecurity provides. Symptomatically, in both the Primorskii and EU tests, the largest reduction in regression coefficients measuring the effects of socioeconomic valuations on hostility took place when threat perception measures were added to the model.

Family Matters

One major persistent difference between the EU and Primorskii results is that acceptance of marriage with migrants was a statistically significant correlate of threat and hostility only in the EU. One plausible contextual explanation – perhaps worth exploring in future research – is that a considerably higher proportion of the EU respondents (55 percent) accepted marriages of their family members with minorities than the proportion of Primorskii's respondents (about 40 percent) who accepted family member marriages with Chinese migrants. Additionally, family unions with migrants or minorities in general were much less of a practical issue in Primorskii than in the EU. Only a handful of such marriages were registered in the 1990s in Primorskii, as compared to multitudes in the EU. Besides, most migrants did not settle down in Primorskii. Chinese migration's symbolic and hypothetical linkage with larger geopolitical threats – such as territorial claims and border conflict – could also conceivably diminish the importance of migrants' marriages as an issue.

6

Los Angeles Ablaze

Antimigrant Backlashes in the Nation of Immigrants

Public opinion data from the Russian Far East and the EU show that the logic of the security dilemma is part and parcel of antimigrant hostility. Whereas antimigrant hostility does not automatically lead to mass violence (as has been the case so far in the Russian Far East and the EU), meta-analysis of social and psychological research strongly suggests that attitudes and behavior are significantly interrelated (Kraus 1995). As we shall see in this chapter, immigration resulting in ethnic balance shifts has been systematically associated with antimigrant hostility and interethnic violence in the world's most prominent "nation of immigrants," the United States. Focusing on hostile response to the "new immigration" from about 1970 to the present and, in particular, on patterns of fatalities in the 1992 Los Angeles riots, this chapter examines the "added value" of the security-dilemma logic with respect to existing explanations of anti-immigrant violence in the United States. Another distinctive feature of this case study is the high levels of ethnic heterogeneity that characterized both the migrant population and migrant-receiving communities of the Greater Los Angeles area. In particular, the case of Black–Korean violence is a case of minority-against-minority violence. While posing a new question as to whether the security-dilemma logic would apply in minority-on-minority relations among ethnically heterogeneous populations, this case has underlying similarities with the Russian and European cases. For while a minority in an interethnic context, the Black communities in question still viewed themselves as incumbents – albeit one group among many – similar to the way that the Russian communities in the Far East or the native communities in the EU representing strong majority populations viewed themselves. In this sense, the case has been selected on the same causal factor – newcomer–incumbent interactions – as the preceding cases were. At the same time, the implications of the multiethnic heterogeneous environment on the social and perceptual logic of the security dilemma are discussed in detail.

In approaching the issue of antimigrant hostility in the United States, I encountered an obstacle precluding opinion data analysis that would parallel survey analyses in Russia and the EU. In the last century, the United States experienced multiple cases of ethnic balance shifts resulting from migration and multiple cases of violent backlashes by incumbent ethnic majorities against the newcomer minorities. The United States is also a country where public opinion research has been widespread, consistent, methodologically rigorous, and transparent. Starting for the most part in the 1950s, immigration and interethnic attitudes have been systematically measured in the ANES and the General Social Survey conducted by the National Opinion Research Center (NORC), as well as in dozens of state-, county-, and city-level surveys (for an extensive overview of the data, see Schumann et al. 1997). And yet, in none of the ANES or NORC or other surveys dealing with immigration and ethnic relations and archived at the Inter-University Consortium for Political and Social Research (ICPSR) and the Roper Center at the University of Connecticut does one find questions capturing respondents' support for aggressive, coercive antiimmigrant actions such as support for wholesale deportation of all immigrants in the EU or support for antimigrant paramilitaries in the Russian Far East. Some related measures in these surveys are worth discussing in detail to flesh out the distinctive contribution of the present study to the literature on intergroup conflict.

The 1986 CBS/*New York Times* survey dealing with immigration (Part 7, N = 1,618) had two items dealing with attitudes toward deportation and the use of armed forces to combat illegal immigration to the United States. The wording of the survey questions, however, precluded me from using these items as indicators of antimigrant hostility, in contrast to Fetzer (2000). The questions about the armed forces asked: "If the U.S. border patrol is unable to stop the flow of illegal aliens from Mexico to the United States, do you think we should use the Army to keep them out, or would this be too drastic a step?" Aside from being suggestive in categorizing the use of the Army as being "too drastic," this wording would elicit a "yes" from respondents who did not necessarily believe that the immigration policy was not tough enough at the time of the survey and who felt that the Army would only be needed if the U.S. border patrol failed. This conditionality would inflate the number of positive responses. In this sense, the question conflates the indicator of support for coercive responding to migration (use of the Army) and the indicator of concern about government capacity (U.S. border patrol is unable to stop the migrant flow). In the Primorskii and EU tests, the first measure only was the dependent variable, while the second measure was one of the independent variables in regression models.

Similarly, on deportation the 1986 CBS/*New York Times* survey asked: "The law requires that illegal aliens be deported. Do you think an exception should be made for those who have lived here for several years without breaking any laws, or not?" While probing attitudes toward a coercive antiimmigrant measure (deportation), this question also focuses respondents' attention on the legal aspects of deportation. In a sense, this would be similar to asking whether someone who committed a felony should be pardoned without trial if he or she does not commit any more crimes for several years. As such, this question is not necessarily about respondents' antimigrant hostility, as it is about respondents' views on the compatibility between crime and punishment. Additionally, the 1986 CBS/*New York Times* poll had no questions that I could use as measures of threat perception, strength of government authority, and the scale of differences between the respondents and the immigrant groups. See the survey description at the ICPSR Web site (http://www.umich.icpsr.org).

Support for deportation was also included in the June 1984 Gallup/*Newsweek* survey (N = 751), but it was phrased in a way that conflated response preferences with perceptions of government capacity and immigration scale: "Some people say that there are too many illegal immigrants living in this country for the authorities to arrest and deport them. They feel we should have an amnesty to let most of them live here legally. Others say that the government should do everything it can to arrest and deport those living in this country illegally. Which view comes closer to your own?" A Merit telephone survey in 1982 asked if respondents believed "the federal government's immigration department should or should not continue to make arrests of illegal aliens at their place of work." In addition to confining itself to a narrow policy measure, the question did not ask if respondents would support the Immigration and Naturalization Service (INS) making *more* arrests and not only in the workplace.

A survey sponsored by the Chicago Council on Foreign Relations and the German Marshall Fund (N = 2,862), had a measure of threat perception arising from immigration: "(I am going to read you a list of possible threats to the vital interest of the United States in the next ten years. For each one, please tell me if you see this as a critical threat, an important but not critical threat, or not an important threat at all.) ... Large numbers of immigrants and refugees coming into the U.S." However, "threats to the vital interest" are not coterminous with threats to the security of the United States or the states where respondents reside (i.e., as in a threat of ethnic violence, riots, disturbances, or war). Such interests may be perceived in economic or cultural terms and therefore reflect individuals' perceptions of immigration's impact on the economy and society of the host state, rather than insecurity. The question on preferences for lower, higher, or same levels of immigration – used most commonly as a proxy for immigration attitudes in survey analysis in the United States – is too ambivalent and therefore inadequate as a measure of antimigrant hostility. This is not only because a person favoring lower immigration levels may think in terms of legislation or economic or social policy rather than in terms of coercive, if not violent, countermeasures. But this is also because this question relates first and foremost – that is, directly and straightforwardly – to perceptions of intergroup population balance and only indirectly and ambiguously to response preferences concerning migration. In other words, someone may think the level of immigration is too high, yet would oppose restrictive countermeasures, perhaps because that same person may derive benefits from immigration, because he or she may believe that measures to limit immigration would backfire, or because of any number of other reasons. And even if response preference is implied in valuation of immigration levels, the nature and the intensity of the preferences will remain indeterminate. Support for anti-immigrant initiatives in California (such as Propositions 187 and 227) does reflect response preferences, but the focus of these preferences is limited to socioeconomic policy and does not capture proclivities for coercive and violent antimigrant measures.

However, the United States is also a place where reliable demographic, socioeconomic, and crime statistics have been widely available – something that enabled scholars to systematically explore the linkages between immigration trends and interethnic violence. Reinterpreting the existing findings, I focus on what happens when the rise of antimigrant hostility is followed by intergroup violence – something one cannot do with opinion data alone. In this sense, the present chapter adds value to the Primorskii and EU survey analyses, not only by focusing on a different migrant-receiving state, but also by exploring the potential impact of antimigrant hostility on intergroup violence. The first goal in this exercise is to identify whether and how violent backlashes by incumbent majority groups against newcomer minority groups relate to the social and psychological bases of the security dilemma. The second goal is to tease out lessons for intergroup conflict prevention in situations where hostility is palpable but no mass violence has yet occurred. Toward this end, I ask what inferences, if any, one may reasonably draw from the pattern of fatalities in the 1992 Los Angeles riots. In examining the role of migration in one of the deadliest single cases of interethnic clashes in the twentieth-century United States, this chapter places the 1992 L.A. riots in the context of rising anti-Latino and anti-Asian sentiments in America since the 1970s and, to start with, in the longer historical context of violent responses to shifting ethnic balances in America's cities since the late nineteenth century.

The Logic of Insecurity: A Missing Link in Explaining Historical Patterns of Antimigrant Hostility in the United States

I found no single study that would first catalog all cases of ethnic balance shifts in a representative sample of cities, towns, counties, or census tracts across the United States over a substantial period of time[1] during the last century or so and then explore if these shifts related to antimigrant hostility and intergroup (interethnic) violence (but see Green et al. 1998 for a study of these patterns in the New York metropolitan area). Without taking stock of demographic trends first and violence second across at least a representative sample of locations, an element of selection on the dependent variable – what one may term the Monday-morning-quarterback logic – undermines the validity of any inference about the relationship between immigration and violence. Yet, even with this flaw, evidence from individual studies suggests that immigration has had a lot to do with interethnic violence in the United States.

As we shall see when this evidence is examined in greater detail, the predominant explanations linking immigration and interethnic violence in the United States have emphasized either the logic of competing interests (especially socioeconomic and political interests) or the logic of clashing identities (especially ethnocultural identities) or some combination thereof. As we shall also see, however, the logic of interests and the logic of identity are both confounded when one juxtaposes research on hostility toward the "new immigration" of the late nineteenth century (Olzak

[1] By this, I mean sufficient time for population balances to shift for which five-to-ten-year coverage would appear reasonable.

1992) against research on hostility toward the "new" Latino and Asian immigration of the late twentieth century (Cornelius 2002). At the same time, the logic of insecurity and fear exaggeration – implicit in the social and psychological logic of the security dilemma – has been a missing link in the analyses of antimigrant hostility in the United States. Yet, as subsequent sections of this chapter will show, it is the logic of insecurity that offers answers to the puzzles confounding both the logic of interests and the logic of identity. A reinterpretation of existing empirical studies suggests that the insecurity logic applies to antiimmigrant backlashes in the American public opinion since the 1970s and in the streets of Los Angeles in 1992. It is not that interests or identities do not matter. They do. But, taken separately, they fall short of explaining why and how interests and identities relate to exaggerated threats and to fear and hostility spiraling out of control.

America's Antimigrant Hostility Puzzle I: The Logic of Economic Competition in 1880–1915 and in 1970–2000

Susan Olzak (1992) provides perhaps the most rigorous and comprehensive assessment of the relationship between immigration patterns and interethnic conflict and protest in the United States over more than three decades at the turn of the twentieth century. Using the newspaper of record, *The New York Times*, Olzak documented 262 events from 1877 to 1914 in seventy-seven major U.S. cities involving threats of violence; property damage; personal injury; takeover of spaces, persons, or buildings; use of blunt weapons (e.g., rocks and clubs); use of lethal weapons (e.g., knife, gun, lynching rope); and killings – all broken down by source and target ethnic groups (Olzak 1992: 242–3). Distinguishing between intergroup conflicts and civil rights protests, these events were summarized as "ethnic collective action" between white natives and African Americans, Chinese, Hispanics, and Eastern and Western Europeans. Olzak also compiled data on immigration rates, wages, economic depressions, event duration, strikes, unionization, business failures, literacy, and other socioeconomic characteristics of city populations. Having analyzed the data with cross-sectional and time-series methods, Olzak found that proportional change in immigration related significantly ($p < 0.01$) to collective ethnic action (Olzak 1992: 78). The latter was associated nonrandomly and positively with immigration rates.

Specifically regarding ethnic "other" newcomers – predominantly African Americans – to seventy-seven major U.S. cities, Olzak found that change in overall immigration rates had a significant effect on anti-Black violence. The higher the annual immigration rate was, the higher was the count of violent acts against African American newcomers. Interpreting Maximum Likelihood and Weibull model estimates, Olzak concluded that the "rate of violence against African-Americans when immigration rose most steeply was about nine times higher than when immigration fell most steeply." By another calculation, the rates of anti–African American violence in U.S. cities "was over three times higher when immigration surged than in the period when immigration remained unchanged from year to year" (Olzak 1992: 126).

Olzak concluded that immigration gave rise to interethnic violence by "niche overlap and competition" with "attempts at competitive exclusion" galvanizing grievances into violence (ibid. 1992: 209).[2] Socioeconomic motivations – especially regarding employment and income – appear to have been the prime mover of niche competition. First, Olzak reported that between 1870 and 1880 "a racial job queue" emerged in American cities because Whites – both the native Whites and White immigrants from South, Central, and Eastern Europe – "held more diverse jobs in cities where the black community was also becoming more numerous" (ibid. 1992: 210). The arrival of African Americans into major cities in large numbers around the turn of the century and in the early 1900s therefore threatened the economic position of Whites, especially the immigrants in low-wage occupations, who, according to Lieberson (1980: 1), had already "piled up in the slums of the great urban centers of the East and Midwest" since the 1880s.

Second, according to Olzak (1992: 211), ethnic collective action increased when and where higher immigration rates were accompanied by higher rates of business failure than elsewhere – that is "competition intensified when the number of newcomers rose and economic opportunities declined." Third, "the founding rate of national labor unions and the number of unions in existence significantly raised the rate of conflicts and violent conflicts against all groups" (ibid. 1992: 212) – strongly suggesting that institutionally mobilized (i.e., unionized) forms of labor competition related to greater intensity of interethnic conflict. Fourth, "dispersion of the foreign-born from segregated occupations raised rates of ethnic conflicts against all groups" (ibid. 1992: 214). Fifth, immigration restrictions on immigrants from Asia and South, Central, and Eastern

[2] In developing her arguments, Olzak drew on theoretical insights of ecological competition theories (notably, Barth 1969) and applied them to interethnic conflict in America.

Europe – reducing the flow of newcomer competitors – was followed by a decline in the frequency of attacks against these groups (ibid: 215). Sixth, city-level analysis of the 1890-to-1914 data showed that "competition affected protest and conflict similarly, even though the two types of collective action typically have distinct goals and grievances" (ibid: 217). Seventh, "despite the fact that southern cities were more likely to experience racial unrest, competition affected rates of lynching and racial violence in northern and southern cities similarly" (ibid.).

As a result of competition, primarily over jobs and income and sometimes for political influence, Olzak concluded – "in direct contrast to models emphasizing that *segregation* of ethnic and racial populations causes ethnic conflict" – that "*desegregation* causes ethnic conflict" (Olzak 1992: 213). One may justifiably infer that were it not for socioeconomic competition, migration and ethnic intermingling would not appear threatening to incumbent majorities facing massive urban migration, antimigrant hostility would not be acute and widespread and interethnic violence would be unlikely to erupt.

Olzak persistently marshaled impressive evidence to rule out ethnocultural explanations of different rates of attacks on African Americans versus Hispanics, Asians, and South, Central, and Eastern Europeans, arguing that "somewhat different aspects of competition intensified the rate of attack on each group" (ibid.: 211). While plausible, this argument raises the possibility that "aspects of competition" were different in the first place precisely because of the different nature of ethnic groups targeted by collective action. At any rate, several findings in the Olzak study suggest that perceived ethnocultural attributes of out-groups had independent effects on interethnic conflict and protest in American cities from 1877 to 1915. For example, Olzak found that about 83 percent of Black/White conflicts were violent as compared to only 43 percent of conflicts between Whites and other newcomer groups (ibid.: 101). Black/White conflicts and protests were also found to be more sizeable than conflicts and protests involving other ethnic dyads. Thus, nearly 20 percent of Black/White events involved thousands of participants, compared with about 10 percent of Chinese/White events and 13 percent of events involving other groups. Olzak's explanation – that African Americans were disproportionately targeted because they were "least powerful to fight back" – would be consistent with the ethnic competition hypothesis, but it is not tested in the study. The analyses provide no measure of perceived capacity of the target groups to "fight back" by groups initiating ethnic conflict and protests.

A similar problem arises regarding the finding that wage increases of common laborers over that period "raised the rate of antiblack conflict," but "depressed the rate of anti-Chinese conflict" (ibid.: 84). While suggesting two contextual explanations consistent with ethnic competition theory – concentration of Chinese settlements in the West and the passage of the Asian Exclusion Act of 1882 – Olzak acknowledges that "further investigation of regional differences in employment and ethnic group distribution" was in order. A more puzzling set of findings is that while *lower* wages were related to more intense White/Chinese conflict in the statistical analysis, Olzak notes that "nearly all anti-Chinese events took place during 1880–82, when real wages of laborers were *high* [italics added by the author] and immigration was rising" (ibid.: 84). A broader, systemic shortcoming of the study design is that it does not control for enthnocultural factors – such as perceived ethnic distance between group dyads or feelings in the host communities toward various ethnic "others."

That these perceptions need to be controlled is suggested by studies that analyzed responses to the latest wave of "new" immigration to the United States. Socioeconomic interests – embedded in niche competition between the incumbent and migrant populations – appear to be a weak predictor of hostility toward "new" Latino immigration from the 1970s to the early 2000s. Wayne Cornelius, Director of the Center for Comparative Immigration Studies at the University of California, San Diego, conducted research suggesting that public attitudes toward immigrants and immigration policy in the United States in the late twentieth and early twenty-first centuries have been driven by "the complex interplay between economic and ethno-cultural factors" (Cornelius 2002: 165). As fear of and hostility toward the "new immigrants" approached its peak in the mid-1990s – signified most notably by the approval of California's antiimmigrant Proposition 187 by 59 percent of the voters in 1994[3] – opinion polls showed that interethnic competition for jobs and incomes with immigrants was not an issue for the overwhelming majority of U.S. and California residents. In nationwide opinion polls, the number of respondents agreeing with the statement that immigrants take jobs from American citizens was 36 percent in the *New York Times* (December 1995) poll, 39 percent in the CBS/*New York Times* (February 1996) poll, and 21 percent in the Princeton Survey Research Associates (March 1996) poll. In the same polls, respectively, 55, 51, and 65 percent of

[3] Proposition 187 restricted access to social services, such as medical care and education, to illegal immigrants.

respondents agreed with the statement that immigrants take jobs Americans don't want (see Cornelius 2002: 170). In California, a statewide survey by the Public Policy Institute of California in April 1998 asked more-specific questions, suggesting to respondents that while immigrants may be hard workers, they are also consuming public services. Even though the questions did not mention that immigrants and immigrant employers also paid taxes that exceeded the cost of public services to immigrants, the majority of respondents (46 percent) said immigrants were a net benefit to California. Most strikingly, from the standpoint of economic niche competition, 66 percent of Latinos and 68 percent of Asians – who as recent immigrants themselves had stronger reasons to fear economic competition from new arrivals than the African and European American residents did – said that immigration benefited California. Economic competition theory also suggested that Blacks in California would be more threatened by Latino and Asian immigrants than Whites, because Blacks were more likely than Whites to seek employment in low-wage service and manual labor sectors. And yet, in the 1998 statewide survey, 45 percent of Blacks but only 37 percent of Whites said immigration was a benefit to California.

More importantly, Cornelius marshaled extensive evidence suggesting that the prevailing perception among Whites of immigration as a burden to California (49 percent in the 1998 poll) had little to do with economic niche competition. The U.S. and California economies, even before the economic expansion of the 1990s, provided multiple economic and social niches for Latino immigrants where they posed little challenge to the native residents. Notwithstanding arguments that in the 1990s low-skilled job opportunities decreased as the American economy became more knowledge-intensive and high-tech, millions of Latino migrants who arrived in the 1980s and 1990s found full employment in what would be considered low-skilled sectors (Cornelius 2002: 166). In Los Angeles, according to Waldinger and Bozorgmehr (1996, cited in ibid.), 85 percent of Mexican men who had no formal education, nevertheless had full-time jobs in 1990. Even recent arrivals to southern California from Mexico and Central America could typically find employment for at least two to three days a week in street-corner labor markets (Cornelius 2002: 166; also see Cornelius and Kuwahara 1998 and Valenzuela 2000). Far from confined to low-wage "mobility traps," the U.S. Census Bureau reported, the new immigrants (including 60 percent of Latinos in California in 1999) found employment in fast-growing, technologically advanced industries (Pastor and Marcelli 2000, cited in Cornelius 2002: 3). Studies by Cornelius (1998), Cornelius and Kuwahara (1998), Smith (1996), and Waldinger (1996) provided evidence that in major immigrant-receiving urban centers of the United States, such as San Diego and New York City, the demand for Latino labor had become structurally embedded and thus principally independent from the business cycle. Businesses consistently hired immigrants during recessions and immigrant labor demand withstood the tightening of border control and immigration restrictions of the mid-1990s. As Cornelius (2002: 167) concluded, "immigrant-dominated labor markets in the United States are highly institutionalized and operate with remarkable efficiency and flexibility. Mature, transborder immigrant social networks linking places of origin in Mexico and Central America with destination cities (and usually with specific employers in those cities) now provide a continuous and easily accessed supply of labor for small and medium-size businesses." Spatial dispersion of Latino population out of California from 1990 to 1998, especially to the Southwest and the South – with a 110 percent increase in North Carolina, 102 percent in Georgia, and 90 percent in Tennessee – has also "been driven by rapid creation of hard-to-fill jobs in industries requiring large amounts of manual labor, such as meatpacking, egg processing, construction, landscaping, restaurants, warehousing, foundries, and carpet manufacturing" (Cornelius 2002: 168).

And yet, despite weak economic competition and despite rapid growth of the U.S. economy in the second half of the 1990s – with unemployment rates dropping to 3–4 percent and companies desperately hunting for new recruits, including immigrants – approximately 50 to 70 percent of Americans in national opinion polls continued to express negative views on immigration (Cornelius 2002: 172). In fact, statistical analysis of survey data in the 1990s consistently revealed that being unemployed had no significant effect on natives' assessment of immigration's impact on the economy or on restrictionist sentiments (Bauer, Lofstrom, and Zimmermann 2000; Citrin et al. 1997; Espenshade and Hempstead 1996). One multivariate analysis of polling data from the United States, France, and Germany in 1986–95 (Fetzer 2000) found that not only one's status as unemployed, but also one's personal income and occupation as manual laborer, did not relate significantly to antiimmigrant views in these three countries. These findings also mirror the results of my Primorskii 2000 and Eurobarometer 1997 studies reported in Chapters 4 and 5. Yet even though immigration was hardly seen as a source of economic competition, the majority of Americans persistently opposed increasing quotas for legal immigrants and supported tougher border enforcement and larger penalties on those who hired illegal immigrants (Espenshade and Belanger 1997).

America's Antimigrant Hostility Puzzle II: Ethnicity, Culture, and the "New" Latino Migration in the Late Twentieth Century

Having shown that the economic logic fails to explain persistent antimigrant sentiments among the American public in the 1990s, Cornelius (2002: 173) offers an alternative explanation – that is, "the influence of *non-economic* factors, especially ethnicity, language, and culture." The ethnocultural argument builds on national survey analysis by Citrin et al. (1997) who found that restrictionist attitudes were significantly linked to negative views of Latinos as an ethnic group (not to be confused with negative views of any group as immigrants). Also, Vidanage and Sears (1995: 13, cited in Cornelius 2002: 174) found that among Los Angeles county Whites in a 1994 poll, "anti-*immigrant* feeling may be largely anti-*Hispanic* feeling."

Perceptions that immigrants fail to learn English – thus preserving their linguistic distinctiveness from the host society – was found to have a significant effect on negative sentiments about immigration among the U.S. general public (Espenshade and Calhoun 1993). Antiimmigrant sentiments in the United States in the 1990s also correlated with the majority public perception that increasing diversity brought by immigration threatened American culture and made it harder to "keep the country united" (Cornelius 2002: 175).[4] In a Princeton Survey Research Associates poll conducted in May 1997, almost three times as many respondents expressed unfavorable opinion toward immigrants from Mexico (34 percent) and Cuba (35 percent) than toward immigrants from Europe (12 percent) (cited in Cornelius 2002: 176).

In California, counties where a majority of voters supported the "English only" Proposition 63 were by and large the same counties where a majority of voters supported Proposition 187 denying access to public service by illegal immigrants (MacDonald and Cain 1998: 296–7, cited in Cornelius 2002: 14). Exit polls in 1994 and 1998 California state elections also showed that support for Proposition 187 and antibilingual

[4] For example, in the *Los Angeles Times* nationwide survey of August 1996, 42 percent of respondents saw immigration as a threat to American culture, compared to 30 percent who saw it as a benefit and 18 percent who believe immigration had no effect on American culture.

education Proposition 227 was more than twice as strong among non-Hispanic Whites (63 percent and 67 percent) than among Latinos (23 percent and 37 percent) (Cornelius 2002: 179). And in the 1998 California Statewide Survey, almost twice as many Latinos (66 percent) and Asians (68 percent) than Whites (37 percent) saw immigrants – the majority of whom happened to be Latinos and Asians – as a benefit to the state (Cornelius 2002: 171). These trends indicate that cultural issues indeed came on top of socioeconomic competition with respect to immigration. After all, migrants who actively learn English would stand a greater chance to get the jobs that the Americans want, creating potentially the "ethnic job queues" that Olzak linked to ethnic violence. The strong insistence on immigrants learning English thus would be illogical if immigration attitudes were shaped predominantly by strategic calculus grounded in individual economic self-interest.

Summarizing the findings of mass survey analyses on immigration in the United States, France, and Germany, Fetzer (2000: 17–18) concluded that "opposition to immigration . . . has as much to do with symbolically delegitimating the values and cultures of immigrant minorities as with preventing foreigners from 'taking natives' jobs.'" According to Fetzer, opposition to immigration has been about "the dominant cultural 'insiders' (e.g., French Catholics, white American Protestants) . . . lashing out at the cultural 'interlopers' (e.g., North African or Turkish Muslims, Latin American Catholics)" (ibid.). In particular, attribution of threat to reluctance of migrants to learn the host countries' languages makes the ethnocultural argument distinct from the economic competition argument. For the latter standpoint, migrants should be seen as a greater threat if they learned the host country's language fast and thus were able to compete for jobs and access to resources and political status with the natives.

And yet, ethnocultural distinctiveness and prejudices – even when considering also that Mexicans comprised the largest proportion of immigrants to the United States in the 1990s – appear to be insufficient to explain anti-Mexican attitudes in America in the 1990s. In theory, the findings that antiimmigrant attitudes are predominantly anti-Hispanic attitudes is not in itself sufficient to claim that antiimmigrant attitudes arise from concerns about cultural identity. The question is whether anti-Hispanic attitudes are driven by perceptions that by their very nature the Hispanics are more "Hispanicized" than, say, the Chinese are "Sinified" or the Americans are "Americanized." Or is it some other dimension of the Mexican immigration that underlies anti-Hispanic attitudes in the first place? Consider, for example, the following counterfactuals implicit in the same data that have been cited in support of the ethnocultural explanation. First, the Princeton Survey Research Associates poll on immigration in May 1997 suggested that ethnocultural distinctiveness in its own right was not necessarily associated with negative sentiments toward immigrants. For example, assuming that physiological proximity to the predominantly non-Hispanic White population of the United States is an ethnocultural factor, then one would have expected the Princeton survey respondents to have more unfavorable opinions of immigrants from Africa, the Caribbean (especially, Haiti and Jamaica), and Asia than of immigrants from the Middle East, Mexico, Cuba, and Central/South America. Contrary to this prediction, however, a significantly larger percentage of the Princeton Survey respondents, on average, expressed more-unfavorable views of the latter group (31 percent) than of the former (21 percent) (Cornelius 2002: 176).

Second, the same poll casts doubt as to the interactive effects between the size of an immigrant group and its ethnocultural distinctiveness. Assuming that immigrants from China, Japan, Korea, and Vietnam are ethnically and culturally equidistant from the majority of U.S. non-Hispanic Whites, one would expect those among the four Asian groups who immigrate to the United States in larger numbers to draw out more-unfavorable attitudes among survey respondents. And yet, in the Princeton survey about the same number of respondents voiced their dislike of the Chinese (19 percent) and the Japanese (18 percent), although the Chinese in the 1980s immigrated into the United States and into California in overwhelmingly larger numbers than the Japanese.[5] One could also expect greater dislike of the Chinese based on the fact that they had been arriving from a less economically advanced country than Japan. Similarly, the same proportion of respondents (25 percent) held unfavorable views of the Koreans and the Vietnamese. Yet, the Vietnamese migrants came in with significantly smaller assets and had lower education levels that the Koreans. Also, the Vietnamese population included a significantly higher proportion of political refugees (the boat people) entitled to government-subsidized education, housing, and other social services. Third, if, indeed, it were the illegal character of immigration that keyed ethnocultural prejudices, then one would expect unfavorable views of the Chinese and the Mexicans to be about the same. Yet, in the Princeton survey of 1997

[5] For example, in Los Angeles County the U.S. census found that there were 245,033 residents of Chinese origin in 1990 compared with 129,736 residents of Japanese origin. See Morrison and Lewis (1994: 28).

nearly twice as many respondents said they disliked immigrants from Mexico (34 percent) than from China (19 percent) (Cornelius 2002: 176). Perhaps one could argue that the Chinese had exhibited greater inclination to assimilate culturally in America. However, just as many Americans became alarmed about salsa outselling ketchup (ibid.: 178) one may reasonably expect Americans to be alarmed by proliferation of Chinatowns and Chinese restaurants – often with service personnel speaking at best rudimentary English. And if one were to explain the larger scope of negative attitudes toward the Mexicans than toward the Chinese by suggesting that the former have been perceived as more hardworking than the latter, then one may wonder if the actual explanation of antimigrant hostility comes down to economic valuations after all. The logic here is straightforward: Groups perceived as "hardworking" are more likely to be stronger competitors for jobs and resources with the natives than groups perceived as lazy.

Fourth, as Cornelius argues persuasively, it is not merely perception of ethnocultural distinctiveness, but belief that immigrants are not going to integrate or assimilate in the host society that could explain antiimmigrant and, in particular, anti-Mexican attitudes in America. And underlying the latter is the suspicion that migrants intend to forge ethnic "fifth columns" that would – intentionally or not – undermine not only the identity, but also national security of the United States. Samuel Huntington of Harvard University – whose arguments about immigrant threat to the American Creed were sketched out in Chapter 1 – is one of the best exponents of the identity–security fusion. This conceptual linkage comes through with striking clarity in Huntington's futuristic scenario in which the United States contemplates going to war in order to protect its energy reserves. However, the ascending Hispanic population uses its newfound political clout to stop the war. The United States then fails to defend its vital national interests. Thus, immigration of Hispanics and their failure to become loyal to their new country directly threatens the U.S. interests, if not national security and survival. Huntington casts this shadow of insecurity to amplify his claims that cultural assimilation is an important political issue. Yet even this type of argument is unsustainable empirically. As de la Garza (2004) shows in his review of research on Latino migration, none of Huntington's claims regarding the alleged resistance of Hispanics to assimilation and the alleged adherence of Hispanics to non-American cultural and political "creeds" holds water. By the early 2000s, exclusive Mexican communities where English is not spoken have largely failed to become a systematic feature of American society and Mexican intermarriage with non-Mexicans had not decreased (ibid.: 110). Similarly, systematic research established that bilingual education in the United States – seen through Huntington's uncertainty prism as the forerunner of security challenges – has been predominantly viewed by Mexican Americans as a means to learn English rather than to retain Spanish (ibid.) And empirical studies cited by Cornelius (2002: 178) indicate that among immigrants from Mexico "virtually all second- and third-generation descendants have good English language skills" (Smith and Edmondson 1997: 378). Portes and Hao (1998) found that while most U.S.-born Latino eighth and ninth graders in Miami and San Diego were fluent in English, fewer than half of them were still fluent in Spanish. And U.S. Census data indicate that the more recently born American residents of Mexican origin were also more likely to speak exclusively English (Smith 1998). These trends suggest that to explain mistrust among Americans about immigrant integration, one has to explain why "the general U.S. public tends to focus on the Spanish-dominant first-generation immigrants in their midst" (Cornelius 2002: 179) rather than on increasingly English-only-speaking second- and third-generation immigrants.

America's Antimigrant Hostility Puzzle III: The Big Picture and the Logic of Insecurity

It is not so much that the logic of interest may have failed to explain some important puzzles about antiimmigrant violence in 1877–1915 or that the logic of identity may have failed to explain some important puzzles about antiimmigrant sentiments in the 1990s. It is the "big picture" juxtaposition of antiimmigrant hostility explanations during these two historical periods that confounds both the logic of interest and the logic of identity simultaneously. Let us suppose that none of the objections I raised previously overrules the principal arguments advanced by Olzak and Cornelius. In that case, we will have to accept that the economic competition logic explains antiimmigrant hostility and violence in 1877–1915, but not persistent antiimmigrant attitudes in the 1990s. Conversely, the ethnocultural logic would explain persistent antiimmigrant attitudes among Americans in the 1990s, but not antiimmigrant hostility in 1877–1915. One inference from this juxtaposition is that both logics are flawed (if only by being secondary to differences in historical context) and that the explanatory power of each one of them is weak. Given the amount of supporting evidence, however, it is more plausible that both the logic of interest and the logic of identity are valid and powerful predictors, but that both are channeled toward antimigrant hostility and decisively mediated by other factors. While accounting for and analyzing all such factors is beyond the scope of this chapter, the findings in Primorskii krai and the EU suggest that the logic of fear exaggeration would be one such powerful factor.

The key perceptual drivers of this insecurity logic – above and beyond the discreet logics of interest and identity – are the sense of emergent anarchy and the effects of uncertainty on valuations of ethnic balance, migrant intent, capacity of migrants to assimilate, and socioeconomic effects of migration. In fact, it is the factors related to the logic of insecurity that appear to make the most convincing case in Cornelius's (2002) explanation of persistent anti-Latino sentiments in the United States in the 1990s. One potent symbolic expression of the insecurity logic is the argument – advanced even by established mainstream historians such as David Kennedy (1996) – that Latino migration threatens to result in a "Chicano Quebec in the Southwest." This symbol is identical to the threat symbols of Chinese migration potentially engendering "Asian Balkans" or "Siberian Israel" in Russia. In fact, "Balkanization" was also evoked in the United States to describe the ostensibly devastating effects of immigration on the nation's ethnocultural identity. These are all symbols of "nested" or "truncated" minorities that give rise to the perceptual logic of the interethnic security dilemma, regardless of the stated intent of the migrants and the natives. These are the symbols of inherent mistrust embedded in this type of demographic intermingling that cues fear exaggeration. And once the logic of fear exaggeration sets in, the security-dilemma theory predicts that seemingly innocuous developments are likely to be interpreted as real threats, and hostile intentions are likely to be ascribed to migrants who have no desire whatsoever to become or represent such "nested minorities."

In Chapters 4 and 5, I dealt with these types of perceptions in the Russian Far East and the EU. In the United States, Cornelius suggests, "Mexicans provoke particular concern" not so much due to "their cultural traditions and Spanish-language use," but because the latter "are constantly being reinforced through continuing, large-scale immigration from Mexico, making them prime candidates for ethnic separatist movements" (Cornelius 2002: 177). Latino separatist movements do not have to exist for the exaggerated suspicions to fester and translate into antiimmigrant hostility. These suspicions would arise from the fact that the U.S.–Mexico border is long and hard to monitor, that Mexicans have tremendous incentives to immigrate to the United States, and that fertility rates among the natives would not offset the inflow of immigrants making the proverbial tipping point in the ethnic balance inevitable. One may recall a stream of media stories in the early 1990s publicizing projections by demographers that by 2020 or so Whites would no longer comprise a majority of the U.S. population. And around 2000, Whites lost their majority status in California, in no small part due to the influx of immigrants from Mexico in the previous three decades. Cornelius (2002: 178) also found studies (including Frey [1996] and Gimpel [1999]) that linked perceptions of Balkanization to "growing spatial inequality and resegregation: increasing differences between poor inner-city neighborhoods flooded with newly arrived immigrants and affluent suburbs populated by the native-born and the minority of immigrants who have achieved economic mobility; out-migration by natives from heavily immigration-impacted states and regions to less-impacted areas."

The logic of uncertainty under the security dilemma would explain why Americans discounted real-world trends showing that the "new" Latino immigrants have been following the traditional assimilation trajectory in the second and third generations, focusing instead on the "dissimilating" first-generation immigrants. The logic of insecurity would also explain why more Americans in the 1990s had unfavorable views of Mexicans than of Chinese, for example, with a broader point that antiimmigrant sentiments would vary by group depending on the salience of exaggerated threats potentially ascribed to any given group of migrants. The insecurity calculus also illuminates why restrictionist sentiments among Americans persisted in the 1990s despite the adoption of tougher immigration laws in 1996 and despite tangible and widely acknowledged economic benefits of migrant labor. At the same time, the logic of risk aversion under uncertainty would also account for the positive role of perceived economic effects in softening antimigrant hostility and preventing hostility from translating into violence.

More generally, while explaining particularly negative perceptions of migration from Mexico, the security-dilemma logic would also explain why antimigrant hostility and violence may be directed at other groups – if perceptions of anarchy, intent, ethnic distinctiveness, and socioeconomic effects coalesce in a particularly intense and explosive fashion. The theory also suggests that the groups most threatened by and hostile toward migrants do not necessarily have to be those that comprise the majority of residents within a nation-state. Collectivities at any level of aggregation – a group of countries, a single country, a subnational region, a province, a state, a county, a city, or a census tract – may face the social conditions giving rise to the logic of fear exaggeration and preemptive retaliation against newcomers.[6] As the analysis that follows indicates, to a large extent such, in fact, was one of the worst cases of intergroup violence in the United States in the twentieth century: the Los Angeles riots of April–May 1992.

The Security Dilemma and the 1992 Los Angeles Riots

The largest outbreak of race-related violence in the United States since the urban riots of the 1960s took place on April 29, 1992, when crowds poured into South Central Los Angeles to protest the acquittal verdict of four White police officers who had been shown hundreds of times on national television beating the African American motorist Rodney King. Violence erupted soon afterward and lasted six days, resulting in fifty-one people being killed, 2,383 injured, and 8,000 arrested. More than 700 businesses were set ablaze, contributing to an estimated $1 billion in property damages (Jacobs 1996; Webster 1992: 23). Television screens and front pages of newspapers across the nation carried horrific images of burning buildings, smoke-coated neighborhoods, unruly mobs, chaotic looting, armed business owners, and trucks unloading units of the National Guard servicemen in riot gear. Summarizing research on the 1992 L.A. riots, Mark Baldassare, professor and chair of the Department of Urban and Regional Planning at the University of California, Irvine, said they were "among the most violent, destructive, and frightening episodes in twentieth century American urban history" (Baldassare 1994: 1).

In numerous publications on these events, I found no studies that examined the 1992 L.A. riots through the lens of the interethnic security dilemma – something that would require systematic and comprehensive testing of the role of anarchy, intent, groupness, and impact perceptions. One major study, however, did undertake rigorous testing of the effects of insecurity associated with the shifting ethnic balance in Los Angeles County on the pattern of fatalities in the 1992 riots. The analysis by Bergesen and Herman (1998), published in the *American Sociological Review* – the flagship journal of the American Sociological

[6] In other words, while in the United States nationwide the focus would be on the relationship between non-Hispanic Whites and the new Latino immigrants, in any given city hostile responding to migration is likely to come from a group whose majority status would be threatened.

Association – focused on the effects of ethnic succession across Los Angeles neighborhoods on riot violence, while controlling for the neighborhoods' economic conditions and ethnic compositions. Data in this study were aggregated at the lowest level available – by census tracts or neighborhoods – capturing much better the demographic and socioeconomic context, or "ecological dynamics," of group relations than previous studies that relied on state-, county-, or city-level data. Focusing on census tracts also provided Bergesen and Herman with a substantially larger number of cases (1,637 census tracts in Los Angeles County) than city- or county-level analyses, enabling the authors to control for a larger number of explanatory variables and making it harder to attribute the findings to chance. Independently of the authors' intent, the study provides an acceptable proxy test of the relationship between the security-dilemma logic and antiimmigrant violence. The authors, essentially, ask whether in the context of emergent anarchy (e.g., street protests in L.A. after the Rodney King verdict), one would observe higher rates of "defensive backlash violence from African Americans in those neighborhoods in which the rate of in-migration by nonblack minorities is increasing" (Bergesen and Herman 1998: 42). Ethnicity of target groups, unemployment, and household income by neighborhood were held constant. It is especially important that the authors set up their study specifically as a test of Olzak's ethnic competition theory – the one positing that competition for employment and housing brought on by immigration of Latinos and Asians into Black neighborhoods would provide the principal behavioral motivation for interethnic riot behavior. Modifying Olzak's arguments, however, Bergesen and Herman stressed the decisive and independent role of "hyper-ethnic succession" as the underlying social mechanism of riot violence. According to them, "[H]ousing and job competition are secondary processes such that by the time a neighborhood has become desegregated enough to foster political and economic competition and Herman did not specify the behavioral microfoundations putatively linking migration rates and violence. While citing extensive previous research (including Bergesen [1977, 1980], Blalock [1967], Bobo and Hutchings [1996], Bobo and Zubrinsky [1996], Olzak [1992], Quillian [1995], Tilly [1969, 1978], and Vanneman and Pettigrew [1972]) that established "an association between prejudice and reactionary collective violence by groups displaced through rapid social change" (ibid.), Bergesen and Herman did not identify the nature of the effect of high rates of in-migration on riot behavior.

How plausible is it that the logic of fear exaggeration – implicit in the interethnic security dilemmas – was one of the crucial behavioral microfoundations linking "hyper-ethnic succession" and violent antiimmigrant behavior? Addressing this question, I reexamined Bergesen and Herman findings, focusing on evidence linking riot violence and the four dimensions of the interethnic security-dilemma logic: perceived anarchy, intent, groupness, and socioeconomic impact.

Emergent Anarchy: Government Incapacity and Social Anomie

The opening paragraph of the Bergesen and Herman article acknowledges the role of the acquittal verdict in the Rodney King case as the immediate trigger of the riots. The added insight of the security dilemma here is that the acquittal of the four White officers sent an unambiguous and powerful signal to the African American community in Los Angeles that government agencies were incapable of protecting their security. The effect of this signal was particularly strong because widely televised videotapes of Rodney King's beatings by the police officers left little doubt that the beating took place. Moreover, the perpetrators were precisely the agents of the government charged with guarding the security of Los Angeles residents. If these government agents committed visible acts of brutality against the people they were supposed to "serve and protect," individuals identifying with the victim would feel unprotected and exposed to violence. They would feel the urge to take matters into their own hands and assume that with no higher authority to regulate conduct they were in the self-help world where preemptive offense is the best form of defense. In Los Angeles, according to Baldassare (1994: 7): "The beating of Rodney King . . . was perceived by many blacks as a validation of their worst fears about police misconduct."[7] The scene was set for the "self-help" mentality to take over, prompting individuals to act preemptively and aggressively in self-defense. In Los Angeles, members of the African American community responded to this signal by immediately gathering in South Central L.A. to protest the verdict, followed by sporadic looting and lashing out at motorists to avenge violence against Rodney King. With law enforcement agencies unable to control the situation, a classic case of emergent anarchy was in place. The breakdown of government authority was a

[7] In fact, Baldassare (1994: 7) presents data suggesting that insecurity among L.A. minorities concerning local police was widespread by the time of the riots: "A quarter of the 8,274 public complaints against the police in the late 1980s were for excessive use of force, and many of these complaints came from minority neighborhoods."

precursor of violent attacks across ethnic lines. It is also important to note that the Rodney King verdict was distinctly exogenous to patterns of demographic change in Los Angeles, making anarchy (breakdown of authority) a discrete independent variable.[8]

The security-dilemma perspective also highlights the point made by Baldassare (1994: 2) that surprise played an important role in engendering anarchy in the streets of L.A.: "No one had expected that a jury viewing this [Rodney King beating] tape would find the four police officers to be not guilty of using excessive force.... The Los Angeles Police Department was unprepared when the personal shock over the trial outcome turned into angry and violent crowd behavior." As subsequent investigations established, temporary breakdown of the chain of command within the L.A. Police Department was among the crucial contributors to police inaction. According to Morrison and Lewis (1994: 44), "[T]he chief of police was attending a fund-raising party in Beverly Hills during the crucial hours, and none of his subordinates seemed willing to commit manpower to the trouble spots even though officers were assembled and ready for action."

Emergent anarchy at the top linked up with powerful "bottom-up" drivers of uncontrolled crowd behavior: social anomie and alienation, especially among young males in South Central Los Angeles. Morrison and Lewis (1994: 35–6) estimated that in this part of L.A. approximately 50,000 unemployed men between the ages of sixteen and thirty-four were "available" to participate in the riots. This group represented "a critical mass of young males who had no regular occupation, little reason to feel bound by social rules, and the physical energy needed to stone, loot, burn, and run from the police" (ibid.: 36). Weak "central authority" – or lack of adult supervision – was widespread within families where a substantial proportion of these males socialized. According to the 1990 census data (Morrison and Lowry 1994: 37), only 44 percent of children in South Central L.A. lived with both parents, and 82 percent of single parents were mothers (hence, lack of male authority role models for boys). Moreover, in South Central L.A. 38 percent of children aged twelve to

[8] For example, critics of the security-dilemma explanation of interethnic violence in the former Yugoslavia have pointed out that it was not necessarily clear in that case whether the decline of government authority engendered ethnic conflict or whether ethnic conflict engendered the decline of government authority. In the case of the L.A. riots, the onset of anarchy clearly preceded the outbreak of violence. Moreover, the Rodney King case centered on Black/White relations, while in the L.A. riots the principal antagonists were Blacks, Asians, and Latinos.

seventeen lived in families where their mother was the only parent. More than 37 percent of South Central's children were born to mothers who had never married. These rates were nearly twice the U.S. average (22 and 20 percent, respectively). And as the *Los Angeles Times* investigation of the riots found out, only a few of those arrested for riot-related felonies came from two-parent families and 89 percent were unmarried. The *New York Times* editorial writer, Bob Herbert, has captured the anarchy- and fear-producing effects of this social environment – clearly persisting at the time this book was written. Herbert found data showing that from the early 1980s to the early 2000s neighborhood violence claimed approximately 10,000 young people in South Los Angeles (the name given to South Central L.A. after the 1992 riots for public relations' purposes). According to Reverend Leonard Jackson, president of the Los Angeles Council of Churches: "The young people have more of a chance dying here in South Central than in a military combat zone. To say that there's a climate of fear is understating it" (quoted in Herbert 2003).

Emergent Anarchy: Shifting Ethnic Balances

The demographic dynamics behind the L.A. riots was the centerpiece of a Bergesen and Herman study. Their findings lend impressive support for the ethnic succession hypothesis. The authors started by demonstrating that the ethnic balance in the Los Angeles area shifted decisively toward Latino population from 1980 to 1990. The share of Latinos in L.A. increased from 28 percent in 1980 to 40 percent in 1990, making Latinos the largest ethnic group in the area. The White population over the same period of time declined from 48 percent to 37 percent. Moreover, while the ethnic balance in L.A. County tipped in Latinos' favor, the proportion of African American population in L.A. declined from 17 to 13 percent. The Asian segment of the L.A. population increased meanwhile from 7 to 13 percent (Webster 1992: 36). Morrison and Lewis (1994: 23) also report that in the 1980s the Anglo population of L.A. County increased by 8 percent, whereas the Hispanic population grew by 62 percent and the Asian population by 110 percent. In contrast, the African American population of the county remained at about the same level, because "the magnitude of black net outmigration from the county was so substantial that it offset much of the black population's natural increase" (Morrison and Lewis 1994: 29). These ethnic trends were thus particularly unfavorable to the Black population in L.A. In 1980, African Americans were a sizeable third-largest group in the area. By 1990, African Americans not only became more outnumbered by the Latinos than they were in 1980, but they were about to be outnumbered by the Asians as well. Based on the complete records of the U.S. Censuses of the Population, Morrison and Lewis (1994: 28), by 1990 there were 992,974 Black residents and 954,485 residents categorized as Asian and Pacific Islanders. And if illegal immigration were to be taken into account, it is most likely that there were already fewer African Americans than Asians in the area by 1990.

Measuring ethnic transition, Bergesen and Herman estimated the rates of Latino and Asian in-migration and African American out-migration by census tract (neighborhood) throughout L.A. County from 1980 to 1990. They also obtained data on the percentages of Whites, Blacks, Asians, Latinos, and foreign-born for each neighborhood. Plotting the demographic data against riot fatalities, Bergesen and Herman showed that most fatalities occurred around the borderline separating a cluster of neighborhoods with a majority Latino population from neighborhoods with a majority Black population. Moreover, the largest cluster of fatalities was located within neighborhoods comprised of at least 40 percent African Americans and 40 percent Latinos – areas that one may consider "contact zones" or "contested areas" (Grimshaw 1960). The only other sizeable cluster of fatalities was in the Koreatown/Pico Union area north of the Latino–Black contact zone – neighborhoods where the rising Asian population could have conceivably raised the specter of ethnic succession among African Americans whose share in the population was much smaller than in adjacent neighborhoods. Showing that ethnic succession took precedence over ethnicity, Bergesen and Herman found that rates of Asian migration into South Central L.A. and Compton areas were not significantly related to riot fatalities – unlike the Koreatown/Pico Union area, where ethnic transition posed a conceivable threat.

Using difference-of-means tests, Bergesen and Herman compared ethnic demographics of neighborhoods that had a fatality with those that had no fatalities. For Los Angeles County as a whole, in census tracts with a riot fatality the percentage of African Americans declined about ten times more than in counties without a fatality (by 11.7 percent versus 1.2 percent, respectively). Neighborhoods where riot deaths occurred also had more than twice as high an increase in Latino/Hispanic population than neighborhoods where no riot deaths took place. The proportion of both Blacks and Latinos in "fatality tracts" was 20 percent higher than in "no-fatality neighborhoods" (Bergesen and Herman 1998: Table 2). Notably, this relationship between ethnic transition and violent deaths is straightforward for the group tipping into the top position (Latinos) and the group tipping into the bottom position (African Americans) in the demographic standings among the four major ethnic groups in L.A. The situation was different in the Koreatown/Pico Union area, but generally consistent with the logic of threat under ethnic succession. In that area, the percentage change from 1980 to 1990 for Blacks, foreign-born, Latinos, and Asians was approximately the same in neighborhoods with and without fatalities. However, fatalities were associated with a faster decline of the White population (by 13.7 percent in fatality neighborhoods versus by 9.6 percent in no-fatality neighborhoods) and with a larger overall percentage of Asians (21.2 percent in fatality neighborhoods versus 17.6 percent in no-fatality neighborhoods). These data associate riot violence with displacement of White residents (representing a group whose numbers "tipped" downward from first into second place by the 1990s) by Asian immigrants (representing a group whose numbers tipped upward from fourth into third place by 1990).

The course of the L.A. riots suggests, however, that the linkage between ethnic transition and interethnic violence was hardly straightforward. The reason why fatalities occurred consistently in mixed Black and Latino neighborhoods was not because Blacks and Latinos fought one another, but because they joined forces and lashed out at members of other ethnic groups, especially Koreans. In fact, according to the *Los Angeles Times* investigation (quoted in Morrison and Lewis 1994: 38), 51 percent of those arrested during the riots were classified as Hispanics and 43 percent of those convicted for riot-related felonies were classified as Latinos. The *Times* also noted that arrest and conviction data most likely underestimated Latino participation in the riots, because "some were turned over to immigration authorities and not processed through the courts." Additionally, their sample of police data excluded juveniles (ibid.).

Also noteworthy is the fact that the ethnic group that emerged as the main target of street violence was not increasing their presence in South Central L.A., where the most intense rioting took place. Asian immigrants did not threaten to physically displace the Blacks from their neighborhoods. While the fastest growing racial group countywide, the Asians did not settle permanently in South Central L.A. Instead, they were economic migrants or a trading minority – very much like Chinese migrants in the Russian Far East, except that in L.A. the Asians migrated across neighborhood borders and not interstate borders. As Morrison and Lewis (1994: 32–3) write, "Asians entered this territory [South Central L.A.] as shopkeepers – Korean and Filipino owners of the multitude of convenience stores who work on the premises stocking shelves and ringing up sales – but made their homes outside South Central's traditional boundaries. Some Japanese, Chinese, and Koreans live inside the northern boundary of South Central, but their numbers [were] not increasing."

The relationship between ethnic succession and interethnic violence therefore has to do with something other than head-on rivalry between groups whose numbers decline and neighboring groups whose numbers increase. Regarding the 1992 L.A. riots, Morrison and Lewis suggest that riot behavior emerged not necessarily from direct competition resulting from ethnic succession, but from the overall sense of insecurity, uncertainty, frustration, tension, and lawlessness arising from shifting ethnic balance. In other words, ethnic transition mattered not directly and mechanically in its own right, but because it contributed to the overall sense of emergent anarchy. In South Central L.A., Black–Latino ethnic tensions emerged throughout the 1980s, even though they did not receive as much media attention as Black–Latino rivalry for political power and patronage jobs (Morrison and Lewis 1994: 32). The record of riot violence in L.A. suggests that rather than leading to clashes between two groups experiencing ethnic tension, a breakdown of government authority could give both groups the incentive and the opportunity to release these tensions by lashing out against a third group. Moreover, the two violence-initiating groups do not necessarily have to nurse common grievances against the groups they both attack – as long as both initiator groups defy government authority. As Morrison and Lewis (1994: 38) concluded, "Hispanics did not particularly share the black grievances but may have lacked allegiance to the established order."

This observation about the different nature of grievances among Blacks and Hispanics – as well as the combination of demographic trends and socioeconomic conditions by census tract in L.A. – challenges Petersen's (2002) emotion-based explanation of ethnic violence. This is despite the fact that Petersen's theory is designed explicitly and specifically to explain which groups become major targets of violence in multiethnic settings. Analyzing cases of interethnic violence in twentieth-century Eastern Europe, Petersen concluded that the strongest emotional factor explaining ethnic targeting was "resentment" – an emotion combining "the feeling that status relations are unjust with the belief that something can be done about it" (ibid.: 256). The most likely targets of ethnic violence would then be groups that are (a) "perceived as farthest up the ethnic status hierarchy," and (b) "can be subordinated through ethnic/national violence" (ibid.) At the same time, Petersen noted, the emotional thrust generated by resentment would be only likely to lead to violence if the dominant group is rapidly dislodged from its privileged position (e.g., top government jobs change hands in favor of lower-status groups), if differences in group status are large, if perceptions change rapidly, and if the status hierarchy is "clearly established." With respect to social conditions in 1992 L.A., hardly any of these criteria applied – no group was rapidly dislodged from its position (at least in the sense that there was no major reshuffling of government appointments or dramatic shifts in overt or covert ethnic-based hiring practices); some perceived differences in group status were present, but overall groups that were smaller than others were not underrepresented in key position by several orders of magnitude, as in the twentieth-century East European cases; political and socioeconomic group status was not rapidly changing; and the ethnic-based status hierarchy overall was opaque. Moreover, groups with different level of grievances about their socioeconomic conditions – the Blacks and Hispanics – participated about equally in attacks on Koreans. Finally, if we consider group size as a factor or as a putative indicator of potential status hierarchies, then nonviolence cooperation should have been a more likely outcome of the L.A. crisis over the Rodney King verdict: The numerical status of Blacks and Asians was approximately equal, with each group at 13 percent of the county population; and most violence occurred within or at the juncture of neighborhoods with approximately equal numerical status (about 40 percent) of Blacks and Hispanics.

Offensive Advantage and Intent Credibility

A major implication of perceived anarchy from the security-dilemma standpoint – even though Bergesen and Herman do not examine it – is that the rising uncertainty and suspicion would prompt the incumbent group (African Americans in the majority Black neighborhoods of L.A.) to ascribe hostile intent to out-groups. With the increasing sense of authority breakdown, the urge to strike preemptively at these out-groups would be likely to spiral out of control. Bergesen and Herman's analysis provides strong circumstantial evidence consistent with the security dilemma's core logic linking capabilities and intentions of any opposite "others." By analogy with the logic of escalating arms races that nobody wants when each side sees the other as increasing offensive rather than defensive capabilities, higher rates of ethnic balance shifting in favor of migrant groups would give rise to more hostile intent ascribed to migrants. This logic mirrors that of the hyperethnic succession theory in that, according to Bergesen and Herman (1998: 47), "it is not just the changing proportion of racial/ethnic groups, but the rate of change in relative group sizes that triggers racial violence."

Using logistical regression analysis, Bergesen and Herman found that the rate of both Black population decline and foreign-born population increase in L.A. County from 1980 to 1990 was a statistically significant predictor of fatalities in the 1992 riots. "The more rapid the change the more likely the fatalities," concluded Bergesen and Herman (ibid.), even when "control variables for economic deprivation [unemployment and income – author] and the relative size of the black and foreign-born populations are in the equation."

But suspicion about intentions of ethnic others has to do not only with uncertainties arising from ethnic succession. As the Primorskii case suggests, the history of intergroup relations shapes reputations of outgroups. These reputations play an independent role in intent assessment. In the 1980s and early 1990s, the Korean traders in South Central Los Angeles acquired a reputation among local African Americans for "low inventory, poor selection, and high prices" – combined with a reputation for unwarranted and disproportionate violence toward Black customers. Two killings of African American customers in South Central L.A. by Korean American merchants in 1991 played a critical part in the emergence of this reputation for violence. In March 1991, a shopkeeper of Korean origin, Soon Ja Do, shot and killed Latasha Harlins, a thirteen-year-old African American girl, following an argument about payment for a container of orange juice. In June 1991, a Korean American merchant at John's Liquor Store shot and killed an African American customer, Lee Arthur Mitchell (Freer 1994: 188). Around 1990, the shooting of Black customers by Korean merchants also took place in Brooklyn, New York; Atlanta; Baltimore; Washington, DC; and Philadelphia (Freer 1994: 177). In L.A., responding to the shootings, African American community leaders organized boycotts of a number of Korean American–owned shops. As Freer (1994: 175) describes it: "Tensions flared on all sides of the conflict; one such boycott lasted for more than 90 days, eventually shutting down the store." These developments contributed to widespread perceptions among the Black community that ethnic Koreans had a general lack of respect for African Americans. In other words, by the early 1990s Koreans developed a reputation among African Americans for abusive behavior toward Blacks.

Offensive "Groupness"

Whereas Bergesen and Herman did not include measures of perceived group distinctiveness among Blacks, Whites, Latinos, and Asians in Los Angeles before the riots, the overall demographic pattern of fatalities shows a distinct interethnic character of violence. The general implication is that group distinctiveness matters, although under conditions of increasing anarchy the finer nuances of interethnic stereotypes – including the ones used in the analysis of the Primorskii 2000 and Eurobarometer 1997 data – become less significant. In the end, it indeed remains unexamined whether those African Americans who held more-entrenched ethnic stereotypes against Latinos and Asians were, in fact, more likely to take part in violent street action in the streets of L.A. than those who held more-benign interethnic views. And yet, the occurrence of the riots along L.A.'s ethnic divides suggests that the negative intergroup sentiments most likely crossed a certain threshold in public opinion – even though such sentiments would have been insufficient in their own right to spark riot behavior.

Freer (1994) noted that perceived cultural differences and ethnic stereotypes – especially between the Blacks and Koreans – have been a major contributor to interethnic hostility and riot behavior. African Americans, for example, complained about poor English-language skills of first-generation Korean American merchants – as illustrated by an angry behavior of a Black customer shopping at a Korean-owned store in Spike Lee's movie "Do the Right Thing." Frustrated by the store owner's inability to understand how many Energizer D batteries he wanted to buy, the customer opens a barrage of verbal abuse, firing a twelve-letter expletive that starts with an "M" and ends with an "R."

The clash of ethnic stereotypes was also captured in a hit song called "Black Korea" (1991) by L.A.-based rapper Ice Cube. In this xenophobia-drenched song, the Black protagonist goes to an Asian American–owned store and describes the two merchants as "oriental one-penny countin' motherf****rs" (complete lyrics are available at http://www.lyricsdomain.com). This ascription of extreme stinginess to the Asian shopkeepers immediately punctuates a cultural and behavioral chasm between them and the Black protagonist. The Asians in the song come through as incapable of bridging this chasm and treating Blacks with respect – and this incapacity is viewed as a damning, rotten quality the Asians possess as a group. The lyrics are noteworthy, however, not just for the sheer rage of anti-Korean expletives, but mostly for the fact that what I defined as hostility in this study – proclivity for aggressive responding – is explicitly wedded to the graphic descriptions of offensive "groupness" of Koreans. This is when the singer threatens the Korean shopkeepers with a nationwide boycott and with burning their stores "down to a crisp" – unless they show respect to Black Americans.

From the Korean American perspective, cultural distance and group stereotypes were also major sources of interethnic tensions and hostility. According to the former executive director of the Korean American Grocers Association, Annie Cho, "Newly arriving immigrants need to be educated about American customs... something as trivial as looking a person in the eye. In Korea to look someone in the eye you are accusing them of something. So to be polite you don't do that. They are trying to be polite in their own way, but in this country that is not what American culture dictates" (quoted in Freer 1994: 190). Yet, more was at play than mismatching behavioral patterns. On the Korean side, too, stereotyping of African Americans – creating the incentives for Koreans to distance themselves from Blacks as a group – had been conditioned by the media and popular culture both in Korea and in the United States. According to Edward Chang (1990: 167), a specialist on ethnic politics and the American Korean community at the University of California, Riverside: "... many Korean immigrants are exposed to American values and culture and thus may come [to the United States] with negative images of blacks. They have learned and accepted the stereotypes of blacks as criminals, welfare recipients, drug addicts, and/or lazy through American movies, T.V. shows, and American Forces Korea Network (AFKN) programs" (quoted in Freer 1994: 191–2).

These vignettes by no means prove that individuals who perceived group differences more intensely than others rioted in larger numbers and/or more actively. Yet, they do suggest that perceptions of intergroup distinctiveness were part of the social context in which the riots erupted. Examining the preriot history of Korean–African American relations, Freer (1994: 182) concluded: "Cultural and racial differences... play a significant role in the creation of 'other.' This 'otherness,' is a critical variable in explaining just how it is that two relatively, but not identically, resource-poor groups can come to view their differences as being more important than their similarities."

Socioeconomic Impact: At the Intersection of Blocked Opportunities

Bergesen and Herman paid careful attention to economic indicators traditionally associated with a sense of heightened vulnerability to economic competition: median household income and unemployment rates from 1980 to 1990. A cursory look at the aggregate data for L.A. County would, in fact, suggest that unemployment and income were at least as plausible predictors of riot violence as ethnic composition and overlap across census tracts. Of the fifty-one riot fatalities, only ten took place in neighborhoods where the median household income in 1990 was above the county average and the unemployment rate was below the county average. Most fatalities took place in neighborhoods where median household income was about half of the county average and where unemployment rates were 1.5 to 2 times as high as the county average. The difference-of-means tests reported by Bergesen and Herman told the same story: For Los Angeles County, neighborhoods with riot fatalities had a mean household income of $21,800 and mean unemployment rate of 13.6 percent compared to $39,080 and 7.3 percent in neighborhoods without a fatality.

However, when Bergesen and Herman held constant the levels of interethnic contact[9] as well as the proportion of Black, Mexican, non-Mexican Hispanic, Asian, and foreign-born in each census tract, they found that fatality patterns had no significant relationship with proportion unemployed and median household income by neighborhood. In other words, in neighborhoods with similar ethnic balances and levels of interethnic contact, variation in unemployment and income rates had no systematic effect on fatality incidence. This finding held for Los Angeles County in general as well as for the South Central L.A./Compton and Koreatown/Pico Union areas in particular (Bergesen and Herman 1998: Table 5).

These results do not necessarily suggest that economic trends and perceptions have little to do with riot-proneness. They do suggest that variation in socioeconomic conditions does not automatically produce equivalent variation in the intensity of grievances, frustration, and proclivity for aggression. Yet, interviews and anecdotal evidence show that – similar to the effects of ethnic balance shifts – socioeconomic conditions in migrant-receiving areas most likely affected proclivities for aggressive responding to newcomers indirectly, by contributing to the general sense of scarcity, mistrust of authorities, social alienation, and uncertainty about the future. In short, socioeconomic impact perceptions mattered because they enhanced insecurity-proneness. Annie Cho pointed out precisely these perceptions when explaining the socioeconomic background of the 1992 L.A. riots: "[T]he economy has been very bad, people are losing jobs, there's a threat of welfare cuts, people are worried about being evicted because they can't pay their rent, so people are

[9] Bergesen and Herman estimated interethnic contact by multiplying population percentages of the two largest ethnic groups in each neighborhood. The closer the percentage of each of these groups to fifty, the larger the value of this measure.

very edgy and their tolerance level has become very low" (Freer 1994: 190).

Importantly, the Black-Latino-Korean conflict in L.A. involved three communities with the most acute sense of blocked opportunities. The reduction of approximately 75,000 relatively well-paying manufacturing jobs in Los Angeles during the 1970s hit the African Americans and Latinos harder than other ethnic groups, because the majority of plant closures took place in predominantly African American and Latino communities (Johnson and Oliver 1989). Steep property price increases in the L.A. area during the 1970s also blocked opportunities for these groups to relocate to more economically developed towns and counties. Among the Korean immigrants, who were mostly middle class and college educated, the sense of blocked opportunity stemmed from laws excluding immigrants from taking professional qualifying exams and English proficiency tests and from limited capital availability for business investment. More than half of Korean immigrants were estimated to bring in assets valued from $60,000 to $250,000 – amounts sufficient to open businesses in economically depressed areas such as South Central L.A., but not in more prosperous and predominantly White L.A. neighborhoods (Freer 1994: 181–2). These general contextual factors were likely to make residents feel negatively about the socioeconomic effect of trade and business across ethnic lines. Blacks and Latinos could blame Korean merchants for bringing in limited, low-quality merchandise at high prices, thus contributing to a depressed lifestyle. Koreans blamed Blacks in particular for failing to work hard and to get themselves off welfare, thus restricting consumer capacity in neighborhoods where Koreans opened businesses.

Conclusion: Insecurity – the Critical Multiplier

Research in the United States on the effects of desegregation and immigration on interethnic hostility and violence has emphasized the logics of interests (socioeconomic and political niche competition), identity (ethnocultural distinctiveness), and ethnic succession (threat to group position). In what way does the security-dilemma approach add value to these explanations?

Overall, the security-dilemma perspective incorporates the logic of ethnic succession, but in addition it emphasizes the role of uncertainty and vulnerability in exaggerating socioeconomic and cultural threats. While recognizing the destabilizing potential of ethnic transitions in their own right, the security-dilemma theory would account for the absence of conflict even when ethnic balances change rapidly. It would also account for hostility and conflict when actual demographic changes are slow and small. The security-dilemma logic is more attuned to *perceptions* of ethnic balance and to the fact that such perceptions would be affected by the public's sense of central authority, by context-specific histories of intergroup relations, by intergroup distinctiveness, by socioeconomic effects of migration, by individual sensitivities to majority–minority status reversal, and by the priming effects of political discourses in the media. From the security-dilemma standpoint, it is not necessarily knowledge that the population balance is likely to change in favor of ethnic others, but suspicion that prospective population changes may lead to majority–minority status reversal that would relate significantly to threat and hostility. Vulnerability to socioeconomic and cultural implications of prospective majority–minority status reversal would further enhance insecurity and proclivity for hostile responding.

For example, in the middle of the twentieth century the number of African Americans in the fourteen largest cities in the United States (those with a population over 1 million) increased much faster than the number of European Americans. From 1940 to 1950, the total White population in these cities grew by about 4 percent, whereas the total Black population grew by 68 percent (Grodzins 1957: 33). In other words, Black populations' rate of increase was more than sixteen times higher than that of the White population. Moreover, ethnic transition or ethnic "tipping" affected thousands of urban neighborhoods (Grodzins 1957). However, for the 1950s – when ethnic tipping was happening on a mass scale – Gottesman and Brown (1999, Chronology) in the *Encyclopedia of Violence in America* record no equivalent of the 1992 L.A. riots or the "long hot summer" of 1967, when racial violence erupted in 150 U.S. cities. At the same time, as Bergesen and Herman noted, the riots that broke out in the 1960s were predominantly "political protest against economic conditions and a struggle to gain political power" rather than a backlash response to ethnic succession. The discrete logic of insecurity, however, would suggest an explanation both for the absence of "long hot summers" in response to Black–White neighborhood tipping in the 1950s and the eruption of interracial violence in the 1960s. The crucial point to be made about the former is that by moving out to the suburbs and by simultaneously imposing effective restrictions against outsiders, the White population reduced insecurity arising from large-scale ethnic balance shifts in urban settings. The Whites essentially followed the strategy of ethnic partition by resegregating themselves in the suburbs. Grodzins

(1957: 33–4), in fact, provides a compelling explanation of what, from the security-dilemma standpoint, would be a major anarchy-reducing factor for the incumbent group:

> . . . the suburban towns have employed restrictive zoning, subdivision and building regulations to keep Negroes out. Some, for example, have set a minimum of two or more acres for a house site, or required expensive street improvements, and have enforced these regulations against "undesirable" developments but waived them for "desirable" ones. A builder in a Philadelphia suburb recently told an interviewer that he would like to sell houses to Negroes, but the town officials would ruin him. He explained: "The building inspectors would have me moving pipes three eighths of an inch every afternoon in every one of the places I was building – and moving a pipe three eighths of an inch is mighty expensive if you have to do it in concrete!"

The deep-seated racial and socioeconomic problems in American cities, however, have not been resolved – but rather enhanced – by White flight. Their persistence suggests that ethnic resegregation is not a good social policy, although it does improve perceived security of the incumbent ethnic group in the short term.

Regarding the 1960s riots, the insecurity logic would prompt one to reexamine the pattern of fatalities – something that Bergesen (1982) analyzed systematically for Newark and Detroit. Bergesen's analysis of police-instigated violence against Blacks – which resulted in the majority of fatalities during the riots – generally concurred with the findings of the National Advisory Commission on Civil Disorders (1968: 335) that "in their anxiety to control disorders, some law enforcement agencies may resort to indiscriminate, repressive use of force against wholly innocent elements of the Negro community" (quoted in Bergesen 1982: 262). The "anxiety to control disorders" leading to indiscriminate use of force corresponds exactly to the security dilemma. The pattern of indiscriminate "lashing-out" by police in Detroit and Newark, according to Bergesen, appears to happen in response to emergent anarchy exemplified by looting. At first, the police lashed out against those looters who had already looted (71 percent of the looters killed by the police were fleeing the premises). After that, police switched to shooting at cars and crowds, mostly at random, killing individuals who were not engaged in criminal activities. Police also randomly strafed apartment houses, something that according to Bergesen (1982: 273) "only resulted in killing women and children within their homes." Moreover, official violence was out of sync with civilian violence. In the 1968 Detroit riots, for example, after the first two days nineteen deaths were instigated by law-enforcement officials and only two were a result of civilian accidental violence (ibid.). This civilian-riot-versus-police-counterriot pattern of violence is consistent with the dynamic aspect of the security dilemma: At the onset of social disorder, fear that protesters would become uncontrollable would urge law enforcement agencies to respond with indiscriminate and disproportionate violence, but it also would urge protesters to act aggressively while the crowds are still around and before law enforcement would block them, split them, or disperse them.

In the security-dilemma searchlight, one also discovers the lack of national surveys on immigration attitudes in the United States that would capture in one questionnaire the respondents' assessment of government capacity to maintain law and order; ethnic balance trends; and, especially, their support for hostile and violent responses to migration. Given the long and bloody record of interethnic and antiimmigrant violence in America, it is counterintuitive that no opinion survey comprehensively evaluating these perceptions has been conducted in the United States to the best knowledge of this author. If this chapter prompts the emergence of such a study, the application of the security-dilemma perspective to immigration studies would have paid off regardless of the validity of other insights discussed in this book.

7

Immigration and Security

How Worst-Case Scenarios Become Self-Fulfilling and What We Can Do About It

As I started to write the conclusion to this book, I noticed that one of my colleagues down the hall in our office building at San Diego State University had a cartoon on her door that succinctly illustrated where immigration phobia may take us if it comes to inform public policy on immigration. The publication date was cut out, but it was clearly done some time after the September 11, 2001 terrorist attacks on the United States. Originally published in *The Miami Herald*, this syndicated cartoon warned that overreaction to post-9/11 threats could reverse the very identity of the United States as a nation of immigrants. In the artist's grim portrayal, the Statue of Liberty had a new inscription, asking the world to give America not the "huddled masses," but metal detectors, frisks, illegal searches, I.D. spot checks, and the "scared people yearning to feel safe." Somehow, after conducting years of comparative research on antiimmigrant hostility I could not dismiss this unflattering dystopia as an artist's fantasy. This chapter scans broader and more nuanced policy implications of immigration phobia, but the concerns that this analysis raises resonate profoundly with the one raised in the Statue of Liberty cartoon. Specifically, it focuses on four major issues: (1) the distinct role of the core security-dilemma perceptions (emergent anarchy and intent offensiveness) in the formation of antimigrant hostility; (2) the added value of the security-dilemma perspective with respect to major existing theories of interethnic conflict; (3) implications of this study for research on early warning and prevention of ethnopolitical conflict; and (4) immigration policy implications.

In Their Own Right: The Discrete Effects of Perceived Anarchy and Migrant Intentions

This project was the first one that used statistical analysis of large-N opinion data to test the perceptual logic of the security dilemma with respect to antimigrant hostility. The findings indicate that migration gives rise to exaggerated threats and hostility when it makes different groups of people proximate and "suddenly . . . responsible for their own security" (Posen 1993: 103). The emphasis on anticipation of emergent anarchy and, as a consequence, on uncertainty about the intentions of ethnic "others" is precisely where the security-dilemma perspective adds value to research on interethnic relations. Previous survey-based analyses of immigration attitudes and interethnic hostility did not include these perceptions.

In the statistical tests of the Primorskii and Eurobarometer data, measures of perceived anarchy and intent offensiveness accounted for between one-third and one-half of the variation in threat and antimigrant hostility that was explained by the security-dilemma model as a whole.[1] These measures were based on survey respondents' perceptions of the strength of government capacity, ethnic balance trends, and migrant intentions. The following findings show that these perceptions came out as prominent threads in the fabric of immigration phobia:

- Perceptions of the Russian government's capacity to resolve interethnic disputes and of Primorskii's isolation from central Russia were statistically significant predictors of a perceived threat of armed interstate conflict between Russia and China.
- Perception of government weakness in the EU member states was significantly related to support for wholesale deportation of all immigrants and their children.
- Perceived size of migrant minorities in host states had statistically significant effects on threat perception and antimigrant hostility in both Primorskii krai and the EU.[2] Moreover, for threat perception, the statistical effects in these two cases were similarly strong despite a wide variation in the *actual* rates of in-migration between the Russian Far East and the EU as well as across the EU member states.

[1] This estimate is easy to make comparing the value of Adjusted R^2 for Model 2 in Tables A.1–A.3 and B.1–B.2.

[2] In both cases, these effects were mediated by respondents' sensitivity to changes in minority group size.

- In the Primorskii 2000 survey, respondents' suspicion that the Chinese nursed territorial claims on Russia was a significant and most consistent predictor of threat and hostility. This finding suggests that migration has the potential to reanimate histories of territorial disputes between the migrant-sending and migrant-receiving states. In the case of the Russian Far East, this history included mixed patterns of settlement, wholesale Russification of Chinese place names, and fierce armed border clashes. Also contributing to "offensive" reputation of migrants were stories about the Chinese guest workers saying, "[W]e are building these things for ourselves;" stories about Chinese maps interpreting the Russian settlement in the Far East as the "ripping away" of historically Chinese territories; and stories of Mao declaring the Arctic Ocean as China's northern frontier.
- In the EU, respondents felt more insecure about immigrants if they disagreed with the statement that not all members of minority groups intended to integrate into the host country. This finding is seemingly counterintuitive, and it contradicts reports about increasing pressure on immigrants across the EU to assimilate or integrate into host societies (e.g., *The Economist*, May 17, 2003). It is consistent, however, with the simultaneous increase in public demands among Europeans – arising from projections of demographic trends into the future – to toughen border controls and immigration restrictions. The statistical analysis indicates that respondents associated "intent to integrate" with increasing probability that more outsiders intended to come and stay in their countries, rather than with proclivity of immigrants already settled in their countries to internalize the norms and values of host societies. This explanation of the EU finding on assimilation preferences also explains one paradoxical result in the Russian Far East. In the Primorskii 2000 survey, the majority of respondents favored Chinese cultural centers and increasing teaching of Chinese language in local schools and university, but at the same time they wanted to ban or never allow Chinese-language media and Chinatowns. This dichotomous position on Chinese culture, however, is understandable considering that cultural centers and language learning are not associated with the emergence of migrant settler communities ("truncated nations," "nested minorities," "fifth columns") to anywhere near the same extent as Chinese media and Chinatowns. These findings suggest that assessment of migrants' intentions to settle and pose threats had a systematic effect on perception of the desirability of cultural integration of migrants within host states. In a way, this finding could be

> characterized as the "assimilation and the security dilemma" placing migrants in a no-win situation: If migrants make attempts to assimilate in local communities, the natives may interpret their efforts as an attempt to gain power and influence at their expense (as the realistic-threat theories would predict). But if migrants refrain from these efforts, they may be seen as intransigent, distant, and disloyal (as the symbolic-threat theories would predict).

In addition, a review of statistical data on demographic and socioeconomic conditions in Los Angeles at the time of 1992 riots (Bergesen and Herman 1998; Morrison and Lewis 1994) shows that the pattern of fatalities was consistent with the logic of the interethnic security dilemma. On the one hand, most deadly violence occurred in mixed Black–Hispanic neighborhoods or at the juncture of predominantly Black and predominantly Hispanic neighborhoods, suggesting that ethnic transition set the stage for the disturbances. On the other hand, the Black rioters lashed out not at Hispanics whose arrival threatened to displace African Americans as the incumbent majority group in areas such as South Central L.A., but at Korean merchants who had a particularly strong reputation among Blacks for hostile intentions toward them. These developments indicate that in ethnic transitions involving several groups, perceived intent offensiveness is likely to be a major ingredient in explaining which of the groups would come under attack.

Identity, Interests, and the Insecurity Multiplier

The logic of insecurity, however, does not play out in isolation from interests and identity concerns among the host populations and the migrants. The logic of insecurity works through and interacts with the logics of identity and interests in the formation of threat and antimigrant hostility. The empirical findings from the Primorskii and Eurobarometer studies and the 1992 L.A. riots case are by no means conclusive in this regard, yet they do yield some insights that are worth exploring further. These insights also speak directly to major existing theories of interethnic relations and spotlight their contributions and limitations in explaining varying threat perceptions and antimigrant hostility.

Prejudice as Perceived Threat to Group Position

The results in Primorskii 2000 and Eurobarometer 1997 surveys indicate that a sense of group position is a strong component of the security-dilemma logic. In the Russian Far East, respondents who felt Russia would lose sovereignty over Primorskii krai if local population were one-quarter Chinese were more likely to support paramilitary anti-immigrant groups than respondents who felt Russia would not lose sovereignty over Primorskii unless the proportion of the Chinese reached at least one-third. Generally, respondents who associated the smaller proportion of prospective Chinese residents with potential loss of Russian sovereignty were more likely than others to hold more intense antimigrant policy preferences. In the EU, a sense that minority group size had "reached its limit" (whatever that limit was in the mind of each respondent) related significantly to insecurity about minorities and support for deportation of all immigrants. Yet, these findings also suggest that in the context of uncertainty and mistrust of migrant intentions – as has markedly been the case in Primorskii – the actual shifts in population size matter less than prospective valuations that may have little or nothing to do with actual migration trends. Even though the actual size of Chinese migration has been rather marginal (estimated at between 1 and 3 percent of the Russian Far East population around 2000–2), hostility against migrants has been more intense than in the EU where immigration happened on a larger scale and literally changed the face of public schools, stores, factories, and soccer teams.

The important difference between the Russian Far East and the EU, however, is that in the former the incumbent ethnic group's decline due to decreasing fertility, increasing mortality, and rising internal out-migration has been considerably more pronounced. Thus, perhaps one insight of the security dilemma is that a strong sense of threat to group position is likely to arise among ethnic incumbents not necessarily when demographic trends suggest that a tipping point in group hierarchies may be fast approaching, but when the size of the incumbent group begins to decline rapidly, increasing sensitivity to even small incursions of ethnic others. This would be especially the case when the sending state has a larger population than the receiving state – in this case, a sense of threat to group position among host populations would be likely to arise even if only a small proportion of migrants expressed any desire to settle in the host country. And as the security-dilemma logic suggests, under these circumstances no amount of claims by migrants about the nature of their intentions would appear credible to the incumbent groups.

In the United States, one implication of the quantitative analysis of demographic and economic conditions in the pattern of fatalities during the 1992 Los Angeles riots is that the logic of anarchy is a powerful catalyst of the "wounded" sense of group position. In a way, anarchy is about the disappearance of credible guarantees that the incumbent group's claim "to certain areas of privilege and advantage" (Blumer 1958: 4) will be upheld. As the Primorskii results show, even a distant and vague anticipation of swamping by migrants is likely to activate a sense of insecurity. And the same findings indicate that when individuals in a host society feel the balance is likely to tip in favor of the out-group, the sense of threat translates into heightened proclivity for aggressive backlashes against migrants. Yet, as the 1992 L.A. case suggests – albeit indirectly – the sense of government failure to protect the incumbent group position is a crucial factor in turning hostility into actual violence. After all, predominantly Black neighborhoods of Los Angeles in the 1980s and 1990s were not the only ones in the United States that bordered on neighborhoods with increasingly predominant Latino and Asian population. Nor was L.A. the only city with a cluster of "ethnic contact zones" in neighborhoods where the proportion of two predominant ethnic groups was about 40 percent each. Yet, mass interethnic violence erupted nowhere else in the United States in the late 1980s or early 1990s. The Rodney King verdict, the unresponsiveness of law enforcement agencies, and the decline of family authority in ethnically mixed neighborhoods had socially destabilizing (anarchy-producing) effects that made the crucial difference.

Social Categorization and Group Identity

The analysis of Primorskii 2000 and Eurobarometer 1997 surveys provides evidence that perception of intergroup difference is a major ingredient of immigration phobia. Perception of Russian–Chinese differences (based on factor analysis of intergroup stereotypes) were by far the strongest predictor of the perceived Chinese migration threat to Russia and Primorskii krai, as well as of armed conflict threat by 2010. In the EU, a belief that newcomer minorities were too different to be fully accepted as members by host societies was by far stronger than other perceptions related to respondents' support for wholesale repatriation of immigrants. The same belief was among the strongest predictors of threat perception in the EU. The only dependent variable that was not significantly associated with perceived group differences was support for antimigrant politicians and paramilitaries in Primorskii. These results show that insecurity is indeed associated with social categorization.

Moreover, in both Primorskii and the EU, threat and antimigrant hostility related more strongly to perceived group differences than to assessment of migrants' capacity to assimilation in host societies. This finding corroborates the results of psychological experiments (as in Dovidio and Gaetner 1998) suggesting that there's a relationship between perceived group distance and a sense of out-group cohesiveness. The greater the sense of group distance, the greater the sense that the "other" is a tightly knit, homogeneous entity – thus threatening to overwhelm the in-group that would, by contrast, appear to be more fragmented than it is in reality.

This study adds value to the social categorization theory, however, by suggesting why out-groups perceived as having intent to integrate or assimilate with the in-group may be perceived as more threatening than out-groups perceived as remaining distant, homogeneous, and inscrutable. To go back to the Eurobarometer study, respondents who believed migrant minorities had intent to integrate in host societies were more supportive of deportation. This finding contradicts the logic of social categorization, but not of the security dilemma. From the security-dilemma standpoint, incumbent groups would consider that if migrants intended to integrate into host states they, by definition, would be there to stay, and, hence, their claim on the host state's resources, territory, and even sovereignty would be more likely. This perception is broadly consistent with retaliatory logic under emergent anarchy and rising fears of the ethnic balance tipping in favor of the newcomers – "[I]f so many of them want to come and stay, we want to send them back."

The security-dilemma perspective in this respect has an insight for comparative immigration studies that the social categorization theory would not provide. Namely, it suggests that host populations are likely to welcome the intent to assimilate on the part of resident immigrant minorities, but oppose such an intent on the part of transient minorities, such as migrant workers, or on the part of prospective immigrant minorities. Thus, the security-dilemma perspective explains why increasing public support for cultural integration of immigrants in EU member states coincided with increasing public support for tighter border controls and restrictions on the entry and settlement of the new arrivals.

Ethnic (Labor Market) Competition

One of the intuitive explanations of antimigrant hostility has to do with competition between incumbent and newcomer groups for jobs, incomes, housing and other socioeconomic and even "symbolic" niches.[3] This

[3] Susan Olzak who developed the ethnic competition theory does argue that competition is not necessarily confined to economic issues, but could also revolve around symbolic valuables. However, in her research Olzak (1992 and elsewhere) focuses predominantly on employment, income, and housing competition. While admittedly, the latter would

study's findings suggest that the logic of socioeconomic competition is an important correlate of interethnic fears and hostility. However, the study also finds that the competitive logic reveals itself not so much through obsession with economic gains of one's group relative to other groups and not even so much through the sense of "realistic threats" to individual socioeconomic conditions, but through the sense of out-groups' socioeconomic impact on one's in-group. Comparison of Russian and Chinese economic gains, personal income, and the sense of unemployment risk among respondents, as well as the respondents' occupation as manual workers had no significant relationship with most measures of threat and antimigrant hostility in this study.[4] In contrast, perception of socioeconomic effects of migration – on jobs, income, and crime in Primorskii and on social benefits, education, and crime in the EU – had consistently strong and significant relationship with threat and hostility.

Looking more closely at the survey questions, the findings suggest that socioeconomic impact perceptions represent the combined effects of relative and absolute gains' valuations. In psychological terms, one may also interpret these perceptions as reflecting individual group member proclivity to maximize both intergroup differences and in-group gains. This is particularly evident regarding the estimated effects of migration on jobs and income opportunities. If these opportunities are perceived as worsening, it implies that competitive pressures are likely to rise – or at least respondents would be more sensitive to the prospect of competition with migrants in the future. Conversely, if job and income opportunities appear to the natives as improving as a result of migration, competitive pressures would matter less. In general, the study suggests economic valuations are likely to affect threat perception not only through the sense of head-on competition between incumbent and newcomer groups, but largely through the overall sense of opportunity among groups. From the security-dilemma standpoint, migration would be more threatening if it raised the sense of uncertainty about one's group's economic opportunities. This uncertainty would increase vulnerability to competition, but it is not something that would necessarily arise out of actual competition for jobs. Thus, in Primorskii krai stories about 4,000 Chinese migrant workers near Pogranichnyi raised fears of imminent Chinese takeover,

have symbolic value in addition to material benefits, the exact role of symbolic factors is hard to isolate using these variables.

4 In the EU, higher personal income and perception that life was improving had a significant relationship with support for deportation – although the relationship was weaker than for most other significant predictors.

yet, when offered, few local Russians wanted to take those 4,000 jobs (Nazdratenko 1999: 21).

In the 1992 L.A. case, the similarity of socioeconomic characteristics between the two largest groups, incumbent Blacks and immigrant Latinos, suggested that racial violence would likely erupt between the two out of competition for low-skill employment. Instead, both groups directed riot violence predominantly against the Korean merchants, who did not compete with either of them for low-skilled manual jobs. In fact, by lashing out at Korean merchants, the young male Blacks and Hispanics were risking to reduce the pool of such jobs available to both groups.

In addition to these considerations, survey analyses also suggest that perceptions of government capacity are likely to relate to perceptions of socioeconomic impact of migration – embedding abstract notions about anarchy and government power in the concrete experiences of everyday life.

Implications for Research on Interethnic Conflict Prevention

Whereas this study has focused predominantly on hostility rather than actual conflict – and the distance between the two is still substantial even though they are interrelated – it has implications for research on early warning and prevention of ethnopolitical violence. The bulk of the early-warning research has been based on data usually aggregated by country (as in the Correlates of War and Minorities at Risk datasets) and on methods derived from event-data analysis[5] (see also Davies and Gurr 1998; Merritt, Muncaster, and Zinnes 1993). The country-level data approach focuses predominantly on long-range trends likely to result in deadly organized violence. The event-data approach seeks to identify short-term (1–3 months out) predictors of mass violent conflict that appear to take policy makers and analysts by surprise. One problem with the first approach is that it paints the picture with too broad a brush and by default provides no indication as to the probability that certain demographic and socioeconomic conditions at the country level would translate into behavioral patterns producing violence. The problem with the second approach is that by the time event-data would generate credible signals of

[5] For example, the Global Event-Data System (GEDS), the Kansas Event-Data Project (KEDS), CASCON, "Sino-Soviet Interaction: Project Triad, 1950–1967," the Conflict and Peace Data Bank (COPDAB), and the World Event/Interaction Survey (WEIS) are all available on the Internet.

impending violence, domestic actors are likely to be strongly committed to staying the course and international actors are unlikely to be able to mobilize for meaningful peacemaking intervention. The reluctance of the Clinton administration to intervene in the conflict in Rwanda despite first-hand evidence several months in advance that mass violence was imminent is one potent illustration of political constraints on early warning's efficacy.

Cognizant of these issues, this study was designed with more modest expectations. Three suggestions appear to be worth developing:

- Given the importance of ethnic transitions in the emergence of interethnic security-dilemma situations, it would be advisable to collect data on ethnic population trends at the country level and in major regions and/or cities within countries. So far, to the best knowledge of this author, data on ethnic transitions are not included in the Minorities at Risk and Correlates of War datasets and are not provided in statistical yearbooks of the United Nations Population Division. The data exist in multiple sources, but they need to be brought together so that implications of ethnic transitions can be studied systematically.
- Policymakers and NGOs could use reliable yet unobtrusive survey instruments to identify social contexts where the proclivity for hostile intergroup action is more likely than in others, where the probability of surprise is higher than in other contexts, yet where such probabilities are expressed not in abstract aggregate data or event counts, but in the voices of living, breathing human beings. Surveys offer the opportunity to develop medium-range assessments that are more context- and situation-specific than aggregate-data assessments, yet sufficiently early to give time for development and implementation of preventive measures.[6] The present study not only provides batteries of questions that are likely to generate assessments of antimigrant hostility in diverse environments, but it also offers some insight as to their effectiveness. Generally, questions about effects of migration on the ethnic balance and sensitivity to shifts in the ethnic balance; about migrants' intent; about group distinctiveness; and about migrants' impact on

[6] I do not assume that governments would actually want to prevent conflicts if they obtain credible signals that they are likely to happen. For this reason, the involvement of NGOs and international organizations is important, in case governments would deploy survey research not to prevent violent conflict, but rather to avoid investing in the necessary preventive measures and to keep it out of the public arena.

employment, income, education, and social services are likely to be the most potent, unobtrusive indicators of threat perception and antimigrant hostility. One is likely to find out more about individual antimigrant attitudes from these questions than from standard sociological variables, such as sex, age, income, education, religion, occupation, place of residence, or employment status of respondents.

The present study also revealed that controlling for the perceived migrant intent would require adding new questions to traditional surveys of immigration attitudes. In the United States, for example, no opinion survey covering immigration attitudes probes respondents' fear of something like "a Chicano Quebec in the Southwest" or asks about the capacity of police to enforce law and order in an equitable fashion. In the Eurobarometer survey, the question I used as a proxy for perceived government weakness was a general one asking whether lack of order was a major problem in their country. More revealing of fear and hostility toward immigrants, however, would be a question about the effects of European institutions on national sovereignty, especially the capacity to control and regulate the cross-border movement of people. At the same time, it appears that the question asking respondents to assess the proportion of migrant minority in the local population is likely to perform about the same as the simpler question on whether the level of immigration is too high, too low, or about acceptable.

The results of the Primorskii and EU studies also suggest indirectly that complex stereotypes and a sense of the "other's" capacity to assimilate with the in-group can be captured with a rather simple survey measure. Statistical results in Primorskii krai relied on factor analysis of Russian respondents' assessment of eleven "typical traits" of ethnic Russians and ethnic Chinese. The Eurobarometer questionnaire simply asked if respondents felt the minority groups were so different that they could never be fully accepted members of the host society. The significance and the strength of relationship between the Primorskii and the Eurobarometer measures of group differences and threat perception were about the same (standardized regression coefficients were .246 for general threat and .231 for armed conflict threat in the Primorskii study and .125 for threat and .229 for hostility in the Eurobarometer study).

- Those conducting policy-relevant research may consider using survey results in scenario-planning exercises to assess conflict-proneness in individual cases. For example, the question on the acceptable proportion of migrants in the host community could be checked against actual population trends and modal perceptions of the current percentage of migrants in the community to project rising tensions. Plotting perceptions of economic effects of migration against socioeconomic trends in migrant-receiving areas would enable informed guesstimates about the effects of these trends on antimigrant hostility. Using secondary survey or focus group data about recognition and interpretation in host communities of past interactions between the migrant-sending and -receiving states would give a clue about the likely nature of perceived offensiveness of migrant intentions from these states. Assembling data banks combining survey data from different parts of the world covering the same correlates of insecurity as this study would lay down the foundation for sophisticated and context-sensitive preventive monitoring and scenario planning, thus identifying prospective hot spots.

Comparative evaluation of factors that engendered interethnic violence in some cases, but not in others, can be used to assess the plausibility of violent conflict in situations where antimigrant hostility is high. For example, in drawing lessons from the present study one may ask: What conditions underlying the 1992 L.A. riots were missing in migration contexts in Primorskii and the EU? Such an analysis would suggest that despite stronger antimigrant sentiments than in California, large-scale anti-Chinese violence is unlikely to erupt in the Russian Far East in response to Chinese migration. Despite fiercely exaggerated estimates of Chinese presence, cross-border migration since the early 1990s failed to produce Chinese permanent settlements sizeable enough to translate into 40–40 mixed neighborhoods with the Russians. No county or neighborhood in Primorskii krai at the time of writing has over 50 percent permanent Chinese population. Sharp ethnic divides between and within neighborhoods have not emerged.

Even though this is a process worth monitoring, it is a kind of process that is likely to be slow and is unlikely to result in ethnic juxtapositions similar to those in L.A. Major Russian Far Eastern cities such as Vladivostok, Khabarovsk, Nakhdoka, or Ussuriisk are no match for the likes of Los Angeles, San Francisco, or Seattle as immigration magnets. Economic opportunities are too limited to attract and sustain hundreds of thousands of immigrants. Migrant labor legislation, contract law, and transparency combined with deep suspicions about China's territorial claims have so far precluded the development of projects – however utopian in design – that would attract mass Chinese migration.[7] This, as everything else, may change over time, but it is more likely to take decades, not years. Regarding Russia's government capacity, the current Russian president, Vladimir Putin, had vigorously pursued the policy of centralization of the Kremlin's authority ever since attaining power in 2000. This policy meant the revival of the Soviet-era type of support for military and law enforcement agencies. But above and beyond practical political considerations, an important distinction between the Russian Far East and the European and American contexts is that the Russian residents experienced not only decades of unrepresentative and increasingly corrupt Soviet rule, but also a major political transition *simultaneously* with the onset of sizeable migration from China. In this situation, it is hard to visualize a scenario where any court decision or political incident could trigger the same sense of betrayal and government failure as the Rodney King verdict did in Los Angeles. Most residents were already accustomed to government inadequacy.

Implications for Immigration Policy

The "ideal type" policy recommendation to reduce the interethnic security dilemma is separation and partition of ethnic groups, including provision of each group with its own government. As we have seen in this study, perceptions associating migration with the security dilemma – emergent anarchy, offensive intent, "groupness," and economic vulnerability – relate significantly to support for exclusionist or "partitionist" responses to migration. Whereas ethnic partition is unavoidable to stop ongoing violent conflicts between ethnic groups and to give them an opportunity to cool off, exclusionism is hardly a viable policy solution with respect to international migration and interethnic migration within states. The overwhelming majority of nation-states are already multiethnic and few governments have the interest or the power to stop interethnic migration entirely, especially within states. A preventive separation of ethnic groups in relatively peaceful settings may cause precisely the conflicts policymakers would seek to avoid. Moreover, as discussed at the beginning of this

[7] Even such projects as the East–West trans-Siberian oil and gas pipelines are not necessarily going to increase Chinese migrant settlement in Russia, because they create short-term, high-paid, and transient jobs rather than long-term "stationary" jobs, as do the manufacturing industries.

book, migration is part of the increasingly interdependent global economy and the emergence of transnational labor markets.

For migration, the security-dilemma approach instead warns against the temptation to implement excessive exclusionist policies and to "securitize" migration by seeking remedy in stricter border controls, tighter law enforcement, and reliance on the military. As this chapter was written, for example, the U.S. Department of Homeland Security proposed to use military surveillance drones such as the Global Hawk to monitor the U.S.–Mexican border (National Public Radio, June 16, 2003, 6:00 News PST). The security dilemma explains that the temptation to militarize immigration policy would arise regardless of the fact that most migrants have no intent to take over host societies, undermine them economically, create ethnic enclaves, or encourage social unrest and insurrection. Importantly, once this "securitizing" mind-set takes hold, assurances and pledges of innocence by migrants or migrant-sending states are unlikely to be trusted by the public and policymakers in migrant-receiving states.

Overcoming this type of mutual suspicion and mistrust is likely to be a difficult and protracted endeavor. Bilateral diplomacy is unlikely to yield quick, satisfactory results. This is illustrated at the time of writing by the ongoing stalemate on U.S.–Mexican dialogue concerning Mexican labor migration to the United States. On the one hand, the president of Mexico, Vicente Fox, has repeatedly made assurances that Mexican workers in the United States were "reliable people" and not a security threat (*Washington Post*, May 27, 2003: A10). While making concessions to Washington's heightened security concerns in the post-9/11 world, Fox appealed to reason: "It's understandable that the worry exists, but we must be pragmatic and objective in evaluating the situation: No terrorists have come from Mexico, and none has been a Mexican." Instead, Fox said, the overwhelming majority of Mexicans were driven to the United States by "a clear dream of work." Not only did these Mexicans contribute to economic prosperity in the United States – especially by supplying low-cost labor for hard-to-fill jobs – but also to America's security. "Many migrants participate in the U.S. Army, participate in the defense of U.S. security," noted Fox. Arguing in favor of legalizing the estimated 4 million illegal Mexican immigrants in the United States, Fox stressed mutual socioeconomic benefits of such a policy move: "We will keep insisting until the final day of this administration that the migration issue can be solved with big opportunities for both countries" (ibid.).

On the other hand, an editorial in the *San Diego Union-Tribune* (May 21, 2003: B8) illustrates why the sense of the security threat caused by Mexican migration in California is unlikely to diminish in response to President Fox's arguments. The editorial complained that while "the American public states in poll after poll that it wants illegal immigration ended and legal immigration reduced," the U.S. Congress, "in thrall of immigration lobbies, does nothing." The editorial expressed the view that legalizing illegal Mexican immigrants in the United States would be dangerous: "We cannot think of a more perfect incentive to attract more illegal immigrants." The logic of the editorial was based on the assumption that illegal migration is a threat in its own right – a perfect reflection of the security-dilemma mind-set. The editorial predictably emphasized security and law enforcement solutions, rather than economic policy solutions to the Mexican immigration problem: "Mexico should understand that the only basis for legalization of Mexicans currently here is to close off permanently the flow of illegals." For U.S. domestic policy, the editorial proposed another exclusionist measure in response to Mexican labor migration: "The first step should be the creation of a Social Security worker registry system of the kind immigration officials have requested for years. Cut off jobs for illegal workers and they will stop coming" (ibid.). At the national level, this type of concern – amplified by conservative groups and opinion leaders – silenced even the sensible proposal by President George W. Bush in early 2004 to reform immigration laws so that willing workers and employers could more easily find one another.

The security dilemma warns, however, that simple exclusionist measures such as border control or worker registration are likely to backfire as long as the economic demand for low-cost migrant labor persists. Given that labor cost differentials are significantly larger than consumer price differentials across borders, this demand is unlikely to abate. Tough exclusionist measures – a knee-jerk response under the security dilemma – would backfire by discouraging return migration, increasing the secretiveness and sophistication of immigrant smuggling networks, driving migrant labor markets underground, and fostering corruption in migrant-receiving states. An enlightened reading of the security-dilemma implications would warn against unilateral migrant exclusionism and reliance on bilateral ad hoc solutions.

In fact, in the searchlight of the security dilemma one can see how securitizing migration may result in diminishing security within host societies that implement antimigrant exclusionist measures in the name of protecting their security. As in the case of spiraling arms races, overrating of security threats arising from migration is likely to generate self-fulfilling prophecies: The more migration is feared as a security threat, the more of a security threat it becomes. As with the arms race, the security dilemma between law enforcement and migrants may lead to the two-sided spirals of violence and insecurity. One way this "spiral dynamic" may arise is summarized in de la Garza's (2004: 93) review of research on immigration and Latino politics in the United States: "[N]egative reactions to future immigration [along the lines of Huntington and Buchanan – author] could lead to the establishment of new barriers to Latino incorporation and the creation of a new and permanent Latino underclass whose very existence would require reexamining Latino–white relations." Ken Ellingwood (2004) – a *Los Angeles Times* correspondent assigned to the U.S.–Mexico border from 1998 to 2002 – painstakingly documented the failure of Operation Gatekeeper launched in the mid-1990s to curb illegal trafficking in drugs and human beings. While removing most illegal migrants from metropolitan centers, such as San Diego, the doubling of the number of border patrol officers and tougher policing of urban centers near the Mexican border empowered precisely the "permanent Latino" underclass whose actions, in de la Garza's (2004: 93) view, "could easily lead to more polarized relations between Latinos and Anglos." Reliance on security-driven policies – such as Operation Gatekeeper – failed to stop illegal immigration, but they have been contributing to "black-marketization" of border-crossing businesses and to the hardening of the smuggler underclass. Reports in the *San Diego Union-Tribune* (August 6, 2002: B1, 3) illustrated this "hardening" process in response to tighter border control between the United States and Mexico. Rather than giving up trafficking in migrants – most of them driven by the age-old desires to improve their well-being, give their children a better life, and escape hardship or injustice – one smuggling ring in the Mexican border city of Tijuana trained operatives to bypass border guards by literally roaring into the United States on the wrong side of the road in specially refurbished cars. These smuggle-mobiles had tires filled with silicone gel, making them impervious to spike strips placed at border crossings to bar drivers from getting into the United States on the wrong side of the road. They had reinforced bumpers to push any oncoming traffic around the border posts out of the way and high-powered beams to stun the drivers of oncoming vehicles and force them to make way for the smugglers. In this way, the global labor market was demonstrating that where there is a will there is a way and straightforward security enhancement would not stop free enterprise. However, once the migrants invest in overcoming barriers to entry into more lucrative labor markets by resorting to illicit, violent methods – such as pushing oncoming cars out of the way on the wrong side of the road and endangering the lives of their drivers – they become the living embodiment of the initial alarmist projections that linked migration with diminishing security. "See," any California resident can now say, "these migrants would not stop at anything, even killing us, to get into the country. We need to get tougher." And the spiral winds upward. In fact, predictably, the emergence of the wrong-side-of-the-road smugglers elicited no strategic reconsideration of migration policy on the part of the responsible government agencies in the United States and Mexico – a reconsideration that would take into account the threat of self-defeating unintended consequences of the security dilemma. Rather – and predictably – officials on both sides of the border immediately responded with suggestions to continue securitizing the border. On the U.S. side, these responses included increasing nighttime surveillance of border crossings and the use of Border Patrol helicopters that could track vehicles far inside the Mexican territory. The Mexican officials proposed to install one more strip of tire shredders and to block potential access points to the wrong side of the road. The only question was what shape the "hardening" of criminal smuggling would take in response to these measures.

On a larger scale – and not as visible and dramatic as the wrong-side-of-the-road high-beam cars – the predominant reliance on security measures in dealing with immigrant-based gangs in California in the mid-1990s started to exhibit the alarming signs of "blowback" in the early 2000s. According to investigative reporting by Ginger Thompson (*The New York Times*, September 26, 2004: 1, 14), in the mid-1990s law enforcement agencies in the United States rounded up and deported approximately 40,000 illegal immigrant members of street gangs a year in response to increasing public alarmism about illegal Latino immigration. The securitizing policies in fact translated into military-style operations targeting migrant communities. The Marine commanders in charge of antiinsurgency operations in Fallujah, Iraq kept coming to Los Angeles to take lessons from local antigang units. The deported gang members – hardened in armed interneighborhood clashes resembling the tribal wars in the developing world – returned by the thousands into poor and poorly governed Central American countries such as Honduras and El Salvador. "Suddenly, one of the poorest corners of the world, which struggles to meet its people's basic needs, was burdened by a superpower's crime plague," wrote Ginger Thompson – a sharp comment pinpointing the social crucible that would further harden deported criminals and pave the way to the transnational recycling of the gangsterized underclass, something that the proponents of the security-driven exclusionism in the United States of the mid-1990s fought hard to root out in the first place. Another spiral, another self-fulfilling prophecy unfolded. Rather than designing large-scale socioeconomic policies to integrate and rehabilitate the deported gang members, the authorities in Honduras and El Salvador resorted to straightforward counterinsurgency measures and zero-tolerance laws known as the "Firm Hand" (*Mano Dura*) strategy. Like in the Los Angeles suburbs, migration again was treated as a security issue. The *Mano Dura* measures included summary arrests and incarceration for between six and twelve years of any returnees who had gang-related tattoos – without investigating whether, in fact, they still had any relationships with the gangs or were still involved in criminal activities. Reports of massive abuse of power by police have been widespread. A government investigation in Honduras – hardly sympathetic to the deportees – found that in 2003 the guards and soldiers at the El Porvenir prison massacred sixty-eight inmates, with fifty-nine of them shot, stabbed, or burned to death and the rest gunned down while running away from the fire and pleading for mercy (ibid.). The net result of responding to migration challenges as if they amounted to insurgency was hardly the desired eradication of criminal gangs. By late 2004, signs were abundant that persistent cross-border securitizing of migration backfired. Thompson's report unambiguously suggested that "with the extraordinary measures by Central American governments driving them away, the rampage has come full circle. The sheer force of illegal immigration has made the Mara Salvatruchas and the 18th Street gang two of the fastest-growing gangs in the United States" (ibid.). Thompson quoted American police officials alarmed by increasing gang violence not only in traditional trouble spots such as Los Angeles and Chicago, but to the previously sedate Washington, DC suburbs; smaller cities such as Durham, North Carolina and Omaha, Nebraska; and small-town areas like Nassau County, New York. The reporter also cited a study by the Northeastern University that recorded a 50-percent increase in gang-related homicides in the United States from 1999 to 2002 – the years following Operation Gatekeeper and the increasing treatment of migration as a security challenge to the United States. The transnational recirculation of increasingly more secretive and ruthless *maras* – the slang word for these gangs derived from a name for swarming ants – is a yet underappreciated illustration that responses rooted in the perceptual logic of the security dilemma are more likely to spread rather than to solve security-related problems arising from migration.

Self-defeating securitizing spirals are difficult to undo. It is difficult to break through plausible deniability that the security-dilemma trap exists. All that any politician or law enforcement agent needs to say is that migrant gang members are inherently criminal, that they have inborn intent to prey on local communities, to profit from terrorizing law-abiding natives. Indeed, with respect to committed criminals – people whose behavior is indeed driven predominantly by intent to do harm to others – the security dilemma does not apply. But the investigation of the immigrant gang world by Ginger Thompson suggests that gangs are multifaceted, complex organisms and most members are not inherently predatory and violent. The trajectory of the two largest L.A. gangs – the Mara Salvatrucha and the Mara 18 – indicates that exclusionism without expulsion – the blocking of opportunities within the receiving communities – was the most likely cause of these groups' shift toward crime and communal violence. Initially, Mara Salvatruchas were not a conglomeration of gangs, but rather of support networks and social clubs that were started by the children of refugees from civil wars in Central America, in which the United States actively backed the anticommunist forces. (Suggesting strongly that the initial emergence of these migrants was itself a result of the security dilemma–based "domino theory" that informed the U.S. Cold War policy of containment.) Mara 18 sprang up in the communities of Mexican immigrants of the 1970s who arrived earlier in search of economic opportunities that did not fully materialize. Moreover, Thompson's interviews with gang members suggest the majority of them yearn to have "normal lives" and start families and deeply resent social ostracism. One typical statement comes from Gustavo Olivera, a twenty-six-year-old former gang member who returned to Honduras: "We want to change. We are fathers and husbands. We want to work to give our families good homes. But the government does not want that." Another deportee, Javier Torres concurred gruesomely: "The government demonizes us for political purposes. We are worth more to them dead than alive."

Another striking example of how securitizing of migration draws perfectly normal, law-abiding residents into "underclass" activities is the story of the Sanctuary movement, which emerged in 1986 in protest to the repatriation by the U.S. government of the refugees fleeing a civil war in El Salvador and Guatemala. Participating in this movement were hundreds of hitherto God- and authority-fearing clerics who put together an illegal underground railroad to smuggle the war refugees to safety in the United States (Bhagwati 2004: 217).

In the post-9/11 context, the excessive securitizing of migration also poses another self-fulfilling prophecy threat to national security: increasing probability of hostile action by migrant diasporas against states that overrate internal threat from migrant diasporas. This is a complex, long-term challenge, but one well worth examining systematically in future studies. Here I outline its basic logic in the light of the immigration security dilemma. Diasporas are an integral part of modern societies, from California to Indonesia. Their members – while feeling some ancestral, cultural, or kin-based affinity to their societies of origin – typically have little time to develop these connections unless they are a core component of their daily work activities (e.g., export-import business, travel services, etc.). In whatever time that remains – judging, among other sources, from my own experience and that of other Russians, Ukrainians, Georgians, and Armenians in the United States with whom I have communicated since the early 1990s – "diaspora" members typically maintain benign, if not to say trivial, connections with their ex-homelands. Most typically say they follow the news from their countries of origin (some may subscribe to cable TV services in their native languages or read the mother-country press on the Web), send money back to their relatives (hence, the ubiquity of Western Union offices in the United States), and communicate with their family and friends (taking advantage of low-cost global telephone networks or Internet-based communications). A smaller number of them may participate in community organizations – such as churches or ethnic-based associations – or practice sports that are more common in their mother country (as evidenced in this author's experience playing in amateur soccer leagues in the United States). In relation to trillions of trillions of benign, routine daily activities, which one may construe as a connection between the diaspora members and the sending states, the percentage of diaspora activities related to violence or terrorism would be infinitesimally small and statistically negligible. However, it is important not to discount that these activities may pose real threats to national security – the point driven home with horrific brutality of the 9/11 attacks. And it is also an inescapable fact that terrorist groups draw on millions of benign diaspora interactions, from money transfers to arranging housing for its members in host countries. The security-dilemma logic, however, suggests that caution should be applied when publicly framing the diaspora challenges to national security precisely in these terms. Despite the vivid destructiveness and flagrant inhumanity of the 9/11 attacks, the migrant communities remain more of a threat to their sending states than to their new homelands. This is the principal argument regarding diasporas made by Weiner and Teitelbaum (2001: 77–8). Radical Islamic fundamentalists based in Germany are more likely to finance their allies in Turkey and Algeria than in Germany; Sinhalese Tamils in the United States target the Sri Lanka government, not the White House; Sikh activists in Canada focus on politics in India, not in Ottawa; and Albanian independence supporters in Switzerland and Italy primarily supported the Kosovo Liberation Front, rather than, say, the Tyrolean separatists. At the same time, Weiner and Teitelbaum (2001: 8) found that "no immigrant community in the United States or Europe has formed a political party directed against its host society, notwithstanding substantial pockets of alienation among many North Africans in France and Turks in Germany." Absence of aggressive immigrant parties is also strikingly surprising considering the spread of aggressive antiimmigrant parties and groups in most migrant-receiving states. The danger in the post-9/11 world is that the attacks on the World Trade Center and the Pentagon make it harder for the natives to comprehend that diasporas pose less threat inside than outside their states and that a greater risk to social stability, in the apt summary of Weiner and Teitelbaum (2001: 77) comes from "a backlash against migrants and refugees, the growth of anti-migrant, anti-foreign sentiment that under some conditions may take a repressive, anti-democratic form." The latter stands to increase grievances within diasporas against receiving states, something that in the long run stands to increase social support within the diasporas to activities, including violence, against host societies.

These developments suggest that the principal policy challenge is how to reduce the temptation and the public pressure to "securitize" immigration control while at the same time to effectively manage migrant flows and unlock the social and economic potential of migration. Toward these ends, this study suggests two general approaches: (1) increasing interactivity among global, interstate, national, and local institutions to foster multilateral rule making on entry, registration, and conditions of stay of migrants; and (2) increasing the use of economic incentives in migration management. Whereas these measures are only general sketches, they do emphasize the importance of mitigating situations in which host populations could plausibly develop exaggerated concerns about the size of migration, the intention of migrants, the migrants' otherness, and a sense of economic vulnerability to migration.

Global Level

Because migration by its very nature is a transnational phenomenon, the sense of anarchy that migration injects into the receiving states is likely to be mitigated if host populations and their governments can appeal to an international body with credible authority to adopt, modify, and enforce the rules that would manage migration flows around the world. With respect to international trade – another phenomenon that makes interstate borders appear permeable – national governments have recourse to the WTO. In the EU, national governments and provincial and local governments within states have recourse to central authority above nation-states through European legislature, the executive offices, and the judiciary. Whereas the freeing of the transnational labor markets stands to deliver momentous gains to the world economy in excess of gains from trade (see Chapter 1), no equivalent international rule-making body on migration and immigration is in place. The United Nations has several international organizations under its umbrella that could play a part in improving global-level management of migratory flows, including the International Organization for Migration, the Intergovernmental Committee for Migration, and the High Commissioner for Refugees. Yet, the world has not seen a concerted effort among the most powerful states to produce the migration-related equivalent of the Bretton Woods system that increased openness to trade and capital flows around the world. Global economy, however, could not be an effective global *market* economy unless capital and commodity markets are not accompanied by institutionalization of international labor markets. This does not have to be a grandiose undertaking of Utopian proportions. In fact, since the early 1990s, a Columbia University economist, Jagdish Bhagwati (2004: 218), argued for the institutionalization of a World Migration Organization that would systematically catalog and compare national "entry, exit, and residence policies toward migrants, whether legal or illegal, economic or political, skilled or unskilled." While specific and manageable, this would also be a potentially threat-assuaging mission.

It would be naïve to expect that any such international body would quickly learn to micromanage migratory flows successfully over the short term – if ever. But that's not the point. The mere knowledge that such a body is "out there" and that rules *potentially* would be enforceable will mitigate the security dilemmas and contribute to a more relaxed policy-making climate where effective context-specific solutions will have a better chance. As in the world trade and tariffs negotiations, such as the Uruguay Round, one would be wise to expect any progress to be slow – but as the media continue to report on the mere fact that the international migration rules are being worked out, the incentive for nation-states to unilaterally toughen migration controls will be reduced. Another powerful influence such an international body could have on desecuritizing migration policy would be through efficient provision of information to migrants about existing employment and business opportunities around the world. The increasing mobility of migrants is likely to reduce the perception in host states that economic migrants would stay permanently, raise the cost of social services, and create distinct ethnocultural enclaves "Balkanizing" host societies.

Interstate Level

The move toward global migration management has a lot to build on in the form of interstate legal and institutional arrangements to manage the cross-border flow of people. Of particular interest are developments such as Euro-regions and the EU's framework agreements on transborder cooperation; border-crossing cards in Mexican cities near the U.S. border; and initiatives promoting fee-based labor migration. Above and beyond their substantive content, these measures are valuable because they recast migration from being a spontaneous, unmanageable, and therefore threatening development into orderly, manageable, and nonthreatening "business as usual." For less developed areas, the Russian and Chinese authorities recently implemented a blueprint for managing cross-border migration geared to preserve the benefits and to reduce the security concerns in the receiving states. At the border town of Pogranichnyi in Primorskii krai – where in the early 1990s former Primorskii governor Nazdratenko warned the Chinese were physically taking over the Russians – a large new building was erected in late 2002. Officially called the Primorskii Trade and Economic Center, the building has two separate border-crossing checkpoints for the entrants from Russia and from China. Any Russian or Chinese resident can enter the trade area without a visa. Once inside, they can buy, sell, or trade goods in this hybrid between the street market and the supermarket. But they can only leave through the same checkpoint through which they entered – the Russians going back to Russia, the Chinese to China. Such projects do not necessarily have to be confined to guarded buildings, but it is plausible that such trade and economic centers straddling state borders will over time graduate toward larger transborder regions where the movement of goods and people will be regulated primarily by economic incentives without causing security threats. After all, the Primorskii Trade and Economic Center has grown out of the ramshackle Chinese markets and haphazard trade off the back of cargo trucks along the potholed side roads near Pogranichnyi.

National Level

One of the lessons from survey analysis in this study is that availability of data on migration by ethnic group is more likely to reduce than to enhance interethnic tensions. The conventional wisdom – sometimes known as "village knowledge" – would suggest that provision of such data in host societies could equally have a calming or destabilizing effect. It may assuage fears that too many outsiders are coming in if their actual number is small, or it may enhance fears if the number is large. But from the security-dilemma standpoint, if the number of migrants is already too large, much less room for threat exaggeration will be available and so the provision of data is unlikely to make tensions worse. However, because the security dilemma predicts that ethnic tensions may arise even when the number of migrants is small relative to the host population – as in the Russian Far East – provision of statistical data on the actual size of migration would stand to reduce threat perception at least among some members of the public. When I traveled to the Russian Far East, I soon established that finding credible and comprehensive information about Chinese migration in media sources easily accessible to the public was impossible. The government official who provided me with the number of Chinese nationals crossing the Russian border in Primorskii for most of the 1990s also told me that he took part in numerous interagency conferences on regulating Chinese migration. Yet, apparently, these conferences failed to make a simple move to make the visa service, migration service, and border service data regularly available to Primorskii media through press releases or other media outreach activities. In the database of over 3,500 press reports in major daily newspapers circulating in Primorskii krai on activities involving the Chinese nationals from 1993 to 2000 (Alexseev 2002), I found no information on the scale of Chinese migration of the kind I was able to obtain from interdepartmental memos in Vladivostok. In the absence of data from authoritative government sources, the newspapers published reports and commentary speculating about the present and future size of Chinese migration. Such speculations undoubtedly contributed to the readers' sense of uncertainty about Chinese migrants and understandably translated into exaggerated fears registered in my Primorskii 2000 survey.

One other important policy lesson from Primorskii is that playing on uncertainty and threat exaggeration is likely to be more attractive to local politicians if they can exploit public fears in the bargaining game over power and economic resources with the central government. This was clearly the case with the former governor of Primorskii krai, Yevgenii

Nazdratenko. After his removal and reappointment in Moscow, the role of the principal anti-Chinese "alarm raiser" in the Russian Far East was assumed by Viktor Ishaev, the governor of the Khabarovskii krai, which became the focal point of Moscow's efforts to govern the Far East under president Putin. In short, center–periphery conflict in migrant-receiving states is a factor to watch when the in-migration rate increases.

Also at the state level, the role of police and law enforcement capacity in general is critical in containing hostility. One of the reasons that the 1992 L.A. riots did not repeat themselves in other U.S. cities has been the lessons that police authorities in other metropolitan areas drew from the riots. Increased police preparedness, training, and interaction with community leaders in troubled neighborhoods have been credited with prevention of social unrest that could conceivably have happened elsewhere (Baldassare 1994; Morrison and Lewis 1994). In the rough and uncertain political and socioeconomic climate of the Russian Far East, police played a stabilizing role in and around the Chinese markets, especially when it abandoned physical expulsion and proceeded to provide "protection" services to Chinese traders. From 1994 to mid-1999, police responded harshly to rising Chinese migration by carrying out street and market sweeps and I.D. spot checks as part of "Operation Foreigner" unleashed by the Primorskii governor. However, these operations failed to reduce the intensity of the perceived Chinese threat to Primorskii's security. The police authorities gradually moved from sweeps to offering official protection for a fee to Chinese traders in exchange for law observance guarantees from the latter. This author witnessed two such protection deals take place at the Ussuriisk market in the fall of 2000. From the vantage point of the Ussuriisk market, these quiet arrangements contributed to a greater sense of security around the Chinese markets than the spot arrests and taking away of Chinese traders that this author witnessed in Vladivostok in May 1999. If legalized and made transparent, this street-level corrupt arrangement between the police and migrant traders in Ussuriisk is likely to reduce the sense of the security dilemma.

Local and Group Levels

The challenge at this level is to create environments in which groups and their members will not feel acutely responsible for their own security. On the everyday basis in contexts where mobilization for intergroup violence is not an issue, this means reducing the sense of economic vulnerability to migrant groups. This is where government agencies – especially those at the local level – could provide financial and legal incentives to encourage joint economic activities between host populations and migrants that would benefit both groups. The former mayor of Vladivostok, Vitalii Cherepkov, offered one practical example of such an approach to me during the gubernatorial election campaign in Primorskii in 2001: "Take those Chinese poachers descending on local rivers and lakes to catch frogs by the thousand. When the public hears these stories, they want to crack down on them and shut down the border. But why won't we instead talk to these poachers and set up joint business ventures with them to breed and harvest frogs in local rivers, lakes, and ponds. Demand for frogs in China is huge, and we can create businesses beneficial to both the local Russians and the Chinese. Instead of looking at one another with hostility, we could share profits." In a sense, the Euroregions represent the practical and successful implementation of this vision on a much larger scale – creating fear-reducing environments with free movement of people and mutually beneficial economic growth. Clearly, a stronger government role will be required to remove anarchy-induced impediments to enlightened self-interest in America's troublesome urban neighborhoods.

Local governments would also help reduce threat perception by publicizing economically beneficial activities of migrants. This is particularly important because negative effects are more likely to be picked up by the media that by default are more likely to focus on rare events, such as crime, and on outstanding problems rather than routine achievements.

The ultimate policy prescription under the security dilemma is that unilateral self-defense policies – such as border closure and mass deportation – will only perpetuate insecurity without necessarily stopping illegal migration. Conversely, policies that would establish fear-reducing environments in migrant-receiving states and promote the role of economic incentives in regulating migrant flows are more likely to alleviate interethnic fears and conflicts that population movements beget.

APPENDIX A

Primorskii 2000 Survey

Regression Results

Survey description, methods, descriptive statistics, coding of variables, factor analysis, and related comments are available at the author's Web pages: http://www-rohan.sdsu.edu/~alexseev.

TABLE A.1. *Regression of Perceived Threat to Russia and Primorskii krai (THRRUPK) on Select Predictors*[a]

Variables (perception measures):	Model 1	Model 2	Model 3	Model 4	Model 5
Block 1: Emerging Anarchy					
Ethnic balance 2010 (CH2010)	**.172 (.067)	**.150 (.067)	*.163 (.064)	**.164 (.063)	**.166 (.065)
Government capacity (FEDHLP)	−.030 (.051)	−.026 (.050)	.018 (.049)	.022 (.050)	.025 (.050)
Primorskii isolation 2010 (ISOL10)	**.149 (.053)	**.140 (.053)	**.118 (.050)	.078 (.053)	.076 (.052)
Military balance 2010 (MLBL10)	.109 (.082)	.102 (.081)	.095 (.077)	.083 (.077)	.078 (.078)
Constant	.759 (.240)				
Block 2: Offensive Intentions					
Intent to settle permanently (INFILT)		−.000 (.130)	−.036 (.123)	−.012 (.121)	−.008 (.124)
Territorial claims (TERCLA)		**.406 (.164)	*.376 (.156)	**.372 (.153)	**.368 (.155)
Constant		1.014 (.271)			
Block 3: Group Distinctiveness					
Support intermarriage (MARCHI)			−.148 (.107)	−.125 (.105)	−.114 (.106)
Chinese ability to assimilate (CHASSM)			−.052 (.043)	−.061 (.042)	−.058 (.043)
Ethnic group difference (DF_SOC)			***.263 (.059)	***.235 (.062)	***.233 (.064)
Constant			1.397 (.381)		
Block 4: Deprivation and Socioeconomic Impact					
Personal income valuation (INCOME)				.093 (.109)	−.107 (.113)
Chinese gains from migration (FGAINCHI)				−.061 (.066)	.071 (.067)
Income opportunity, crime (JOBSEC)				**.161 (.055)	**.150 (.057)
Scale of benefits to local Russians (BEN00)				*.090 (.055)	*.091 (.055)
Constant				.658 (.329)	

Block 5: Controls					
Status reversal sensitivity (CHPROP)					.067 (.068)
Ideological/party preference (PARTY)					.013 (.081)
Sensitivity to territorial losses (EXPAND)					.059 (.069)
College education (COLLEGE)					−.077 (.151)
Russian Orthodox believer (ORTHRU)					.019 (.132)
Constant					.768 (.341)
R^2 =	.064	.088	.186	.237	.244
F =	4.06	3.75	5.83	5.39	3.96
(df)	(4,235)	(6,236)	(9,230)	(13,226)	(18,221)
$P(R^2)$ =	.0017	.0007	.0000	.0000	.0000
Change in R^2 =	–	.024	.098	.051	.051
Adjusted R^2 =	.048	.065	.154	.193	.182

[a] Significance: * = $p < .05$, ** = $p < .01$, *** = $p < .001$ (one-tailed). Unstandardized coefficient (B) and its standard error (in parentheses) reported. Multicollinearity diagnostics: Tolerance varied from .757 (DF_SOC) to .949 (MARCHI); VIF varied from 1.053 (MARCHI) to 1.320 (DF_SOC) in the complete model, suggesting acceptable low levels of multicollinearity.

TABLE A.2. *Regression of Perceived Threat of Russia–China Armed Conflict (ARMC10) on Select Predictors*[a]

Variables (perception measures):	Model 1	Model 2	Model 3	Model 4	Model 5
Block 1: Emerging Anarchy					
Ethnic balance 2010 (CH2010)	**.218 (.086)	*.171 (.084)	**.186 (.083)	**.190 (.081)	**.190 (.084)
Government capacity (FEDHLP)	*.113 (.065)	*.110 (.063)	*.152 (.064)	*.116 (.065)	*.112 (.065)
Isolation of Primorskii 2010 (ISOL10)	**.202 (.068)	**.191 (.066)	**.170 (.065)	**.175 (.067)	**.176 (.068)
Military balance 2010 (MLBL10)	.100 (.104)	.104 (.102)	.099 (.100)	.107 (.100)	.105 (.101)
Constant	−1.243 (.307)				
Block 2: Offensive Intentions					
Intent to settle permanently (INFILT)		**−.358 (.161)	**−.391 (.159)	*−.335 (.157)	*−.329 (.161)
Territorial claims (TERCLA)		***.664 (.204)	***.635 (.202)	**.615 (.198)	**.594 (.201)
Constant		−1.037 (.341)			
Block 3: Group Distinctiveness					
Support intermarriage (MARCHI)			−.127 (.137)	−.107 (.136)	−.096 (.138)
Chinese capacity to assimilate (CHASSM)			−.040 (.055)	−.052 (.054)	−.048 (.055)
Ethnic group difference (DF_SOC)			***.266 (.076)	***.302 (.080)	***.283 (.083)
Constant			−1.170 (.344)		
Block 4: Deprivation and Socioeconomic Impact					
Personal income valuation (INCOME)				.128 (.142)	.098 (.147)
Chinese gains from migration (FGAINCHI)				*−.182 (.085)	*−.174 (.087)
Income opportunities, crime (JOBSEC)				.024 (.072)	.027 (.057)
Scale of benefits to local Russians, (BEN00)				*.141 (.071)	*.142 (.072)
Constant				−1.363 (.426)	

Block 5: Controls					
Status reversal sensitivity (CHPROP)					.013 (.089)
Ideological/party preference (PARTY)					.096 (.105)
Sensitivity to territorial losses (EXPAND)					.018 (.090)
College education (COLLEGE)					.085 (.196)
Russian Orthodox believer (ORTHRU)					−.112 (.172)
Constant					−1.32 (.442)
R^2 =	.079	.138	.194	.235	.240
F =	5.06	6.22	6.14	5.39	3.88
(df)	(4,235)	(6,233)	(9,230)	(13,226)	(18,221)
P (R^2) =	.0003	.0000	.0000	.0000	.0000
Change in R^2 =	–	.059	.056	.041	.005
Adjusted R^2 =	.064	.116	.162	.191	.178

[a] Significance: * = p < .05, ** = p < .01, *** = p < .001 (one-tailed). Unstandardized coefficient (B) and its standard error (in parentheses) reported. Multicollinearity diagnostics: Tolerance varied from .757 (DF_SOC) to .949 (MARCHI); VIF varied from 1.053 (MARCHI) to 1.320 (DF_SOC) in the complete model, suggesting acceptable low levels of multicollinearity.

TABLE A.3. *Regression of Militant Hostility (HSTMILIT) on Select Predictors*[a]

Variables (perception measures):	Model 1	Model 2	Model 3	Model 4	Model 5	Model 6
Block 1: Emerging Anarchy						
Ethnic balance 2010 (CH2010)	*.123 (.067)	.101 (.067)	*.111 (.067)	*.113 (.067)	.103 (.066)	.083 (.072)
Government capacity (FEDHLP)	–.031 (.051)	–.026 (.051)	–.004 (.052)	–.000 (.053)	.007 (.053)	.004 (.055)
Isolation of Primorskii 2010 (ISOL10)	**.148 (.053)	**.140 (.053)	**.126 (.053)	.087 (.055)	.083 (.055)	.072 (.056)
Military balance 2010 (MLBL10)	.022 (.081)	.017 (.082)	.014 (.081)	.022 (.082)	.013 (.082)	.000 (.085)
Constant	.685 (.240)					
Block 2: Offensive Intentions						
Intent to settle permanently (INFILT)		–.006 (.131)	–.025 (.130)	–.008 (.129)	–.004 (.130)	–.007 (.135)
Territorial claims (TERCLA)		**.381 (.166)	*.360 (.165)	*.355 (.163)	*.329 (.163)	*.285 (.171)
Constant		.921 (.275)				
Block 3: Group Distinctiveness						
Support intermarriage (MARCHI)			–.100 (.112)	–.075 (.111)	–.041 (.111)	–.024 (.115)
Chinese ability to assimilate (CHASSM)			–.017 (.044)	–.022 (.045)	–.011 (.045)	–.003 (.046)
Ethnic group difference (DF_SOC)			**.159 (.062)	**.124 (.065)	.093 (.067)	.061 (.070)
Constant			.823 (.281)			
Block 4: Deprivation and Socioeconomic Impact						
Personal income valuation (INCOME)				.066 (.117)	.028 (.119)	.016 (.123)
Chinese gains from migration (FGAINCHI)				.006 (.070)	.014 (.070)	.031 (.071)
Income opportunity, crime (JOBSEC)				*.118 (.059)	*.102 (.059)	.082 (.062)
Scale of benefits to local Russians (BEN00)				*.124 (.058)	*.120 (.058)	*.109 (.060)
Constant				.559 (.349)		

Block 5: Controls						
Status reversal sensitivity (CHPROP)					*.131 (.071)	*.120 (.074)
Ideology/party preference (PARTY)					.130 (.085)	.128 (.087)
Sensitivity to territorial loss (EXPAND)					.063 (.073)	.052 (.076)
College education (COLLEGE)					.148 (.159)	.161 (.165)
Russian Orthodox believer (ORTHRU)					.077 (.139)	.073 (.144)
Constant					.753 (.357)	
Block 6: Threat						
Threat to Russia, Primorskii (THRRUPK)						*.131 (.073)
Constant						.642 (.373)
R^2 =	.045	.066	.100	.138	.169	.182
F =	2.784	2.766	2.84	2.785	2.498	2.384
(df)	(4,235)	(6,233)	(9,230)	(13,226)	(18,221)	(19,203)
$P(R^2)$ =	.0129	.0060	.0016	.0005	.0005	.0007
Change in R^2 =	–	.021	.034	.038	.031	.013
Adjusted R^2 =	.029	.042	.065	.089	.101	.106

[a] Significance: * = p < .05, ** = p < .01, *** = p < .001 (one-tailed). Unstandardized coefficient (B) and its standard error (in parentheses) reported. Multicollinearity diagnostics: Tolerance varied from .728 (DF_SOC) to .942 (MARCHI); VIF varied from 1.062 (MARCHI) to 1.374 (DF_SOC) in the complete model, suggesting acceptable low levels of multicollinearity.

APPENDIX B

Eurobarometer Survey No. 47.1 (1997)

Regression Results

Survey description, methods, descriptive statistics, coding of variables, factor analysis, and related comments are available at the author's Web pages: http://www-rohan.sdsu.edu/~alexseev.

TABLE B.1. *Regression of Minority Threat (EB47V340) on Select Predictors, Eurobarometer 47.1 (1997)*[a]

Variables:	Model 1	Model 2	Model 3	Model 4	Model 5	Model 6
Block 1: Emerging Anarchy						
Ethnic balance (EB47V348)	***.212 (.010)	***.204 (.010)	***.127 (.010)	***.069 (.010)	***.046 (.011)	***.044 (.011)
Government weakness (EB47V39)	***.056 (.014)	***.056 (.014)	**.031 (.014)	.008 (.013)	.005 (.013)	.002 (.013)
Constant	1.211 (.019)					
Block 2: Offensive Intentions						
Intent to integrate (EB47V370)		***.109 (.019)	***.078 (.018)	*.035 (.017)	.023 (.017)	.025 (.017)
Constant		1.098 (.027)				
Block 3: Group Distinctiveness						
Family union accepted (EB47V398)			***.150 (.014)	***.093 (.014)	***.084 (.014)	***.081 (.014)
Ethnic group difference (EB47V372)			***.238 (.015)	***.153 (.015)	***.131 (.015)	***.128 (.015)
Constant			.655 (.033)			
Block 4: Deprivation and Socioeconomic Impact						
Personal income valuation (EB47V464)				.000 (.002)	.000 (.002)	−.001 (.002)
Unemployment risk (EB47V250)				.002 (.014)	.006 (.014)	.013 (.014)
Life improvement (EB47V248)				.004 (.008)	.000 (.009)	−.005 (.009)
Impact on social benefits (EB47V333)				***.148 (.015)	***.127 (.015)	***.127 (.015)
Impact on education (EB47V331)				***.156 (.014)	***.148 (.014)	***.150 (.014)
Impact on crime (EB47V408)				***.147 (.015)	***.135 (.015)	***.133 (.015)
Constant				.374 (.044)		

(continued)

TABLE B.1. *(continued)*

Variables:	Model 1	Model 2	Model 3	Model 4	Model 5	Model 6
Block 5: Controls: Perceptions						
Minority size sensitivity (EB47V369)					***.123 (.016)	***.119 (.017)
Ideological identification (EB47V440)					.000 (.003)	.000 (.003)
Pride in own nationality (EB47V254)					*–.012 (.007)	**–.016 (.007)
Constant					.395 (.051)	
Block 5: Controls: Attributes						
Education level (EB47V445)						**.005 (.002)
Blue-collar worker (EB47V455)						–.019 (.021)
Christians (EB47V463)						.023 (.015)
Gender (EB47V447)						.007 (.013)
Immigrant ancestry (EB47V327)						.027 (.020)
Constant						
R^2 =	.094	.100	.182	.252	.261	.263
F =	244.6	175.3	210.9	144.6	119.1	88.8
(df)	(2,4738)	(3,4737)	(5,4735)	(11,4729)	(14,4726)	(19,4721)
P (R^2) =	.0000	.0000	.0000	.0000	.0000	.0000
Change in R^2 =	–	.006	.082	.070	.009	.002
Adjusted R^2 =	.093	.099	.181	.250	.259	.260

[a] Significance: * = $p < .05$, ** = $p < .01$, *** = $p < .001$ (one-tailed). Unstandardized coefficient (B) and its standard error (in parentheses) reported. Multicollinearity diagnostics: Tolerance varied from .621 (EB47V369) to .971 (EB47V327); VIF varied from 1.030 (EB47V327) to 1.610 (EB47369) in the complete model, suggesting acceptable low levels of multicollinearity.

TABLE B.2. *Regression of Antimigrant Hostility (EB47V382) on Select Predictors, Eurobarometer 47.1 (1997)*[a]

Variables:	Model 1	Model 2	Model 3	Model 4	Model 5	Model 6
Block 1: Emerging Anarchy						
Ethnic balance (EB47V348)	***.137 (.008)	***.142 (.009)	***.075 (.009)	***.056 (.009)	***.045 (.009)	***.040 (.009)
Government weakness (EB47V39)	***.052 (.012)	***.052 (.012)	**.033 (.011)	*.024 (.011)	*.021 (.011)	*.019 (.011)
Constant	1.569 (.016)					
Block 2: Offensive Intentions						
Intent to integrate (EB47V370)		***−.066 (.016)	***−.093 (.015)	***−.104 (.015)	***−.107 (.015)	***−.108 (.015)
Constant		1.638 (.023)				
Block 3: Group Distinctiveness						
Family union accepted (EB47V398)			***.094 (.012)	***.073 (.012)	***.068 (.012)	***.060 (.012)
Ethnic group difference (EB47V372)			***.236 (.012)	***.204 (.013)	***.195 (.013)	***.183 (.013)
Constant			1.258 (.028)			
Block 4: Deprivation and Socioeconomic Impact						
Personal income (EB47V464)				***.006 (.002)	***.006 (.002)	***.006 (.002)
Unemployment risk (EB47V250)				−.005 (.012)	−.002 (.012)	.002 (.012)
Life improvement (EB47V248)				**.022 (.008)	**.018 (.007)	*.016 (.008)
Impact on social benefits (EB47V333)				***.040 (.013)	**.031 (.013)	.021 (.013)
Impact on education (EB47V331)				***.048 (.012)	***.045 (.012)	**.034 (.012)
Impact on crime (EB47V408)				***.052 (.013)	***.047 (.013)	**.034 (.013)
Constant				1.106 (.038)		

(continued)

TABLE B.2. *(continued)*

Variables:	Model 1	Model 2	Model 3	Model 4	Model 5	Model 6
Block 5: Controls: Perceptions						
Minority size sensitivity (EB47V369)					**.043 (.014)	*.030 (.014)
Ideological identification (EB47V440)					**–.007 (.003)	**–.007 (.003)
Pride in own nationality (EB47V254)					***–.019 (.006)	***–.021 (.006)
Constant					1.195 (.045)	
Block 5: Controls: Attributes/Threat						
Education level (EB47V445)						.002 (.001)
Blue-collar workers (EB47V455)						–.013 (.018)
Christians (EB47V463)						.011 (.013)
Gender (EB47V447)						.015 (.011)
Immigrant ancestry (EB47V327)						**.043 (.018)
Threatened by minorities (EB47V340)						***.083 (.013)
Constant						1.071 (.056)
R^2 =	.060	.063	.156	.171	.175	.186
F =	150.3	106.2	175.6	88.8	71.8	53.7
(df)	(2,4738)	(3,4737)	(5,4735)	(11,4729)	(14,4726)	(20,4720)
P (R^2) =	.0000	.0000	.0000	.0000	.0000	.0000
Change in R^2 =	–	.003	.093	.015	.004	.011
Adjusted R^2 =	.059	.062	.156	.169	.173	.182

[a] Significance: * = $p < .05$, ** = $p < .01$, *** = $p < .001$ (one-tailed). Unstandardized coefficient (B) and its standard error (in parentheses) reported. Multicollinearity diagnostics: Tolerance varied from .621 (EB47V369) to .971 (EB47V327); VIF varied from 1.030 (EB47V327) to 1.610 (EB47369) in the complete model, suggesting acceptable low levels of multicollinearity.

APPENDIX C

A Journey into Fear

The Immigration Phobia Self-Test

If you made it all the way to this point, please take a few minutes to obtain your own personal immigration phobia score – your fear, hostility, and exaggeration ratings. To take this journey into the world of your own fears and latent hostilities, please complete the questionnaire, following the instructions as you go along. The scores for each response and their effects on the total score are derived, in part, from regression analysis of opinion surveys in this study. Some effects are estimated interactively, reflecting the security-dilemma theory. So, grab a writing implement and jot down your answers to each question. You may want to do it on a separate sheet of paper, especially if you want to expose your friends or students to the same test later or you hesitate to reveal these scores to any outsider who may lay hands on this book. For a better diagnosis, it is important that you

(a) Answer the questions as quickly as possible (preferably within ten seconds of reading and understanding the question);
(b) Don't go back and forth revising your answers;
(c) Resist the temptation to second-guess the effect of each answer on your final score;
(d) Don't rely on your memory; write down your responses to each question.

If this is clear, you are ready to answer the questions. After you are done, go to the Answer Key.

The Immigration Phobia Test

1. How much authority does your government have when it comes to resolving conflicts among different groups of people in your community?
   a. Unlimited authority; it can resolve all conflicts easily
   b. Limited, but substantial, authority
   c. Sometimes a lot, sometimes none
   d. Limited authority, although sometimes it can be effective
   e. Practically no authority
   f. Don't know
   g. Refuse to answer
2. Is maintaining order in your country a problem for your government?
   a. Never a problem
   b. Occasionally a problem
   c. Sometimes it is, sometimes it is not
   d. Often it is an important problem
   e. It is a constant and serious problem
   f. Don't know
   g. Refuse to answer
3. How many migrants do you think are entering your country these days:
   a. Too few
   b. A small number
   c. A substantial number, but well within our limits
   d. Close to the limit of what we can accept
   e. Too many
   f. Don't know
   g. Refuse to answer
4. In what way is the number of the foreign-born in your country, as a share of the total population, most likely to change over the next ten years or so?
   a. Stay about the same or decrease
   b. Increase by no more than 25 percent
   c. Increase by no more than 50 percent
   d. Increase by no more than 75 percent
   e. Double
   f. Triple

g. Increase ten times
h. Don't know
i. Refuse to answer

5. How many migrants do you think would support the claims of their governments or other foreign entities to sovereignty over parts of our territory?
   a. None at all
   b. Some sizeable number, but not most of them
   c. Most of them might
   d. Don't know
   e. Refuse to answer
6. Do you feel that migrants are, as a rule, more unpredictable in their behavior than the native residents of your home country?
   a. Not at all
   b. Somewhat
   c. Very much so
   d. Don't know
   e. Refuse to answer
7. Do you think migrants intend to learn the language, customs, and norms of behavior considered appropriate in your home country?
   a. Yes, most of them do
   b. Some do, some don't
   c. Most of them do not
   d. Don't know
   e. Refuse to answer
8. Do you think the migrants are more loyal to their home country or to their new country?
   a. To their new country
   b. About the same
   c. To their home country
   d. Don't know
   e. Refuse to answer
9. Talking about some typical human qualities, how much do you think most migrants differ – in a good or a bad way – from the natives when it comes to being:

   9.1 Polite
      a. Not at all
      b. Somewhat
      c. A lot

d. Completely
e. Don't know
f. Refuse to answer

9.2 Selfish
a. Not at all
b. Somewhat
c. A lot
d. Completely
e. Don't know
f. Refuse to answer

9.3 Messy
a. Not at all
b. Somewhat
c. A lot
d. Completely
e. Don't know
f. Refuse to answer

9.4 Honest
a. Not at all
b. Somewhat
c. A lot
d. Completely
e. Don't know
f. Refuse to answer

10. What proportion of the native population in your home country benefits economically from migration?
a. Practically everyone
b. Between 60 percent and 80 percent
c. About half
d. Between 20 percent and 40 percent
e. Less than 20 percent
f. Almost no one
g. Don't know
h. Refuse to answer

11. How determined are the migrants to compete for good jobs with the native residents?
a. Not determined
b. Determined, but less than the natives are
c. As determined as the natives are

d. More determined than the natives
e. Don't know
f. Refuse to answer

12. Do you think immigration creates problems for our public education?
a. No
b. Somewhat
c. A lot
d. Don't know
e. Refuse to answer

13. Do you think globalization weakens your national government?
a. Not at all
b. Somewhat
c. A lot
d. Don't know
e. Refuse to answer

14. Compared to other people in your country, how would you rank your family income, on a scale from 1 (highest) to 10 (lowest)?
1 2 3 4 5 6 7 8 9 10
Don't know
Refuse to answer

15. Do you have college education, and if so, how many years of study have you completed?
a. More than four years
b. Between two and four years
c. Two years or less
d. None
e. Don't know
f. Refuse to answer

The Test Key

Step 1

Assign the following scores to each of your answers. No score is assigned for either "Don't know" or "Refuse to answer" responses.

Questions:		Your score:
1.	a = 0, b = 1, c = 2, d = 3, e = 4	________
2.	a = 0, b = 1, c = 2, d = 3, e = 4	________
3.	a = 0, b = 1, c = 2, d = 3, e = 4	________
4.	a = 0, b = 1, c = 2, d = 3, e = 4, f = 5, g = 6	________
5.	a = 0, b = 2, c = 4	________
6.	a = 0, b = 2, c = 4	________
7.	a = 0, b = 2, c = 6	________
8.	a = 0, b = 2, c = 6	________
9.1	a = 0, b = 1.5, c = 2.75, d = 4	________
9.2	a = 0, b = 1.5, c = 2.75, d = 4	________
9.3	a = 0, b = 1.5, c = 2.75, d = 4	________
9.4	a = 0, b = 1.5, c = 2.75, d = 4	________
10.	a = 0, b = 1, c = 2, d = 3, e = 4, f = 5	________
11.	a = 0, b = 2, c = 4, d = 6	________
12.	a = 0, b = 2, c = 4	________
13.	a = 0, b = 1, c = 2	________
14.	The number you selected	________
15.	a = 1, b = 4 c = 7 d = 10	________

Step 2

Calculate your weighted scores for each cluster of the security-dilemma indicators.

1. Sum of your scores for questions 1–4, plus 13 × 6 = ________
2. Sum of your scores for questions 5–8 × 2 = ________
3. Sum of your scores for questions 9.1–9.4 × 6 = ________
4. Sum of your scores for questions 10–12 × 5 = ________
5. Sum of your scores for questions 14 and 15 = ________

Your total immigration phobia score is the sum of the above: ________
(Self-check: Your maximum score is 351 or 351 minus the sum of maximum weighted scores possible for questions you answered as "don't know" or refused to answer.)

Step 3

Using your weighted score, you can now assess your proclivity to overrate threat in terms of the U.S. Department of Homeland Security classification of threat alerts after the September 9, 2001 terrorist attacks on the United

States. This test estimates what your likely *perceived* threat will be when the *actual* threat level is low ("Green").

Your score:[1]	**Your Immigration Phobia Rating:**
0–89	Green
90–179	Yellow
180–269	Orange
270–351	Red

[1] Adjust these ranges proportionately to a different maximum possible score if you chose "don't know" or "refuse to answer" on any question.

References

Achen, Christopher H. 1996. "Social Psychology, Demographic Variables, and Linear Regression: Breaking the Iron Triangle in Voting Research." *Political Behavior* 14: 195–211.

Alexseev, Mikhail A., ed. 1999. *Center-Periphery Conflict in Post-Soviet Russia: A Federation Imperiled.* New York: St. Martin's Press.

______ 2001. "Socioeconomic and Security Implications of Chinese Migration in the Russian Far East." *Post-Soviet Geography and Economics* 42: 95–114.

______ 2002. "Desecuritizing Sovereignty: Economic Interest and Responses to Political Challenges of Chinese Migration in the Russian Far East." In John D. Montgomery and Nathan Glazer, eds., *Sovereignty under Challenge: How Governments Respond*, 261–89. New Brunswick, NJ: Transaction Publishers.

______ 2003. "Economic Valuations and Interethnic Fears: Perceptions of Chinese Migration in the Russian Far East." *Journal of Peace Research* 40: 89–106.

Allen, Christopher and Jorgen S. Nielsen. 2002. "Summary Report on Islamophobia in the EU after the 11 September 2001." Vienna: European Monitoring Center on Racism and Xenophobia.

Allport, Gordon W. 1979 [1954]. *The Nature of Prejudice.* Reading, MA: Addison-Wesley.

Anderson, Benedict. 1991. *Imagined Communities: Reflections on the Origins and Spread of Nationalism.* London: Verso Press.

Asher, Herbert B. 1983. *Causal Modeling*, 2nd ed. Newbury Park, CA: Sage Publications.

Asia Intelligence Wire. 2002. "Europe in Grip of Siege Mentality" (August 13).

Associated Press. 2002. "Europe Copes with Immigration Fears," File: h0529155.600 (May 29).

Averill, J. 1973. "Personal Control over Aversive Stimuli and Its Relation to Stress." *Psychological Bulletin* 80: 226–303.

Azar, Edward and John W. Burton, eds. 1986. *International Conflict Resolution: Theory and Practice.* Boulder, CO: Lynne Rienner.

Azar, Edward and Nadia E. Farah. 1984. "Political Dimensions of Conflict." In Nazli Choucri, ed. *Multidisciplinary Perspectives on Population and Conflict.* Syracuse, NY: Syracuse University Press.

Baklanov, P. Ya. 1999. "Geograficheskie, sotsial'no-ekonomicheskie i geopoliticheskie faktory migratsii kitaiiskogo naseleniia v raiony rossiiskogo Dal'nego vostoka" [Geographic, socioeconomic and geopolitical factors of Chinese migration in the regions of the Russian Far East]. Paper presented at the Roundtable, "Prospects for the Far East Region: The Chinese Factor," Institute of History, Archeology, and Ethnography of the Far Eastern Branch, Russian Academy of Sciences, Vladivostok, June 28.

Baldassare, Mark. 1994. "Introduction." In Mark Baldassare, ed., *The Los Angeles Riots: Lessons for the Urban Future*, 1–17. Boulder, CO: Westview Press.

Banister, Judith. 2001. "Impacts of Migration to China's Border Regions." In Myron Weiner and Sharon Stanton Russell, eds., *Demography and National Security*, 256–304. New York: Berghahn Books.

Barbieri, Katherine and Gerald Schneider. 1999. "Globalization and Peace: Asssessing New Directions in the Study of Trade and Conflict." *Journal of Peace Research* 36: 387–404.

Barth, Fredrick, ed. 1969. *Ethnic Groups and Boundaries.* Boston: Little, Brown.

Bauer, Thomas K., Magnus Lofstrom, and Klaus F. Zimmermann. 2000. "Immigration Policy, Assimilation of Immigrants, and Natives' Sentiments Towards Immigrants: Evidence from 12 OECD Countries," Discussion Paper No. 187, Institute for the Study of Labor (IZA), Bonn, Germany (http://www.iza.org).

BC STATS. 2004. *Statistics Canada, Labor Force Survey (Annual Averages).* Vancouver. (http://www.bcstats.gov.bc.ca/data/dd/handout/lfsmetro.pdf).

Bergesen, Albert. 1977. "Neo-Ethnicity as Defensive Political Protest." *American Sociological Review* 42: 823–5.

______. 1980. "Official Violence During the Watts, Newark, and Detroit Race Riots of the 1960s." In P. Lauderdale, ed., *A Political Analysis of Deviance*, 138–74. Minneapolis: University of Minnesota Press.

______. 1982. "Race Riots of 1967: An Analysis of Police Violence in Detroit and Newark." *Journal of Black Studies* 12: 261–74.

Bergesen, Albert and Max Herman. 1998. "Immigration, Race, and Riot: The 1992 Los Angeles Uprising." *American Sociological Review* 63: 39–54.

Bhagwati, Jagdish. 2004. *In Defense of Globalization.* New York: Oxford University Press.

Blalock, Herbert M. 1967. *Toward a Theory of Minority-Group Relations.* New York: Wiley.

Blumer, Herbert. 1958. "Race Prejudice as a Sense of Group Position." *Pacific Sociological Review* 1: 3–7.

______. 1965. "The Future of the Color Line." In J. C. McKinney and E. T. Thompson, eds., *The South in Continuity and Change*, 322–36. Durham, NC: Seeman.

Bobo, Lawrence. 1999. "Prejudice as Group Position: Microfoundations of a Sociological Approach to Racism and Race Relations." *Journal of Social Issues* 55: 445–72.

Bobo, Lawrence and Camille L. Zubrinsky. 1996. "Attitudes on Residential Integration: Perceived Status Differences, Mere In-Group Preference, or Racial Prejudice." *Social Forces* 74: 883–909.

Bobo, Lawrence and Vincent L. Hutchings. 1996. "Perceptions of Racial Group Competition: Extending Blumer's Theory of Group Position to a Multiracial Social Context." *American Sociological Review* 61: 951–72.

Bookman, M. Z. 1994. *Economic Decline and Nationalism in the Balkans*. New York: St. Martin's Press.

Brewer, M. B. 1979. "Intergroup Bias in the Minimal Intergroup Situation: A Cognitive-Motivational Analysis." *Psychological Bulletin* 86: 307–24.

Brika, Jean Ben, Gerard Lemaine, and James S. Jackson. 1997. "Racism and Xenophobia in Europe." Eurobarometer Opinion Poll no. 47.1. First results presented at the Closing Conference of the European Year Against Racism. Luxemburg, December 18–19. Brussels: European Commission, Directorate General V.

Brody, Richard and Paul Sniderman. 1977. "From Life Space to Voting Place: The Relevance of Personal Concerns for Voting Behavior." *British Journal of Political Science* 7: 377–90.

Brown, Michael E. 1997. *Nationalism and Ethnic Conflict*. Cambridge, MA: MIT Press.

Brown, Rupert. 1995. *Prejudice: Its Social Psychology*. Cambridge: Blackwell.

Buchanan, Patrick J. 2002. *The Death of the West: How Dying Populations and Immigrant Invasions Imperil Our Country and Civilization*. New York: Thomas Dunne Books.

Burns, Peter and James G. Gimpel. 2000. "Economic Insecurity, Prejudicial Stereotypes, and Public Opinion on Immigration Policy." *Political Science Quarterly* 115: 201–26.

Butfoy, Andrew. 1997. *Common Security and Strategic Reform: A Critical Analysis*. New York: St. Martin's Press.

Butterfield, Herbert. 1951. *History and Human Relations*. London: Collins.

Buzan, Barry. 1991. *People, States, and Fear: An Agenda for International Security Studies in the Post-Cold War Era*, 2nd ed. London: Harvester Wheatsheaf.

Campbell, Angus, Philip E. Converse, Warren E. Miller, and Donald E. Stokes. 1960. *The American Voter*. New York: Wiley.

Caplan, Nathan S. and Jeffrey M. Paige. 1968. "A Study of Ghetto Rioters." *Scientific American* 219: 14–21.

Castles, S. and G. Kosack. 1973. *Immigrant Workers and Class Structure in Western Europe*. London: Oxford University Press.

Chandler, Charles R. and Yung-mei Tsai. 2001. "Social Factors Influencing Immigration Attitudes: An Analysis of Data from the General Social Survey." *Social Science Journal* 38: 177–88.

Chang, Edward Taehan. 1990. "Korean–Black Conflict in Los Angeles: Perceptions and Realities." In Kwang Chung Kim and E. H. Lee, eds. *Dreams and Realities*. Institute of Korea.

Checkel, Jeffrey T. 2004. "IR Theory and Epochal Events: Between Paradigm Shifts and Business-as-Usual." In John Tirman, ed., *The Maze of Fear: Security and Migration After 9/11*, 240–50. New York: New Press.

Chernov, Dmitrii. 2003. "Kitatiskaia bolezn' Dal'nego Vostoka: Diaspora zhivet po svoim zakonam." [The Chinese Disease of the Russian Far East: The Diaspora Lives According to Its Own Laws]. *Vremia novostei* (February 19): 6. Eastview. (http://dlib.eastview.com).

Choucri, Nazli. 1974. *Population Dynamics and International Violence.* Lexington, MA: D. C. Heath.

Citrin, Jack, Beth Reingold, and Donald P. Green. 1990. "American Identity and the Politics of Ethnic Change." *Journal of Politics* 52: 1124–54.

Citrin, Jack, Donald P. Green, Christopher Muste, and Cara Wong. 1997. "Public Opinion Toward Immigration Reform: The Role of Economic Motivations." *Journal of Politics* 59: 858–81.

Clark, Rebecca L., Jeffrey S. Passel, Wendy N. Zimmermann, and Michael Fix. 1994. *Fiscal Impacts of Undocumented Aliens: Selected Estimates for Seven States.* Washington, DC: Urban Institute.

Cohen, S., D. C. Glass, and S. Phillips. 1979. "Environment and Health." In H. E. Freeman, S. Levine, and L. G. Reeder, eds., *Handbook of Medical Sociology.* Englewood Cliffs, NJ: Prentice-Hall.

Collins, Alan. 1998. "The Ethnic Security Dilemma: Evidence from Malaysia." *Contemporary South East Asia* 20: 261–78.

______. 2004. "State-Induced Security Dilemma: Maintaining the Tragedy." *Cooperation and Conflict* 39: 27–44.

Connor, Walker. 2001. "From a Theory of Relative Economic Deprivation towards a Theory of Relative Political Deprivation." In Michael Keating and John McGarry, eds., *Minority Nationalism and the Changing World Order*, 114–36. New York: Oxford University Press.

Cook, Stuart W. 1962. "The Systematic Analysis of Socially Significant Events: A Strategy for Social Research." *Journal of Social Issues* 18: 66–84.

Cornelius, Wayne A. 1998. "The Structural Embeddedness of Demand for Mexican Immigrant Labor: New Evidence from California." In Marcelo Suarez-Orozco, ed., *Crossings: Mexican Immigration in Interdisciplinary Perspective*, 115–55. Cambridge: Harvard University Press.

______ 2001. "Death at the Border: Efficacy and Unintended Consequences of U.S. Immigration Control Policy." *Population and Development Review* 27: 661–85.

______ 2002. "Ambivalent Reception: Mass Public Responses to the 'New' Latino Immigration to the United States." In Marcelo Suarez-Orozco, ed., *Latinos in the 21st Century: Mapping the Research Agenda*, 165–89. Berkeley: University of California Press.

Cornelius, Wayne A., with Yasuo Kuwahara. 1998. *The Role of Immigrant Labor in the U.S. and Japanese Economies: A Comparative Study of San Diego and Hamamatsu, Japan.* La Jolla: Center for U.S.–Mexican Studies, University of California, San Diego.

Dabin, P. 1980. "Community Friction in Belgium: 1830–1980." In W. Philipps Davison and Leon Gordenker, eds., *Resolving Nationality Conflicts: The Role of Public Opinion Research.* New York: Praeger.

Davies, John L. and Ted Robert Gurr, eds. 1998. *Preventive Measures: Building Risk Assessment and Crisis Early Warning Systems*. New York: Rowman and Littlefield.

de la Garza, Rodolfo O. 2004. "Latino Politics." *Annual Review of Political Science* 7: 91–123.

de la Garza, Rodolfo O. and L. DeSipio. 1998. "Interests Not Passions: Mexican American Attitudes toward Mexico and Issues Shaping U.S.–Mexico Relations." *International Migration Review* 32: 401–22.

Devine, P. and A. J. Elliot. 1995. "Are Stereotypes Really Fading? The Princeton Trilogy Revisited." *Personality and Social Psychology* 56: 5–18.

Diamond, Jeff. 1998. "African–American Attitudes Toward United States Immigration Policy." *International Migration Review* 32: 451–70.

Diener, Ed and Carol Diener. 1995. "The Wealth of Nations Revisited: Income and Quality of Life." *Social Indicators Research* 36: 275–84.

Dovidio, J. F. and S. L. Gaetner. 1998. "Intergroup Bias: Status, Differentiation, and a Common In-Group Identity." *Journal of Personality and Social Psychology* 75: 109–20.

Downs, Anthony. 1957. *An Economic Theory of Democracy.* New York: Harper & Row.

Doyle, Michael W. 1999. "War and Peace in Cambodia." In Barbara F. Walter and Jack Snyder, eds., *Civil Wars, Insecurity, and Intervention*, 181–220. New York: Columbia University Press.

Easterlin, Richard A. 1974. "Does Economic Growth Improve the Human Lot? Some Empirical Evidence." In Paul A. David and Melvin W. Reder, eds., *Nations and Households in Economic Growth: Essays in Honor of Moses Abramovitz.* New York: Academic Press.

Eberstadt, Nicholas. 1991. "Population Change and National Security." *Foreign Affairs* 70: 115–31.

The Economist. 2002. "The Longest Journey: A Survey of Migration" (November 2): 1–16.

Ellingwood, Ken. 2004. *Hard Line: Life and Death on the U.S.–Mexico Border.* New York: Pantheon.

Esman, Milton, 1994. *Ethnic Politics*. Ithaca, NY: Cornell University Press.

Espenshade, Thomas J. and Charles A. Calhoun. 1993. "An Analysis of Public Opinion Toward Undocumented Immigration." *Population Research and Policy Review* 12: 189–224.

Espenshade, Thomas J. and Katherine Hempstead. "Contemporary American Attitudes Toward U.S. Immigration." *International Migration Review* 30: 535–70.

Espenshade, Thomas J. and Maryann Belanger. 1997. "U.S. Public Perceptions and Reactions to Mexican Migration." In Frank D. Bean, Rodolfo de la Garza, Bryan R. Roberts, and Sydney Weintraub, eds., *At the Crossroads: Mexican Migration and U.S. Policy*, 227–61. New York: Rowman and Littlefield.

Esty, Daniel C., Jack Goldstone, Ted Robert Gurr, Barbara Harff, Pamela T. Surko, Alan N. Unger, and Robert S. Chen. 1998. "The State Failure Project: Early Warning Research for U.S. Foreign Policy Planning." In John L. Davies and Ted Robert Gurr, eds. *Preventive Measures: Building Risk*

Assessment and Crisis Early Warning Systems, 27–38. Boulder, CO: Rowman and Littlefield.

European Monitoring Center on Racism and Xenophobia. 2001. "Anti-Islamic Reactions in the EU after the Terrorist Acts Against the USA." A Collection of Country Reports from RAXEN National Focal Points (NFPs). Second Report: Reactions from September 25 to October 19.

Europe Intelligence Wire. 2002. "Europe: Satellites to Watch on Refugees" (July 21).

Favell, Adrian and Andrew Geddes. 2000. "Immigration and European Integration: New Opportunities for Transnational Mobilization?" In Ruud Koopmans and Paul Statham, eds., *Challenging Immigration and Ethnic Relations Politics: Comparative European Perspectives*, 407–28. New York: Oxford University Press.

Fearon, James D. and David D. Laitin. 1996. "Explaining Interethnic Cooperation." *American Political Science Review* 90: 715–35.

Fetzer, Joel S. 2000. *Public Attitudes Toward Immigration in the United States, France, and Germany*. New York: Cambridge University Press.

Figueiredo, R. J. P. de, Jr. and Barry B. Weingast. 1999. "The Rationality of Fear: Political Opportunism and Ethnic Conflict." In Barbara F. Walter and Jack Snyder, eds., *Civil Wars, Insecurity, and Intervention*, 261–302. New York: Columbia University Press.

Fiorina, Morris P. 1981. *Retrospective Voting in American National Elections*. New Haven: Yale University Press.

Forbes, H. D. 1997. *Ethnic Conflict. Commerce, Culture and the Contact Hypothesis*. New Haven: Yale University Press.

Fosset, Mark A. and K. Jill Kielcolt. 1989. "The Relative Size of Minority Populations and White Racial Attitudes." *Social Science Quarterly* 70: 820–35.

Frank, Robert H. 1985. *Choosing the Right Pond: Human Behavior and the Quest for Status*. New York: Oxford University Press.

Frank, Robert H. and Cass R. Sunstein. 2001. "Cost-Benefit Analysis and Relative Position." *University of Chicago Law Review* 68: 323–72.

Freedman, Lawrence. 1991. "Demographic Change and Strategic Studies." In Lawrence Freedman and John Saunders, eds., *Population Change and European Security*, 7–21. London: Brassey's.

Freeman, Gary. 1998. "The Decline of Sovereignty? Politics and Immigration Restriction in Liberal States." In Christian Joppke, ed., *Challenges to the Nation-State: Immigration in Western Europe and the United States*, 86–108. Oxford: Oxford University Press.

Freer, Regina. 1994. "Black–Korean Conflict." In Mark Baldassare, ed., *The Los Angeles Riots: Lessons for the Urban Future*, 175–203. Boulder, CO: Westview Press.

Frey, William H. 1996. "Immigration, Domestic Migration, and Demographic Balkanization in America: New Evidence for the 1990s." *Population and Development Review* 22: 741–63.

Fussell, Elizabeth and Douglas S. Massey. 2004. "The Limits to Cumulative Causation: International Migration from Mexican Urban Areas." *Demography* 41: 151–71.

Gel'bras, Vil'ia. 1999. "Kitaiskoe zemliachestvo v Moskve" [The Chinese Community in Moscow]. *Aziia I Afrika Segodnia* 11 (December): 34–9

Gerstle, Gary. 2004. "The Immigrant as Threat to American Security: A Historical Perspective." In John Tirman, ed., *The Maze of Fear: Security and Migration After 9/11*, 87–8. New York: The New Press.

Gibson, James L. and Amanda Gouws. 2000. "Social Identities and Political Intolerance: Linkages within the South African Mass Public." *American Journal of Political Science* 44 (2) (2000): 278–92.

Giles, Michael W. and Kaenan Hertz. 1994. "Racial Threat and Partisan Identification." *American Political Science Review* 88: 317–26.

Gilpin, Robert. 1998. "Three Ideologies of Political Economy." In Charles W. Kegley, Jr. and Eugene R. Witkopf, eds. *The Global Agenda: Issues and Perspectives*, 277–95. Boston: McGraw-Hill.

Gimpel, James G. 1999. *Separate Destinations: Migration, Immigration, and the Politics of Places*. Ann Arbor: University of Michigan Press.

Glaser, Charles L. 1997. "The Security Dilemma Revisited." *World Politics* 50: 171–201.

Glaser, James M. 1994. "Back to the Black Belt: Racial Environment and White Racial Attitudes in the South." *Journal of Politics* 56: 21–41.

Goldscheider, Calvin. 1995. *Population, Ethnicity, Nation-Building*. Boulder, CO: Westview Press.

Gordon, C. and A. Arian. 2001. "Threat and Decision Making." *Journal of Conflict Resolution* 45: 196–215.

Gorsuch, Richard L. 1983. *Factor Analysis*. Hillsdale, NJ: Lawrence Erlbaum.

Goskomstat Rossii. 1998. *Sotsial'naia sfera gorodov I rayonov Primorskogo kraia* [Social Sphere in Cities and Counties of Primorskii krai]. Vladivostok: Primorskii Goskomstat.

______. 1999. *Sbornik: Sostav naseleniiaPrimorskogo kraia po polu I vozrastu na 1 ianvaria 1999 g.* [Data Collection: Population of Primorskii krai by Gender and Age as of January 1, 1999]. Vladivostok: Rosstatagenstvo.

______. 2000a. *Sotsial'naia sfera gorodov I rayonov Primorskogo kraia* [Social Sphere in Cities and Counties of Primorskii krai]. Vladivostok: Primorskii Goskomstat.

______. 2000b. *Primorskii krai v 1999 godu (statisticheskii yezhegodnik)* [Primorskii krai in 1999: A Statistical Yearbook]. Vladivostok: Primorskii Goskomstat.

______. 2001. *Primorskii krai v 2000 godu (statisticheskii yezhegodnik)* [Primorskii krai in 2000: A Statistical Yearbook]. Vladivostok: Primorskii Goskomstat.

______. 2003. *Osnovnye itogi vserossiiskoi perepisi naseleniia 2002 goda* [Principal Findings of the 2002 Russia Population Census]. Moscow. (http://www.goskomstat.ru).

Gottesman, Ronald and Richard Maxwell Brown. 1999. *Violence in America: An Encyclopedia*. New York: Scribner's.

Green, Donald P., Dara Z. Strolovitch, and Janelle S. Wong. 1998. "Defended Neighborhoods, Integration, and Racially Motivated Crime." *American Journal of Sociology* 104: 372–403.

Grimshaw, Allen D. 1960. "Urban Racial Violence in the United States: Changing Ecological Considerations." *American Journal of Sociology* 64: 109–19.

Grodzins, M. 1957. "Metropolitan Segregation." *Scientific American,* 197: 33–41.

Gurr, Ted Robert. 1970. *Why Men Rebel.* Princeton: Princeton University Press.

———. 1993. *Minorities at Risk.* Washington, DC: U.S. Institute of Peace Press.

———. 2001. *People Versus States.* Washington, DC: U.S. Institute of Peace Press.

Hall, E. T. 1962. "Space and Organization as a Factor in Mental Health." *Landscape*: 26–9.

Hanson, Stephen E. 1996. *Time and Revolution: Marxism and the Design of Soviet Institutions.* Chapel Hill: University of North Carolina Press.

Hardin, Russel. 1995. *One for All: The Logic of Group Conflict.* Princeton: Princeton University Press.

Hazarika, Sanjoy. 2001. "A Question of Outsiders: Bangladesh, Myanmar, and Bhutan." In Myron Weiner and Sharon Stanton Russell, eds., *Demography and National Security*, 228–55. New York: Berghahn Books.

Herbert, Bob. 2003. "Where Fear Rules the Street." *New York Times* (June 9): A31.

Herd, Graeme. 1998. "Russia: Systemic Transformation or Federal Collapse?" *Journal of Peace Research* 36: 259–69.

Herz, John H. 1950. "Idealist Internationalism and the Security Dilemma." *World Politics* 2: 157–9.

———. 1966. *International Politics in the Atomic Age.* New York: Columbia University Press.

———. 2003. "The Security Dilemma in International Relations: Background and Present Problems." *International Relations* 17 (4): 411–16.

Hirsch, Fred. 1976. *Social Limits to Growth.* Cambridge, MA: Harvard University Press.

Hollifield, James F. 1992. *Immigrants, Markets, and States: The Political Economy of Postwar Europe.* Cambridge, MA: Harvard University Press.

Homer-Dixon, Thomas. 1994. "Environmental Scarcities and Violent Conflict: Evidence from Cases." *International Security* 19: 5–40.

Hood, M. V. and Irwin L. Morris. 1997. "Amigo o Enemigo? Context, Attitudes, and Anglo Public Opinion Toward Immigration." *Social Science Quarterly* 78: 309–23.

Horowitz, Donald L. 1985. *Ethnic Groups in Conflict.* Berkeley: University of California Press.

Hoskin, Marylin. 1991. *New Immigrants and Democratic Society.* New York: Praeger.

Hossack, James. 2001. "Europe on Standby over Fears of Asylum Seekers." Agence France Presse via NewsEdge Corporation (February 26).

Huddy, Leonie and David O. Sears. 1995. "Opposition to Bilingual Education: Prejudice or the Defense of Realistic Interests." *Social Psychology Quarterly* 58: 133–43.

Hughes, Michael. 1997. "Symbolic Racism, Old-Fashioned Racism, and Whites' Opposition to Affirmative Action." In Steven A. Tuch and Jack K. Martin, eds., *Racial Attitudes in the 1990s: Continuity and Change*, 45–75. Westport, CT: Praeger.

Human Rights Watch, International Catholic Migration Committee, and the World Council of Churches. 2001. "NGO Background Paper on the Refugee and Migration Interface." Presented to the UNHCR Global Consultations on International Protection, Geneva, June 28–9. (http://www.hrw.org/campaigns/refugees/ ngo-document/ngo_refugee.pdf).

Huntington, Samuel P. 1996. *The Clash of Civilizations and the Remaking of World Order.* NewYork: Simon & Schuster.

______. 1997. "The Erosion of American National Interests." *Foreign Affairs* 76: 28–49.

______. 2000. *Reconsidering Immigration: Is Mexico a Special Case?* Center for Immigration Studies. (http://www.cis.org/articles/2000/back1100.html).

______. 2004a. *Who Are We? The Challenges to America's National Identity.* New York: Simon & Schuster.

______. 2004b. "The Hispanic Challenge." *Foreign Policy* (March/April): 30–9.

International Organization for Migration. 2001. *Trafficking in Migrants. International Organization for Migration Quarterly Bulletin* 23 (April).

Ivakhniouk, Irina. 2004. "Illegal Migration: Russia." *European Security* (Spring) 13: 35

Jackman, Mary. 1978. "General and Applied Tolerance: Does Education Increase Commitment to Racial Education?" *American Journal of Political Science* 22: 302–24.

Jacobs, Ronald N. 1996. "Civil Society and Crisis: Culture, Discourse, and the Rodney King Beating." *American Journal of Sociology* 5: 1238–72.

Janowitz, Morris. 1983. *The Reconstruction of Patriotism: Education for Civic Consciousness.* Chicago: University of Chicago Press.

Jervis, Robert. 1976. *Perception and Misperception in International Politics.* Princeton: Princeton University Press.

______. 1978. "Cooperation Under the Security Dilemma." *World Politics* 30: 167–214.

Johnson, James H., Jr. and Melvin L. Oliver. 1989. "Interethnic Minority Conflict in Urban American: The Effects of Economic and Social Dislocations." *Urban Geography* 10: 449–63.

Jones, Brian D. 1999. "Military Intervention in Rwanda's 'Two Wars': Partisanship and Indifference." In Barbara F. Walter and Jack Snyder, eds., *Civil Wars, Insecurity, and Intervention*, 116–45. New York: Columbia University Press.

Kahneman, Daniel and Amos Tversky. 1979. "Prospect Theory: An Analysis of Decision under Risk." *Econometrica* 47: 263–91.

Karlusov, V. and A. Kudin. 2002. "Kitaiskoe prisutstvie na rossiiskom Dal'nem Vostoke: istoriko-ekonomicheskii analiz." *Problemy Dal'nego Vostoka* 5: 76–87.

Kaufman, Stuart J. 1996. "Spiraling to Ethnic War: Elites, Masses, and Moscow in Moldova's Civil War." *International Security* 21: 108–38.

______. 2001. *Modern Hatreds.* Ithaca, NY: Cornell University Press.

Kaufmann, Chaim D. 1999. "When All Else Fails: Evaluating Population Transfers and Partition as Solutions to Ethnic Conflict." In Barbara F. Walter and Jack Snyder, eds., *Civil Wars, Insecurity, and Intervention*, 221–60. New York: Columbia University Press.

Kelly, William R. and Omer R. Galle. 1984. "Sociological Perspectives and Evidence on the Links Between Population and Conflict." In Nazli Choucri, ed., *Multidisciplinary Perspectives on Population and Conflict*, 91–122. Syracuse, NY: Syracuse University Press.

Kinder, Donald R. and D. Roderick Kiewiet. 1978. "Economic Discontent and Political Behavior: The Role of Personal Grievances and Collective Economic Judgments in Congressional Voting." *American Journal of Political Science* 23: 495–527.

Kinder, Donald R. and David O. Sears. 1996. "Prejudice and Politics: Symbolic Racism Versus Racial Threats to the Good Life." *Journal of Personality and Social Psychology* 40: 414–31.

King, Gary, Robert Keohane, and Sifney Verba. 1994. *Designing Social Inquiry: Scientific Inference in Qualitative Research*. Princeton: Princeton University Press.

Kinloch, Graham. 1974. *The Dynamics of Race Relations: A Sociological Analysis*. New York: Vintage Books.

Kluegel, J. R. and Eliot R. Smith. 1983. "Affirmative Action Attitudes: Effects of Self-Interest, Racial Affect, and Stratification Beliefs on White's Views." *Social Forces* 61: 797–824.

Kontorovich, Vladimir. 2000. "Can Russia Resettle the Far East?" *Post-Communist Economies* 12: 365–84.

Koopmans, Ruud and Paul Statham, eds. 2000. *Challenging Immigration and Ethnic Relations Politics: Comparative European Perspectives*. New York: Oxford University Press.

Koslowski, Rey. 2002. "Human Migration and the Conceptualization of Pre-Modern World Politics." *International Studies Quarterly* 46: 375–99.

Kraus, Stephen J. 1995. "Attitudes and the Prediction of Behavior: A Meta-Analysis of the Empirical Literature." *Personality and Social Pscyhology Bulletin* 21: 58–75.

Krebs, Ronald R. and Jack S. Levy. "Demographic Change and the Sources of International Conflict." In Myron Weiner and Sharon Stanton Russell, eds., *Demography and National Security*, 62–80. New York: Berghahn Books.

Kritskii, Ye., M. Nistotskaia, and V. Remmler. 1996. "Krasnodarskii krai: Problema turok-meskhetintsev," [Krasnodar Territory: The Problem of Meskhetian Turks]. In *Set' etnologicheskogo monitoringa i rannego preduprezhdeniia konfliktov, Bulleten'* [The Network of Ethnological Monitoring and Early Warning of Conflict, Bulletin] No. 11 (December).

Laitin, David. 1998. *Identity in Formation: The Russian-Speaking Populations in the Near Abroad*. Ithaca, NY: Cornell University Press.

———. 1999. "Somalia: Civil War and International Intervention." In Barbara F. Walter and Jack Snyder, eds., *Civil Wars, Insecurity, and Intervention*, 146–80. New York: Columbia University Press.

Laitin, David and James D. Fearon. 1999. "Weak States, Rough Terrain, and Large-Scale Ethnic Violence Since 1945." Paper presented at the annual meeting of the American Political Science Association, Atlanta, Georgia, September 2–5.

Lake, David and Donald Rothchild. 1996. "Containing Fear: The Origins and Management of Ethnic Conflict." *International Security* 21: 41–75.

______, eds. 1998. *The International Spread of Ethnic Conflict: Fear, Diffusion, and Escalation*. Princeton: Princeton University Press.

Lanoue, David J. 1994. "Retrospective and Prospective Voting in Presidential-Year Elections." *Political Research Quarterly* 47: 193–205.

Larin, Viktor. 1998. *Kitai i Dal'nii Vostok Rossii v pervoi polovine 90-kh: Problemy regional'nogo vzaimodeystviia*. Vladivostok: Dal'nauka.

Lazarus, R. S. 1966. *Psychological Stress and the Coping Process*. New York: McGraw-Hill.

Levy, Jack S. 2002. "Daniel Kahneman: Judgment, Decision, and Rationality." *PS: Political Science and Politics* 35: 271–3.

Lewis-Beck, Michael S. 1986. "Comparative Economic Voting: Britain, France, Germany, Italy." *American Journal of Political Science* 30: 315–46.

Lieberson, Stanley. 1961. "A Societal Theory of Race and Ethnic Relations." *American Sociological Review* 66: 902–10.

Lipset, Seymour M. 1960. *Political Man*. Garden City, NY: Doubleday.

Lischer, Sarah Kenyon. 1999. "Causes of Communal War: Fear and Feasibility." *Studies in Conflict and Terrorism* 22: 331–55.

Lockerbie, Brad. 1991. "The Influence of Levels of Information on the Use of Prospective Valuations." *Political Behavior* 13: 223–35.

MacDonald, Karin and Bruce E. Cain. 1998. "Nativism, Partisanship, and Immigration: An Analysis of Prop. 187." In Michael Preston, Bruce E. Cain, and Sandra Bass, eds., *Racial and Ethnic Politics in California*, vol. 2, 277–304. Berkeley: Institute of Government Studies Press, University of California, Berkeley.

Martin, Terry. 2001. "Stalinist Forced Relocation Policies: Patterns, Causes, and Consequences." In Myron Weiner and Sharon Stanton Russell, eds., *Demography and National Security*, 305–40. New York: Berghahn Books.

Massey, Douglas, Jorge Durand, Nolan J. Malone. 2002. *Beyond Smoke and Mirrors: Mexican Immigration in an Era of Free Trade*. New York: Russell Sage Foundation.

McFaul, Michael, Nikolai Petrov, and Andrei Riabov, eds., *Predislovie* [Introduction], in *Parlamentskie vybory 1999 goda – Biulleten' 1* [Parliamentary Elections of 1999 – Bulletin 1], Michael McFaul, Nikolai Petrov, and Andrei Riabov, eds. (http:pubs.carnegie.ru/elections/Bulletins/bulletin0199.asp).

McLaren, Lauren M. 2002. "Public Support for the European Union: Cost/Benefit Analysis or Perceived Cultural Threat?" *Journal of Politics* 64: 551–66.

______. 2003. "Anti-Immigrant Prejudice in Europe: Contact, Threat Perception, and Preferences for the Exclusion of Migrants." *Social Forces* 8: 909–36.

Mendelberg, Tali. 2001. *The Race Card: Campaign Strategy, Implicit Messages, and the Norm of Equality*. Princeton: Princeton University Press.

Mercer, Jonathan. 1995. "Anarchy and Identity." *International Organization* 49: 229–52.

Merritt, Richard L., Robert G. Muncaster, and Dina A. Zinnes. 1993. *International Event-Data Developments: DDIR Phase II*. Ann Arbor: University of Michigan Press.

Miasnikov, V. S. 1996. *Dogovornymi stat'iami utverdili: Diplomaticheskaia istoriia russko-kitaiskoi granitsy XVII–XX vv.* [Affirmed by Treaty Articles: A Diplomatic History of the Russian–Chinese Border in the 17th–20th Centuries]. Moscow: Russian Academy of Sciences.

Miller, Elisa and Stephanopoulos, Soula, eds. 1997. *The Russian Far East: A Business Reference Guide.* Seattle, WA: Russian Far East Update.

Morgenthau, Hans J. 1948. *Politics Among Nations: The Struggle for Power and Peace.* New York: Knopf.

Morrison, Peter A. and Ira S. Lewis. 1994. "A Riot of Color: The Demographic Setting." In Mark Baldassare, ed., *The Los Angeles Riots: Lessons for the Urban Future*, 19–46. Boulder, CO: Westview Press.

Myrdal, Gunnar. 1957. *Rich Lands and Poor.* New York: Harper & Row.

National Advisory Commission on Civil Disorders. 1968. *Report.* New York: Bantam.

Nazdratenko, Ye. 1999 *I vsia Rossiia za spinoi...* [And All of Russia Behind Our Back...]. Vladivostok: Ussuri.

Ned Lebow, Richard. 1985. "The Soviet Offensive in Europe: The Schlieffen Plan Revisited." *International Security* 9: 44–78.

Newton, L. Y. 2000. "Why Some Latinos Supported Proposition 187: Testing Economic Threat and Cultural Identity Hypotheses." *Social Science Quarterly* 81: 180–93.

O'Balance, Edgar. 1995. *Civil War in Bosnia 1992–1994.* New York: St. Martin's Press.

Oliver, J. Eric and Janelle Wong. 2003. "Intergroup Prejudice in Multiethnic Settings." *American Journal of Political Science* 47: 567–82.

Olzak, Susan. 1989. "Labor Unrest, Immigration and Ethnic Conflict in Urban America, 1880–1914." *American Journal of Sociology* 94: 1303–33.

———. 1992. *The Dynamics of Ethnic Competition and Conflict.* Palo Alto, CA: Stanford University Press.

Osaki, Keiko. 2003. "The International Migrant Stock: A Global View." Paper presented at the Workshop on Approaches to Data Collection and Data Management, International Organization for Migration, Geneva (September 8–9).

Page, Benjamin I. 1977. "Elections and Social Choice: The State of the Evidence." *American Journal of Political Science* 21: 639–68.

Palmer, Douglas L. 1998. "A Detailed Regional Analysis of Perceptions of Immigration in Canada." Executive Summary, Strategic Research and Review, Citizenship and Immigration Canada (June). (http:www.cic.gc.ca).

———. 1999. "Canadian Attitudes and Perceptions Regarding Immigration: Relations with Regional Per Capita Immigration and Other Contextual Factors." Executive Summary, Strategic Research and Review, Citizenship and Immigration Canada (August). (http:www.cic.gc.ca).

Parhe, Kathleen. 1995. "Village Prose Writers and the Question of Siberian Cultural Identity." In Stephen Kotkin and David Wolf, eds., *Rediscovering Russia in Asia: Siberia and the Russian Far East*, 108–19. Armonk, NY: M. E. Sharpe.

Pastor, Manuel, Jr. and Enrico A. Marcelli. 2000. "Social, Spatial, and Skill Mismatch Among Immigrants and Native-Born Workers in Los Angeles." Working

Paper No. 1, Center for Comparative Immigration Studies, University of California, San Diego. (http://www.ccis-ucsd.org).

Perov, Sergei. 2004. "Get Out of Here, Go Where You Please! – Meskhetian Turks Are Emigrating from Russia to the U.S. En Masse." *Noviye Izvestia* (July 22): 2.

Petersen, Roger D. 2002. *Understanding Ethnic Violence: Fear, Hatred, and Resentment in Twentieth Century Eastern Europe.* New York: Cambridge University Press.

Pettigrew, Thomas F. 1971. *Racially Separate or Together?* New York: McGraw-Hill.

______. 1980. "Prejudice." In S. Themstrom, A. Orlov, and O. Handlin, eds. *The Harvard Encyclopaedia of American Ethnic Groups*, 820–9. Cambridge, MA: Belknap Press.

______. 1998. "Intergroup Contact Theory." *Annual Review of Psychology* 49: 65–85.

Pogranichnaia Sluzhba Rossii, Tikhookeanskoe Oblastnoe Regional'noe Upravlenie (TORU) [Border Service of the Russian Federation, Pacific District Administration of the Russian Border Service, Press Service]. 1999. *Spravka o migratsii grazhdan Kitaia v Rossiiu i tret'i strany cherez yeye terriroriiu v 1998–99 gg.* [Memorandum on Migration of Chinese Citizens to Russia and Other Countries Through Its Territory in 1998–1999], Vladivostok.

Portes, Alejandro and Lingxin Hao. 1998. "*E Pluribus Unum:* Bilingualism and the Loss of Language in the Second Generation." *Sociology of Education* 71: 269–94.

Posen, Barry. 1993. "The Security Dilemma and Ethnic Conflict." In Michael E. Brown, ed., *Ethnic Conflict in International Politics.* Princeton: Princeton University Press, 103–25.

Posner, Richard A. 2000. "Cost-Benefit Analysis: Definition, Justification, and Comment on Conference Papers." *Journal of Legal Studies* 29: 1153, 1166–7.

Prislin, Radmila, Wendy M. Limbert, Evamarie Bauer. 2000. "From Majority to Minority and Vice Versa: The Asymmetrical Effects of Losing and Gaining Majority Position within a Group." *Journal of Personality and Social Psychology* 79: 385–96.

Proshansky, Harold M. 1984. "Population Change and Human Conflict: The Individual Level of Analysis." In Nazli Choucri, ed., *Multidisciplinary Perspectives on Population and Conflict*, 59–90. Syracuse, NY: Syracuse University Press.

Quillian, Lincoln. 1995. "Prejudice as a Response to Perceived Group Threat: Population Composition and Anti-Immigrant and Racial Prejudice in Europe." *American Sociological Review* 60: 586–611.

Rabbie, Jacob M., J. C. Schot, and L. Visser. 1989. "Social Identity Theory: A Conceptual and Empirical Critique from the Perspective of a Behavioral Interaction Model." *European Journal of Social Psychology* 19: 171–202.

Radio Free Europe/Radio Liberty. 2001. *Russian Federation Report*, no. 3, vol. 5, January 31.

Reuveny, Rafael, 2001. "Bilateral Import, Export, and Conflict/Cooperation Simultaneity." *International Studies Quarterly* 45: 131–58.

Reymond, R. and K. G. Joreskog. 1993. *Applied Factor Analysis in the Natural Sciences*. New York: Cambridge University Press.

Rieder, Jonathan. 1985. *Canarsie: The Jews and Italians of Brooklyn against Liberalism*. Cambridge, MA: Harvard University Press.

Roe, Paul. 1999. "The Intrastate Security Dilemma: Ethnic Conflict as 'Tragedy'?" *Journal of Peace Research* 36: 183–202.

———. 2000. "Former Yugoslavia: The Security Dilemma That Never Was?" *European Journal of International Relations* 6: 373–93.

Rose, A. 1969. *Migrants in Europe*. Minneapolis: University of Minnesota Press.

Rosenau, James N. 1997. *Along the Domestic-Foreign Frontier*. Cambridge: Cambridge University Press.

Schafer, Mark. 1999. "Cooperative and Conflictual Policy Preferences: The Effect of Identity, Security, and Image of the Other." *Political Psychology* 20: 829–44.

Schelling, Thomas C. 1960. *The Strategy of Conflict*. Cambridge, MA: Harvard University Press.

Schissel, Bernard, Richard Wanner, and James S. Friederes. 1989. "Social and Economic Context and Attitudes Toward Immigrants in Canadian Cities." *International Migration Review* 23: 289–308.

Schloenhardt, Andreas. 2001. "Migrant Trafficking and Regional Security." *Forum for Applied Research and Public Policy* 16: 83–8.

Schmeidl, Susanne. 1997. "Exploring the Causes of Forced Migration: A Pooled Time-Series Analysis, 1971–1990." *Social Science Quarterly* 78: 284–308.

Schuman, Howard, Charlotte Steeh, Lawrence Bobo, and Maria Krysan. 1997. *Racial Attitudes in America: Trends and Interpretations*. Cambridge, MA: Harvard University Press.

Sears, David O. 1988. "Symbolic Racism." In P. A. Katz and D. A. Taylor, eds., *Eliminating Racism: Profiles in Controversy*, 53–84. New York: Plenum.

Sears, David O., Carl P. Hensler, and Leslie K. Speer. 1979. "Whites' Opposition to 'Busing': Self-Interest or Symbolic Politics?" *American Political Science Review* 73: 369–84.

Sidorkina, Z. I. 1997. *Demograficheskie protsessy i demograficheskaia politika na rossiiskom Dal'nem Vostoke* [Demographic Processes and Demographic Politics in the Russian Far East]. Vladivostok: Dal'nauka.

Simon, Julian L. *The Economic Consequences of Immigration*, 2nd ed. Ann Arbor: University of Michigan Press.

Skeldon, Ronald. 2000. "Myths and Realities of Chinese Irregular Migration," Migration Research Series, No. 1, Geneva: Interantional Organization for Migration. (http://www.iom.int/documents/publication/en/mrs_1_2000.pdf).

Slack, J. Andrew and Roy R. Gordon. 2001. "Population Dynamics and Susceptibility for Ethnic Conflict: The Case of Bosnia and Herzegovina." *Journal of Peace Research* 38: 139–61.

Smith, James P. 1998. "Progress Across the Generations." Paper presented at the Annual Meeting of the American Economic Association, Chicago, January.

Smith, James P. and Barry Edmonston, eds. 1997. *The New Americans: Economic, Demographic, and Fiscal Effects of Immigration*. Washington, DC: National Academy Press.

Smith, Robert C. 1996. "Mexicans in New York: Membership and Incorporation of a New Immigrant Group." In Gabriel Haslip-Viera and Sherrie L. Baver, eds., *Latinos in New York*, 57–103. Notre Dame, IN: University of Notre Dame Press.

Sniderman, Paul M. and Philip E. Tetlock. 1986. "Symbolic Racism: Problems of Motive Attribution in Political Analysis." *Journal of Social Issues* 42: 129–50.

Sniderman, Paul M., Pierangelo Peri, Rui J. P. de Figueiredo, Jr., and Thomas Piazza. 2000. *The Outsider: Prejudice and Politics in Italy*. Princeton: Princeton University Press.

Snyder, Jack L. 1985. "Perceptions of the Security Dilemma in 1914." In Robert Jervis, Richard Ned Lebow, and Janice Gross Stein, eds., *Psychology and Deterrence*, 153–79. Baltimore: Johns Hopkins University Press.

Snyder, Jack L. and Robert Jervis. 1999. "Civil War and the Security Dilemma." In Barbara F. Walter and Jack Snyder, eds., *Civil Wars, Insecurity, and Intervention*, 15–37. New York: Columbia University Press.

Solnick, J. and David Hemenway. 1998. "Is More Always Better? A Survey on Positional Concerns." *Journal of Economic Behavior and Organization* 37: 373, 378–81.

Sorenson, Marianne and Harvey Krahn. 1996. "Attitudes Toward Immigrants: A Test of Two Theories." *Alberta Journal of Educational Research* 42: 2–18.

Soysal, Yasmin. 1994. *Limits of Citizenship: Migrants and Postnational Membership in Europe*. Chicago: University of Chicago Press.

Spence, Jacqueline M. 1996. "The European Union: 'A View from the Top': Top Decision Makers and the European Union." A report of the EOS Gallup Europe survey. Brussels: European Commission.

Stein, Robert M. 1990. "Economic Voting for Governor and U.S. Senator: The Electoral Consequences of Federalism." *Journal of Politics* 52: 29–53.

Stephan, John L. 1994. *The Russian Far East: A History*. Stanford: Stanford University Press.

Suttles, Gerald D. 1972. *The Social Construction of Communities*. Chicago: University of Chicago Press.

Suzuki, Motoshi and Henry W. Chappell, Jr. 1996. "The Rationality of Economic Voting Revisited." *Journal of Politics* 58: 224–36.

Tajfel, Henri. 1970. "Experiments in Intergroup Discrimination." *Scientific American* 223: 96–102.

______. 1981. *Human Groups and Social Categories: Studies in Social Psychology*. Cambridge: Cambridge University Press.

Tajfel, Henri and John C. Turner. 1986. "The Social Identity Theory of Intergroup Behavior." In Stephen Worchel and William G. Austin, eds., *Psychology of Intergroup Relations*, 7–24. Chicago: Nelson-Hall.

Tapinos, Georges. 1978. "The World in the 1980s: Demographic Perspectives." In Georges Tapinos and Phyllis T. Piotrow, eds., *Six Billion People: Demographic Dilemmas and World Politics*. New York: McGraw-Hill.

Tarasenko, Pavel. 1999. "Migratsionnye protsessy, ikh vliianie ne kriminogennuiu obstanovku v krae i o dopolnitel'nykh merakh po uporiadocheniiu prebyvaniia i osedaniia inostrannykh grazhdan na territorii Primorskogo kraya." [Migration Processes, Their Impact on Criminal Situation in the *Krai*, and Additional Measures for Regulating the Visits and Settlement of Foreign Nationals in Primorskii Krai]. Paper presented at the Roundtable, "Prospects for the Far East Region: The Chinese Factor," Institute of History, Archeology, and Ethnography of the Far Eastern Branch, Russian Academy of Sciences, Vladivostok. June 28.

Tayler, Jeffrey. 2000. "Another French Revolution: In Marseilles, Europe Confronts Its North African Future." *Harper's Magazine* (November): 58–66.

Teitelbaum, Michael S. and Jay Winter. 1998. *A Question of Numbers: High Migration, Low Fertility, and the Politics of National Identity.* New York: Hill and Wang.

Thalhammer, Eva, Vlasta Zucha, Edith Enzenhofer, Brigitte Salfinger, and Gunther Ogris. 2001a. "Attitudes Toward Minority Groups in the European Union: A Special Analysis of the Eurobarometer 2000 Opinion Poll on Behalf of the European Monitoring Centre on Racism and Xenophobia," Vienna, Austria. (http://www.sora.at).

______. 2001b. "Attitudes Toward Minority Groups in the European Union: A Special Analysis of the Eurobarometer 2000 Opinion Poll on Behalf of the European. Monitoring Centre on Racism and Xenophobia. Technical Report," Vienna, Austria. (http://www.sora.at).

Thornton, Judith and Charles Ziegler, eds. 2002. *Russia's Far East: A Region at Risk?* Seattle: University of Washington Press.

Thucydides. 1972. *History of the Peloponnesian War.* Rex Warner, trans. London: Penguin.

Tienhaara, Nancy. 1974. "Canadian Views on Immigration and Population: An Analysis of Post-War Gallup Polls." Ottawa: Information Canada.

Tilly, Charles. 1969. "Collective Violence in European Perspective." In Ted Robert Gurr and H. Graham, eds., *Violence in America*, 4–42. New York: Signet Books.

______. 1978. *From Mobilization to Revolution.* Reading, MA: Addison Wesley.

Tirman, John, ed. 2004. *The Maze of Fear: Security and Migration after 9/11.* New York: New Press.

Tirtosudarno, Riwanto. 2001. "Demography and Security: Transmigration Policy in Indonesia." In Myron Weiner and Sharon Stanton Russell, eds., *Demography and National Security*, 199–227. New York: Berghahn Books.

Tkacheva, A. 2000. *Demograficheskaia Situatsiia na Dal'nem Vostoke Rossii v 20–30-e gody XX v.* [Demographic Situation in the Far East of Russia in the 1920s and 1930s]. Vladivostok: Dal'nevostochnyi gosudarstvennyi tehnicheskii rybohoziastvennyi universitet.

Toronto Urban Development Services. 2000. "Employment in Toronto 1999." Toronto: Toronto Urban Development Services. (http://www.city.toronto.on.ca/torontoplan/employintor.pdf).

Turner, John C. with Michael A. Hogg. 1987. *Rediscovering the Social Group: A Self-Categorization Theory.* New York: Blackwell.

Turner, John C. and H. Giles. 1981. *Intergroup Behavior.* Chicago: University of Chicago Press.

United Nations. 2001. *World Population Prospects: The 2000 Revision, Volume III: Analytical Report.* New York: United Nations.

———. 2002a. *International Migration Report 2002*. New York: United Nations. (http://www.un.org/esa/population/publications/ittmig2002/2002 ITTMIGTEXT22-11.pdf).

———. 2002b. *World Population Prospects: The 2002 Revision. Annex Tables*. New York: United Nations.

United Nations High Commissioner for Refugees. 1998. *Refugees and Others of Concern to UNHCR. 1997 Statistical Overview.* Geneva UNHCR. (http://www.unhcr.ch/cgibin/texis/vtx/home/opendoc.pdf?tbl = STATISTICS& id = 3bfa31e54page = statistics).

———. 2002. *Statistical Yearbook 2001: Refugees, Asylum-Seekers, and Other Persons of Concern – Trends in Displacement, Protection and Solutions*. New York: United Nations.

United Nations Population Fund. 1993. *The State of the World Population Report*. New York: United Nations.

United States, Census Bureau. 2002. *Global Population Profile*. Washington, DC: U.S. Census Bureau.

United States, Department of State. 2003. "Estimates of the Unauthorized Immigrant Population Residing in the United States: 1990 to 2000." Executive Summary (January 31). Washington, DC: U.S. Department of State. (http://www.state.gov/s/ct/rls/pgtrpt/2003/33771.htm).

Uslaner, Eric M. 1989. "Looking Forward and Looking Backward: Prospective and Retrospective Voting in the 1980 Federal Elections in Canada." *British Journal of Political Science* 19: 495–513.

Valenzuela, Abel. 2000. "Working on the Margins: Immigrant Day Labor Characteristics and Prospects for Employment." Working Paper No. 22, Center for Comparative Immigration Studies, University of California, San Diego. (http://www.ccis-ucsd.org).

Van Evera, Stephen. 1995. "Nationalism and the Causes of War." In Charles A. Kupchan, ed., *Nationalism and Nationalities in the New Europe*, 146–74. Ithaca, NY: Cornell University Press.

Vanneman, Reeve D. and Thomas Pettigrew. 1972. "Race and Relative Deprivation in the Urban United States." *Race* 13: 461–86.

Vaughan, Graham M., Henri Tajfel, and Jennifer Williams. 1981. "Bias in Reward Allocation in an Intergroup and an Interpersonal Context." *Social Psychology Quarterly* 44: 37–42.

Vidanage, Sharmaine and David O. Sears. 1995. "The Foundations of Public Opinion Toward Immigration Policy: Group Conflict or Symbolic Politics?" Paper presented at the Annual Meeting of the Midwest Political Science Association, Chicago, April 6–8.

Ville de Montreal [Montreal City Government]. 1997. "The Montreal Economy," 10 (3) (3rd Quarter). (http://www2.ville.montreal.qc.ca/economtl/97t3/bul97q3.htm).

Vitkovskaya, Galina. 1998. *Migratsiia naseleniia v postsovetskikh gosudarstvakh: annotirovannaia bibliografiia rossiiskikh izdanii 1992–1997* [Migration in Post-Soviet States: An Annotated Bibliography of Russian Publications, 1992–1997]. Moscow: Carnegie Endowment for International Peace.

Vitkovskaya, Galina, Zhanna Zayonchkovskaya, and Kathleen Newland. 2000. "Chinese Migration into Russia." In Sherman W. Garnett, ed., *Rapprochement or Rivalry: Russia–China Relations in a Changing Asia.* Washington, DC: Carnegie Endowment for International Peace.

Vonk, Roos. 2002. "Effects of Stereotypes on Attitude Inference: Outgroups Are Black and White, Ingroups Are Shaded." *British Journal of Social Psychology* 41: 157–67.

Waever, Ole, Barry Buzan, Morten Kelstrup, and Pierre Lemaitre. 1993. *Identity, Migration and the New Security Agenda in Europe.* London: Pinter.

Waldinger, Roger. 1996. *Still the Promised City? – Blacks and Immigrants in Post-Industrial New York.* Cambridge, MA: Harvard University Press.

Waldinger, Roger and Mehdi Bozorgmehr, eds. 1996. *Ethnic Los Angeles.* New York: Russell Sage Foundation.

Walter, Barbara F. and Jack Snyder, eds. 1999. *Civil Wars, Insecurity, and Intervention.* New York: Columbia University Press.

Watts, Meredith W. 1996. "Political Xenophobia in the Transition from Socialism: Threat, Racism, and Ideology Among East German Youth." *Political Psychology* 17: 97–126.

Webster, William H. 1992. "The City in Crisis: A Report by the Special Advisor to the Board of Police Commissioners on the Civil Disorder in Los Angeles." Los Angeles: Special Advisor Study [601 S. Figueroa St., Suite 3425, Los Angeles, CA 90017].

Weiner, Myron. 1971. "Political Demography: An Inquiry into the Political Consequences of Population Change." In National Academy of Sciences, Office of the Foreign Secretary, ed., *Rapid Population Growth: Consequences and Policy Implications.* Baltimore: Johns Hopkins University Press.

______. 1995. *The Global Migration Crisis.* New York: HarperCollins.

______. 1996. "Nations Without Borders." *Foreign Affairs* 75: 127–31.

Weiner, Myron and Michael S. Teitelbaum. 2001. *Political Demography, Demographic Engineering.* New York: Berghahn Books.

Weingast, Barry. 1994. "Constructing Trust: The Political and Economic Roots of Ethnic and Religious Conflict." Unpublished manuscript.

Wendt, Alexander. 1992. "Anarchy Is What States Make of It: The Social Construction of Power Politics." *International Organization* 46: 391–425.

Wheeler, Nicholas and Kenneth Booth. 1996. "Logics of Security." Unpublished manuscript.

Williams, Robin M. 1947. *Reduction of Intergroup Tension.* New York: Social Science Research Council.

______. 1996. "Prejudice Reduction or Self-Selection? A Test of the Contact Hypothesis." *Sociological Spectrum* 16: 43–60.

Wilson, Thomas C. 2001. "Americans' Views on Immigration Policy: Testing the Role of Threatened Group Interests." *Sociological Perspectives* 44: 485–501.

Wishnik, Elizabeth. 2000. "Russia in Asia and Asians in Russia." *SAIS Review* 20: 87–101.

Wolfers, Arnold. 1962. *Discord and Collaboration.* Baltimore: Johns Hopkins University Press.

Woodward, Susan L. 1999. "Bosnia and Herzegovina: How Not to End Civil War." In Barbara F. Walter and Jack Snyder, eds., *Civil Wars, Insecurity, and Intervention*, 73–115. New York: Columbia University Press.

Zevelev, Igor. 2001. *Russia and Its New Diasporas.* Washington, DC: United States Institute of Peace Press.

Zimmermann, Warren. 1995. "Migrants and Refugees? A Threat to Security?" In Michael S. Teitelbaum and Myron Weiner, eds., *Threatened Peoples, Threatened Borders: World Migration and U.S. Policy*, 88–116. New York: W. W. Norton.

Index